D0966807

COURTS, LAW, and JUSTICE

COURTS, LAW, and JUSTICE

GENERAL EDITOR
William J. Chambliss
George Washington University

KEY ISSUES IN *Crime* AND PUNISHMENT

Los Angeles | London | New Delhi
Singapore | Washington DC

Los Angeles | London | New Delhi
Singapore | Washington DC

FOR INFORMATION:

SAGE Publications, Inc.
2455 Teller Road
Thousand Oaks, California 91320
E-mail: order@sagepub.com

SAGE Publications India Pvt. Ltd.
B 1/I 1 Mohan Cooperative Industrial Area
Mathura Road, New Delhi 110 044
India

SAGE Publications Ltd.
1 Oliver's Yard
55 City Road
London EC1Y 1SP
United Kingdom

SAGE Publications Asia-Pacific Pte. Ltd.
33 Pekin Street #02-01
Far East Square
Singapore 048763

Vice President and Publisher: Rolf A. Janke
Senior Editor: Jim Brace-Thompson
Project Editor: Tracy Buyan
Cover Designer: Candice Harman
Editorial Assistant: Michele Thompson
Reference Systems Manager: Leticia Gutierrez
Reference Systems Coordinator: Laura Notton

Golson Media
President and Editor: J. Geoffrey Golson
Author Manager: Lisbeth Rogers
Layout and Copy Editor: Stephanie Larson
Proofreader: Mary Le Rouge
Indexer: J S Editorial

Copyright © 2011 by SAGE Publications, Inc.

Printed in the United States of America.

Library of Congress Cataloging-in-Publication Data

Key issues in crime and punishment / William Chambliss, general editor.

v. cm.

Contents: v. 1. Crime and criminal behavior — v. 2. Police and law enforcement — v. 3. Courts, law, and justice — v. 4. Corrections — 5. Juvenile crime and justice.

Includes bibliographical references and index.

ISBN 978-1-4129-7855-2 (v. 1 : cloth) — ISBN 978-1-4129-7859-0 (v. 2 : cloth) — ISBN 978-1-4129-7857-6 (v. 3 : cloth) — ISBN 978-1-4129-7856-9 (v. 4 : cloth) — ISBN 978-1-4129-7858-3 (v. 5 : cloth)

1. Crime. 2. Law enforcement. 3. Criminal justice, Administration of. 4. Corrections. 5. Juvenile delinquency. I. Chambliss, William J.

HV6025.K38 2011

364—dc22   2010054579

11 12 13 14 15 10 9 8 7 6 5 4 3 2 1

Contents

Introduction: What Makes an Act a Crime?   xiii
William J. Chambliss, General Editor

1. **Asset Forfeiture**   1
   Types of Asset Forfeiture   2
   Asset Forfeiture in American History   2
      Recent History: Acts and Legislation   3
   Asset Forfeiture and Police Budgets   5
   Pro: Arguments Supporting Asset Forfeiture   6
      Funding Police and Saving Taxpayers   7
      Restoration to Victims   8
   Con: Arguments Against Asset Forfeiture   8
      The Taint Doctrine   9
      Constitutional Rights and Pivotal Cases   9

2. **DNA Evidence**   13
   History of DNA Typing in Criminal Justice   14
      Specialized Processes to Enhance DNA Testing   15
   The Misunderstood Science of DNA Testing   16
   DNA Storage   17
   Developing Felon Databases of DNA   18
   Conducting a Mass Screening of Ordinary Citizens   18
   Admissibility of DNA Evidence:
      History and New Tests   19
   Current Legal and Ethical Issues   20
      Who Should Be in the Database?   20
      Database and Familial Searches   20
      Touch/Transfer/Low-Level DNA Samples   21
      Post-Conviction Testing: Access and Timeliness   22
   Pro: Support for Expanding DNA Databases   24
   Con: Opposition to Expanding DNA Databases   25
      DNA Dragnets   26
   Future of DNA Evidence and New Scientific Techniques   27

3. Double Jeopardy   **31**

History of the Double Jeopardy Rule   32

The Attachment of Jeopardy   33

Same Offense   34

Exceptions to the Double Jeopardy Clause   35

     Separate Sovereignties   35

     Petite Policy   36

     Government Appeal   37

     Termination Without Acquittal or Conviction   38

     Application in Non-Criminal Proceedings   38

Pro: Arguments in Favor of Double Jeopardy   39

Con: Arguments Against Double Jeopardy   40

4. Drug Laws   **45**

Drugs: The Stalled Movement for Decriminalization   46

History: Changing Frames for Drug Laws   46

     The 1960s and 1970s: Cultural Strife and Moral Dissonance   47

From the Reagan Era Onward   48

Pro: The Prophylactic Features of Criminalization   49

Con: Criticism of the War on Drugs   50

Hints of a Slowly Shifting Drug Policy   52

     Challenging the Punitive Approach to Drug Enforcement   52

     International Parallels   54

Conclusion   55

5. DUI Penalties   **61**

Relevant Databases   62

Effects or Influences of Drugs on Driving   63

Control of Impaired Drivers   63

Measuring Blood Alcohol Content   64

Implied Consent Laws and Administrative Sanctions   65

Zero Tolerance Laws   66

Standard Criminal Penalties for DUI   67

Nontraditional DUI Penalties   67

     Locking the Ignition   68

Pro: Arguments for Strong Impaired-Driving Laws   69

Con: Enforcement and Sanctions Are Inadequate   70

Questionable Deterrence   71

6. **Exclusionary Rules** 75

    Building the Exclusionary Rules 76

        Fourth Amendment Context 76

        Fifth Amendment Context 78

        Sixth Amendment Context 78

        Fruit of the Poisonous Tree 79

    Limiting the Exclusionary Rules 80

        The Current State of the Exclusionary Rule 83

    Pro: Arguments in Support of the Exclusionary Rule 83

    Con: Arguments Opposing the Exclusionary Rule 85

7. **Expert Witnesses and Hired Guns** 89

    Quality of the Science 91

    Expert Witnesses in Criminal Cases 92

        Psychiatric/Psychological Evaluation 92

        Physical Evidence Evaluation 93

        Medical/Biological Evidence Evaluation 94

        Documentary and Computer Evidence Evaluation 94

        Acoustical Evidence Evaluation 95

        Traffic Accident Reconstruction 95

        Financial Evaluation 96

    Hired Guns 96

    Pro: Arguments in Favor of Using Expert Witnesses 97

    Con: Arguments Opposing the Use of Expert Witnesses 98

    Conclusion 99

8. **Eyewitness Testimony and Accuracy** 101

    History of Eyewitness Identification Research 102

        The Research of Loftus and Wells 102

        DNA Testing and Factors in Eyewitness Error 103

    Pro: Variables Leading to Accurate Eyewitness Testimony 104

        Estimator Variables 105

        System Variables 106

    Con: Variables Leading to Mistaken Eyewitness Testimony 107

        Estimator Variables 108

        System Variables 109

        Lineup Presentation Method 110

        Administrator's Behavior 111

    Conclusion 112

9. **Gun Control Laws**   117
    History of Gun Control and Gun Rights   117
    Foreign Examples of Gun Control   119
    Gun Control Laws and the Constitution   120
      Recent Landmark Cases   122
    Types of Gun Control Laws   123
      Keeping Guns out of the Hands of Criminals   123
      Waiting Periods   124
      Safe Storage and Distance   124
    Major Federal Gun Control Initiatives   125
    Gun Rights Legislation: Conceal and Carry   125
    Gun Laws: The Empirical Evidence   127
    Pro: Arguments in Favor of Gun Control   127
    Con: Arguments in Opposition to Gun Control   128
    Conclusion   128

10. **Insanity Defense**   133
    Procedures Involved in the Defense   134
    History of the Defense   135
      The *M'Naghten* Test   135
      Irresistible Impulse   136
      The *Durham* Test   136
      American Law Institute Test   137
      Guilty but Mentally Ill   137
      Insanity Defense Reform Act of 1984   138
      Post-Traumatic Stress Disorder and Postpartum Psychosis   139
      The Supreme Court Gets Involved   140
    Pro: Arguments in Support of the Insanity Defense   140
    Con: Arguments Against the Insanity Defense   142
      A Case in Point   143

11. **Jury System**   145
    Mechanics of the Jury System   146
    History of the Jury System   147
    The Supreme Court Shapes the American Jury System   149
      Fair Cross-Section Requirement   151
    Pro: Arguments in Support of the American Jury System 153
    Con: Criticisms of the American Jury System   154

12. Mandatory Sentencing   159
    A Brief History of Mandatory Sentencing   160
    Describing Mandatory Sentencing Today   161
    Rationale for Mandatory Sentencing   162
    Effectiveness of Mandatory Sentencing   163
    Pro: Arguments for Mandatory Minimum Sentencing   165
      Protecting the Public   165
      Sentencing Equity   166
    Con: Arguments Against Mandatory Minimum Sentencing   167
      Discretion and Bias   168
      Rigid and Expensive   169
    Future Issues in Mandatory Sentencing   170

13. Miranda Rights   173
    The Law Prior to *Miranda*   174
    Ernesto Miranda   176
    The *Miranda* Ruling   177
      Court Specifies the Language of the Warnings   178
    The Aftermath   179
      Congress, the Court, and the Problem of *Miranda*   180
    Subsequent Caselaw   181
    Berghuis v. Thompkins: A Critical Change   183
    Pro: Arguments in Support of the *Miranda* Ruling   184
    Con: Criticism of the *Miranda* Ruling

14. Plea Bargaining   186
    The Development and Spread of Plea Bargaining   188
      Plea Bargaining in America and Internationally   188
    Pro: Arguments in Support of Plea Bargaining   189
      The Issue of Coercion   190
      In the Shadow of Trials   191
      Plea Bargains as Contracts   192
      Substantive Justice   193
    Con: Arguments in Opposition to Plea Bargaining   194
      Diverging From the Shadow of Trials   194
      The Contract View Fails the Public   195
      Hawks and Doves   196
      Result of an Overadversarial System   197

15. Polygraphs   **201**

History of the Polygraph   201

    Polygraph Groundbreakers: Larson and Reid   202

Procedures of the Polygraph   203

The Use of Polygraphs in the Criminal Justice System   204

The Admissibility of Polygraphs in Criminal Cases   205

    Daubert and *Scheffer*: A Split in the Federal Circuits   205

    The Exception: New Mexico   207

Pro: Supporting the Validity of the Polygraph   208

    Rehabilitation and Recidivism   208

Con: Questioning the Validity of the Polygraph   209

    The Error Rate   209

    Poor Research Standards   210

    No Uniform Training Standards or Procedures   211

16. Restorative Justice   **215**

Basic Premises of Restorative Justice   216

    Conflict as Property   217

    The Work of Braithwaite and Zehr   217

History of Restorative Justice   219

    Victim-Offender Reconciliation Programs   219

    Victims' Rights Movements and

       Indigenous Justice   220

Restorative Justice Interventions   221

    Victim-Offender Mediation   222

    Family Group Conferencing   222

    Sentencing Circles   223

    Community Restorative Boards   223

    Restorative Community Service   223

Pro: Arguments in Support of Restorative Justice   224

    Offender Agreements and Recidivism   225

Con: Arguments Against Restorative Justice   226

    Whose Justice?   226

    Due Process, Fair Sentencing, and Mainstreaming   226

17. Sentencing Disparities   **231**

Inconsistencies in the Research   232

    Methodological Flaws in Sentencing Research   232

    Variables Used in Sentencing Research   233

    Theoretical Premises of Sentencing Disparity   234

Ethnicity and Disparity in Sentencing   235
Disparities in Sentencing and Sentencing Guidelines   236
RDS and the War on Drugs   238
   Crack Versus Powder   238
Pro: Positive Outcomes of Racial Disparity Research   240
Con: Negative Outcomes of Racial Disparity Research   241

18. **Sex Offender Registry**   243
The History of Sex Offender Legislation   244
Contemporary Sex Offender Registry Legislation   245
   Wetterling Act and Megan's Law   245
   Inconsistent Procedures, Specific Types of Information 246
   Sex Offender Levels   246
   Updated Legislation   247
   The Tier System   248
The Legality of Sex Offender Legislation   250
   Two Cases of Constitutional Challenge   251
Pro: Arguments in Support of Sex Offender Registration   252
Con: Arguments Against Sex Offender Registration   253

19. **Three-Strikes Laws**   257
The History and Development of Three-Strikes Laws   258
   The Klaas Murder   259
The Legality of Three-Strikes Laws   260
Pro: Arguments in Support of Three-Strikes Laws   261
   The Deterrent Effect   262
Con: Arguments Against Three-Strikes Laws   264
   Burdensome Costs and Racial Disparities   264

20. **Victim Rights and Restitution**   269
Victim Rights Overview   270
Restitution Overview   271
Typical Victim Rights   272
   Receiving Information and Notification   272
   Reasonable Protection and Separate Waiting Areas   272
   Availability of Transportation   273
   Participation and Attendance in the Justice Process   273
Restitution and Return of Property   273
Victim Services and Applying for Victim Compensation   274
Expectation of Compliance and Legal Remedies   274

State Legislation for Victim Rights and Restitution   275
Federal Legislation for Victim Rights and Restitution   275
Proposed Victim Rights Amendment   277
Pro: Arguments for Constitutional Victims' Rights   278
Con: Arguments Against Constitutional Victims' Rights   279
Conclusion   281

Index   283
About the General Editor   317

Introduction

What Makes an Act a Crime?

What makes an act a crime? "Thou shalt not kill" certainly does not apply to the law. One may kill in self defense, if under duress, or to protect your own property. Law enforcement officers and executioners may kill another human being, as can soldiers under orders. Furthermore, at a bare minimum, for an act to be a crime, it must be the result of an overt act or omission to act when one is legally responsible to do so; must be intentional (in most but not all cases); must have caused harm; and must have a causal relationship between the act and the harm.

Even knowing these principles, however, does not mean that no one is ever found guilty and punished for acts that do not meet these criteria. The roles in the criminal justice system, from police to judges, are filled by fallible human beings; no set of rules or principles can guarantee that role, and that occupants will not find ways to circumvent them.

The chapters in this volume cover a wide range of topics, including drug and gun control laws, as well as numerous chapters that discuss the ins and outs of the justice system once suspected offenders are arrested, during the trial process, and during sentencing.

The chapter *Drug Laws* (Dombrink) gives a historical overview of American drug policy, including changing drug laws over time and the movement to have drugs decriminalized. He explains the pros and cons of current drug policies, international efforts, and the recent changes in America to reduce drug-related crime and harm. *Gun Control Laws* (McGuire) looks at gun control laws in America and discusses America's unique culture and history, which has led to gun control laws being highly contested by many Americans.

Legal issues pertaining to the investigative process once a suspected offender has been taken into custody are reviewed. *Miranda Rights* (Candela) discusses suspects' rights prior to and since the landmark *Miranda* decision, which address an individual's Fifth Amendment rights. In addition to discussing the *Miranda v. Arizona* case, Candela details the pros and cons of *Miranda* and how court cases have since limited *Miranda*. Scott-Hayward's chapter *Polygraphs* and Inman and Beck's chapter *DNA Testing* explain the impact that technology has had on the investigation process, how polygraphs and DNA testing works, and to what degree the information obtained through polygraph and DNA testing has been allowed in criminal trials.

Legal and procedural issues during the prosecution of suspected offenders are also covered in this volume. Binnall's *Exclusionary Rules* outlines the development of the legal doctrine that enables courts to exclude certain pieces of evidence from trial due to unconstitutional police and/or investigation tactics, its constitutional basis, and limitations to the doctrine as ruled by the courts. This chapter shows the impact investigations can have on prosecutions, and that court decisions can have on both investigations and prosecutions. Similarly, Steele's chapter *Double Jeopardy* examines the Fifth Amendment of the U.S. Constitution, which states, "... nor shall any person be subject for the same offense to be twice put in jeopardy of life or limb ..." and discusses how court interpretations, over time, have impacted the justice system. Campbell's chapter *Plea Bargaining* reviews the development and spread of plea bargaining, including different types of plea bargaining, reasons for their use, and the consequences of plea bargaining. Binnall's *Jury System* discusses the development of the American jury system as well as the mechanics and laws pertaining to juries.

This volume also contains extensive information about sentencing and punishments for crimes, including different types of offenses such as sex offenses and DUI. Grimes's chapter on *Three-Strikes Laws* and Fearn's *Mandatory Sentencing* chapter on mandatory minimums both help the reader understand the intended purposes of these laws, the variation of these laws across time and states, and the sociopolitical environment from which these laws developed. Evans's chapter *Sex Offender Registry* analyzes society's attempts to monitor and control sex offenders, especially following the highly publicized kidnappings, murders, and rapes of children such as Jacob Wetterling, Polly Klaas, and Megan Kanka. This chapter also discusses the ongoing debate over whether or not sex offense registries are constitutional or effective.

Finally, Wood's chapter *Restorative Justice* looks at the role the victim plays during the prosecutorial process. Although the U.S. Constitution guarantees rights to suspects and convicted offenders, there are no constitutional rights specific to victims. Wood discusses how society and the justice system have changed over time, which has led to a call by victims' rights activists for changes in the justice system to allow victims to be more involved and protect them from being "re-victimized by the system."

Although the topics of this volume are quite varied, the authors all provide detailed overviews of the development of the justice system and give consideration to the contrasting leading opinions that support or denounce the laws and policies used during the investigative, prosecutorial, and sentencing processes.

William J. Chambliss
General Editor

1

Asset Forfeiture

Stephen A. Bishopp
John L. Worrall
University of Texas at Dallas

Asset forfeiture is loosely defined as the confiscation of property by the state of proceeds or instruments of a crime. It is a government practice deeply rooted in history, one that continues to be the subject of much contention today. It has become an integral part of the war on crime, shaped law enforcement practices, and led to a variety of legislative changes over the past several decades.

The debate over asset forfeiture centers on the necessity of finding a balance between the desire to control crime and the need to protect citizens' civil rights. Asset forfeiture is touted as a tool used by law enforcement to address the daunting task of controlling criminal activity. It is meant to serve as deterrent against organized crime and drug trafficking. However, asset forfeiture is seen by many as a Draconian approach to crime control. This is partly because it creates the opportunity and financial motivation for law enforcement to follow the money, not the crime.

Understanding the key issues underlying the forfeiture debate is vital, including the early history of asset forfeiture, as well as the various benefits and drawbacks associated with the practice. Asset forfeiture is beneficial because it targets criminal profits, is not as difficult as securing a criminal conviction, and funds law enforcement activities (e.g., by funding task forces). To its detriment, forfeiture can create a profit motive for law enforcement; may lead to circumvention of state law through a practice known as equitable sharing; has at its core a questionable taint doctrine; may threaten people's rights; does not require a criminal charge or conviction; and requires a lower standard of proof.

Types of Asset Forteiture

Historically, there have been two basic types of asset forfeiture, in rem and in personam. Property seized in personam occurs as a result of a person being found guilty of a criminal offense. Such property can be confiscated and is utilized primarily as a penalty for a crime. In contrast, in rem forfeiture is a civil proceeding and results in a judgment against a person's property. In effect, the property itself is found guilty, or part of a criminal enterprise, and as such it is subject to seizure. A salient difference between criminal and civil proceedings is the burden of proof required to establish guilt. A criminal trial traditionally requires a judge or a jury to find guilt beyond a reasonable doubt. The government must be able to prove, with the same standard of proof required of a criminal conviction, that the defendant's property is a forfeitable asset. In contrast, a civil trial only requires a preponderance of the evidence. This means that the government must only convince a judge with 51 percent certainty that property is subject to forfeiture. In comparison, criminal trials, proof beyond a reasonable doubt requires at least 95 percent certainty.

Asset Forfeiture in American History

Asset forfeiture has a long history that predates the American colonies. In feudal times, offenses designated as felonies or treasons were considered offenses against the king and required repayment to the crown. This repayment came in the form of forfeited lands or goods, which were immediately seized upon conviction. Eventually, the vigorous use of asset forfeiture by England against the American colonies was partly responsible for the wording of the Fifth, Sixth, and Eighth Amendments to the U.S. Constitution. Since then, the Supreme Court has held that there is no significant constitutional limit to the government's use of civil asset forfeiture.

The use of civil proceedings in asset forfeiture cases began primarily with the Navigation Act of 1651. This act allowed England to seize ships and property of merchants who were in violation of its provisions. The Navigation Act was a means by which England was able to control world trade through the use of statutes that made shipping practices illegal, or deemed a particular type of cargo as contraband. This allowed for the seizure of ships or cargo in rem rather than in personam, thereby avoiding the higher burden of proof associated with criminal proceedings.

Some of America's first asset forfeiture statutes were meant to protect against illegal shipping and piracy in violation of American admiralty laws. Much like English law, a merchant had the opportunity to defend his ship and his cargo (or himself if charged with crime by customs officials); however, contraband cargo was automatically found guilty and was immediately seized.

From the mid-1800s through the mid-1900s, various laws were enacted and government agencies created to regulate and collect funds from the supplying, shipping, and distribution of many drugs and narcotics. For instance, heroin, cocaine, morphine, and marijuana were all once legally shipped, bought, and used throughout the United States. The federal government profited from the taxation and fee collection from drugs and drug-related activity. Doctors were required to have licenses to administer or prescribe certain drugs, and licensing fees were payable to the various government agencies. During this time period, drugs were tightly regulated, but not criminalized, and there was no threat of forfeiture for violating the drug laws.

Recent History: Acts and Legislation

There have been many recent legislative developments in the forfeiture arena. For example, two important pieces of legislation introduced in 1970 had the intent of removing profitability from organized crime and illegal drug activity: (1) the Comprehensive Drug Abuse Prevention and Control Act and (2) the Racketeering Influenced and Corrupt Organizations Act (RICO). The first drug-related asset forfeiture laws were enacted as part of The Comprehensive Drug Abuse Prevention and Control Act. Through utilization of this act, the government was able to seize property involved in criminal activity, such as any equipment or assets used in the making or distributing of contraband, or purchased with money gained from illegal drug activity. This act also categorized certain drugs at various levels of dangerousness and began the process through which many substances were banned, which effectively extended the reach of asset forfeiture laws. Increased penalties and newly prohibited drugs were added to the controlled substance list, allowing for the use of asset forfeiture statutes in more cases.

While this act struck specifically at the supposed drug problem, RICO was aimed particularly at curbing the Mafia and its infiltration into legitimate business. It provided law enforcement with a means by which it could broadly define a series of crimes as organized crime.

In 1984, a new weapon was added to the arsenal of state and federal law enforcement agencies, namely the Comprehensive Crime Control Act (CCA). One of the key purposes of the CCA was to create an incentive for federal and local law enforcement agencies to pool their resources and become more effective in controlling crime. The CCA also allowed local agencies to share in the profits associated with drug forfeitures. State laws could (and some did) impose restrictions on the percentage of money the agency could obtain from forfeited assets. Some states did not permit their law enforcement agencies to keep any of the forfeiture proceeds. However, with the passing of the CCA, local agencies could ask federal officials to adopt the case. Law enforcement could then share in profits that were in excess of what it was allowed to keep under state law. This practice came to be known as *equitable sharing.*

In 2000, fear of potential abuses of equitable sharing led to the passage of the Civil Asset Forfeiture Reform Act (CAFRA). This was an effort by lawmakers to address perceived flaws in federal asset forfeiture laws. Prior to CAFRA, if property was subject to forfeiture, it was the owner's responsibility or burden to prove the property innocent. As a result of the act, a uniform, innocent owner defense was required in all federal forfeiture proceedings. Furthermore, the owner of forfeited property no longer needs to post bond in order to get his or her day in court. CAFRA also made adjustments to time constraints concerning notification of the seizure and potential forfeiture of property. The allotted time for a property owner to make notification of intent to challenge the forfeiture action was extended to 60 days from the original 20 days.

Despite the shift in the burden of proof from the owner to the government, the standard of proof remains the same. The lower standard of proof in civil court systems facilitates the government's ability to gain from civil forfeitures via in rem proceedings. Federal officials need only prove that they have a preponderance of the evidence by demonstrating with 51 percent certainty that the property is forfeitable. Property can also be immediately seized without trial or hearing upon probable cause that it was in some way used in the commission or as a conveyance in criminal conduct. No further investigation needs to be completed, since there is no need to prove that the property owner has committed an offense in order to seize their property.

Property cannot invoke its right to a presumption of innocence; the property owner must take the steps necessary to initiate a trial or hearing to have the property returned.

CAFRA also failed to address a number of other fundamental concerns. Equitable sharing is still permissible and continues to be used by police agencies. State and local agencies can still thwart more restrictive state asset forfeiture laws and allow the agency to profit handsomely from forfeitures through equitable sharing. Additionally, there is no requirement for states to change their laws to reflect federal law changes created by CAFRA. Restrictions placed on the amount of funds, if any, can still be easily sidestepped, and proceeds beyond what the state would normally allow can still be collected. This means that police agencies at the state and local level may continue to collect up to 80 percent of the proceeds from civil asset forfeitures. While CAFRA may have made some headway in protecting citizens' property from forfeiture to the government, it may not have gone far enough to properly protect citizens against civil asset forfeiture abuses.

Asset Forfeiture and Police Budgets

Asset forfeiture is used in a manner that buttresses the budgets of law enforcement agencies. Studies have shown that monetary issues guide civil asset forfeiture activities. Results from an extensive survey of municipal and county law enforcement executives revealed that many law enforcement agencies are dependent on civil asset forfeiture as a necessary budgetary supplement. Some agencies have had their budgets cut or reduced based on prior asset forfeiture money obtained by the police; therefore, continued procurement of seized assets to bolster police coffers becomes necessary.

Police agencies use the money obtained through forfeiture proceedings to finance various operational needs such as equipment and training. Asset forfeiture is a means by which law enforcement agencies can replenish the budgetary void created by combating crime. While it is not the only context in which asset forfeiture occurs, the most notable instance of filling a void created by criminal investigations occurs during drug investigations. Police agencies commit equipment and train personnel with the necessary means to combat drug-related offenses. Money and property seized during drug-related investigations is often used to replenish police budgets strained because of resources spent on investigating drug offenses.

Asset forfeiture continues to be sanctioned at all levels of government through various laws, policies, and programs. Proponents tout its usefulness as a law enforcement tool, while those against it see it as a government intrusion that is fiscally motivated and capriciously applied. Whether forfeiture is driven by profit-seeking or is a genuine tool used to reduce crime remains somewhat unclear. The forceful confiscation of one's personal property without the benefit of a criminal trial is either an overly zealous attempt by the government to make a profit, or a creative tool aimed at deterring criminal activity by targeting its pecuniary underpinnings.

Pro: Arguments Supporting Asset Forfeiture

The primary purpose of asset forfeiture statutes is to cripple organized criminal and drug-related activity by removing the motivations for it, namely money. Asset forfeiture becomes an important tool for law enforcement because it allows them to directly target the proceeds of criminal activity and raise the risks. Asset forfeiture may thus be an effective deterrent to criminal activity, making it easier for law enforcement to remove the profit from organized criminal and drug-related activity.

Asset forfeiture further facilitates the targeting of criminal profits by allowing law enforcement to expand the items it is able to seize. Law enforcement is authorized to seize equipment, conveyances, homes, property, vehicles, and any other items that are in some way tied to proceeds generated from criminal activity. This greatly increases law enforcement's ability to undercut criminal profits.

Asset forfeiture utilizes the civil court system, which is considerably easier than having to obtain a criminal conviction before seizure. In the civil court system, the burden of proof is, once again, a preponderance of the evidence. Since this is lower than the criminal requirement of proof beyond a reasonable doubt, forfeiture is easier to pursue in some respects than a criminal conviction. Law enforcement agencies are still required to have probable cause to believe the property is in some way connected to a crime, but there is no need to go through the rigorous motions of building a criminal case. Because of this, law enforcement is able to get to the financial core of organized criminal or drug-related activity and can do so with the use of fewer resources. Because of the ease with which property can be forfeited in a civil proceeding and the large amount of money and property available for seizure, the use of asset forfeiture has led to an increase in drug arrests.

Racketeering and money laundering are examples of specific crimes against which asset forfeiture is useful. Historically, the Mafia was proficient at using legitimate businesses in order to launder or otherwise hide money gained from a wide range of illegal ventures. Business leaders would ignore or look the other way and allow money from Mafia proceeds to be filtered through the business. Civil asset forfeiture gave law enforcement a new tool to confront the Mafia. Using RICO's civil asset forfeiture provisions, these business owners could be held accountable for the actions of the Mafia, thereby opening up an ostensibly legitimate business to liability. The RICO provision is broad, which enhances its use as a law enforcement tool.

Funding Police and Saving Taxpayers

Asset forfeiture activity also provides funds to help law enforcement agencies fulfill their missions. Law enforcement, particularly at the state and local level, generates its funding through numerous sources. Writing tickets, applying for grants, and receiving monies from private individuals and organizations are a few examples. Asset forfeiture adds to this list and is one of the many ways in which law enforcement is legally able to obtain needed resources. For instance, police departments need training, equipment, and money in order to continue the war on crime. Law enforcement agencies have been able to purchase training facilities, helicopters, weapons, and vehicles, and provide essential training with the proceeds of forfeited assets.

More importantly, because of asset forfeiture, the taxpaying public bears less of the financial burden of supporting law enforcement budgets.

Some states require forfeited assets be used to fund functions not related to law enforcement. Depending on the restrictiveness of the state law, all or a percentage of the proceeds may be deposited into a general fund. Out of this general fund, several state-level programs and agencies may be financially supported. These include education, public assistance programs, corrections, state Medicaid programs, and transportation. Asset forfeiture may thus serve to minimize taxpayer burdens and provide an opportunity for these various public agencies to have their budgets supplemented.

In federal forfeiture cases, the money and property is deposited into the Asset Forfeiture Fund. Several federal law agencies with the Department of Justice have access to this fund. The Federal Bureau of Investigations, the U.S. Marshals Service, the Postal Service, the Drug Enforcement Agency, Immigration Customs Enforcement, the U.S. Parks Police, and the U.S. Attorney's Office all stand to benefit from the forfeiture of seized assets. The proceeds from the Asset Forfeiture Fund are also used for administrative and investigative costs associated with asset forfeiture, third-party payments, and payments to equitable sharing.

Restoration to Victims

Asset forfeiture has been used in some cases to seize property, money, and other assets in order to redistribute as much as possible to the victims of financial schemes. Forfeiture has proven useful in recent high-profile cases, notably those involving Bernie Madoff and Schott Rothstein. Madoff's Ponzi scheme took an estimated $65 billion from unsuspecting clients, whereas Rothstein illegally acquired $1.2 billion from numerous investors.

Con: Arguments Against Asset Forfeiture

Much of the controversy concerning civil asset forfeitures pertains to law enforcement motivations. For example, harsh criticism has been levied against police agencies because there is evidence to suggest some may be addicted to a policing-for-profit scheme. Furthermore, empirical research indicates that some police agencies are financially predatory and motivated by budgetary concerns rather than controlling crime. These arguments are particularly disquieting in light of the War on Drugs. Drug use has fluctuated wildly during the last three decades; however, drug arrest rates have increased steadily. At the least, this suggests law enforcement efforts are not clearly related to drug use. Critics feel that the only real explanation for continuing to devote vast amounts of manpower and resources to drug enforcement is to fill agency coffers through civil asset forfeiture.

The pursuit of money and property for budgetary reasons provides police agencies with the ability and motivation to select targets. Critics posit that because the illicit drug trade generates vast, nearly immeasurable income, and because forfeiture laws cover proceeds traceable to drug transactions, the targeting of those who have the most to forfeit becomes an irresistible temptation. This raises inequality concerns. Those who have the money and property to turn over to police agencies do so to avoid incarceration. In essence, they buy their way out of jail. On the other hand, those who are arrested and have little or no property to subject to civil asset forfeiture are punitively jailed.

Law enforcement officials realize the financial benefit and profits that come from seizing property rather than making arrests. Recognizing this potential for an iniquitous law enforcement motivation to target specific types of criminals for their property (i.e., drug dealers suspected of possessing large sums of money and property), some state laws restrict the amount of assets a police agency may keep. The most restrictive states do not allow their police agencies to keep any of the proceeds. Equitable sharing and adoption laws, however, allow state and federal authorities to work jointly and circumvent more restrictive state laws, thus permitting them to profit from civil asset forfeiture to a greater extent than restrictive state laws may allow. Police agencies that are not permitted to keep any of the proceeds may request that federal authorities adopt the seizure. Afterward, through equitable sharing, such agencies can get back as much as 80 percent of the proceeds. In this way, state laws intended to protect against targeting are effectively rendered null and void by equitable sharing and adoption practices.

The Taint Doctrine

Significantly expanding the amount of property that can be seized, the taint doctrine allows law enforcement to use civil asset forfeiture to obtain money and proceeds that are not directly linked to criminal activity. Essentially, any property that was used to facilitate or was the result of criminal activity can be subject to asset forfeiture proceedings. Because guilt can be attached to all property that may in some way be connected to illegal activity, critics feel this contributes to overreaching on the part of law enforcement. The taint doctrine further exacerbates negative connotations of asset forfeiture because it can be applied to a wide variety of criminal conduct. Financial holdings, as well as personal, real, and even intellectual property tied to criminal activity by mere probable cause, can be seized and potentially forfeited to the government.

Constitutional Rights and Pivotal Cases

Civil asset forfeiture is also viewed by its many opponents as a violation of the rights of citizens. This owes partly to how the practice has affected innocent owners. In one case, *Bennis v. Michigan* (1996), a woman's husband was found with a prostitute inside the family car. The police seized the car as an instrument used in the commission of a crime. The wife, who was co-owner of the vehicle with her husband, was completely innocent of any criminal activity, yet her property was taken from her. The federal government and most states have since put in place protections for innocent owners, but *Bennis* illustrates one of the key problems that has plagued forfeiture for some time.

Critics further argue that asset forfeiture violates several constitutional provisions. For instance, some have claimed that forfeiture constitutes cruel and unusual punishment. Critics point to *United States v. Bajakajian* (1998) as an egregious example of the government forfeiting property in excess. Hosep Bajakajian was leaving the United States on a trip when he was stopped by U.S. Customs officials. They found $357,144 on his person, which he had failed to claim as required by law. The Customs officials seized his cash and sought forfeiture of the entire amount. The Supreme Court held that the government could not seek forfeiture for failing to declare the money. In other words, the penalty levied on Bajakajian violated the Eighth Amendment.

Critics also claim that forfeiture, especially civil forfeiture, is tantamount to double jeopardy, in violation of the Fifth Amendment. Unfortunately, this argument has not succeeded. The leading case is *United States v. Ursery* (1996). In that case, Guy Ursery was arrested for growing marijuana in his house. He was tried and convicted criminally. In addition to the criminal conviction, civil asset forfeiture proceedings were initiated and his property was seized. The Supreme Court held that even though the civil forfeiture proceedings were the result of the same criminal activity for which a criminal sanction was imposed, civil forfeiture was not a part of the punishment. The Supreme Court also held that civil asset forfeiture is a remedial action against property and therefore does not constitute punishment.

Some support for critics' claims that asset forfeiture violates constitutional rights can be found in *United States v. James Daniel Good Real Property* (1993). In that case, the Supreme Court held that civil asset forfeiture can violate due process when authorities do not give notice of what is happening and fail to provide opportunity for a hearing before the seizure of real property. In contrast, the Supreme Court held in *City of West Covina v. Perkins* (1999) that due process was not violated when the city failed to provide instructions on how those whose property was seized could recover their property; law enforcement need only give notice to property owners that their property has been seized.

Critics also believe that once property is seized, owners' rights are further hampered by the burden of proof required in civil forfeiture proceedings. Some find it surprising that the burden of proof for a successful forfeiture is no more than a preponderance of the evidence. The government's position that this is a proper requirement for civil proceedings is highly criticized because asset forfeiture is often used as a proxy for punishment for those engaged in criminal activity. Critics assert that because of the appearance of punishment, the standard should be the same as for criminal trials. The Supreme Court has recognized the quasi-punitive nature of asset forfeiture—for example, in the case of *One 1958 Plymouth Sedan v. Pennsylvania* (1965). A proposal to have the burden of proof lifted to "clear and convincing" was proposed, but it ultimately failed. Such a low burden of proof continues to leave property owners susceptible.

See Also: 3. Double Jeopardy; 4. Drug Laws; 16. Restorative Justice; 20. Victim Rights and Restitution.

Further Readings

Baicker, Katherine, and Mireille Jacobson. "Finders Keepers: Forfeiture Laws, Policing Incentives, and Local Budgets." *Journal of Public Economics*, v.91 (2007).

Baumer, Eric P. "Evaluating the Balance Sheet of Asset Forfeiture Laws: Toward Evidence-based Policy Assessments." *Criminology and Public Policy*, v.7/2 (2008).

Bishopp, Stephen A., and John L. Worrall. "Do State Asset Forfeiture Laws Explain the Upward Trend in Drug Arrests?" *Journal of Crime and Justice*, v.32/2 (2009).

Blumenson, Eric, and Eva Nilsen. "Policing for Profit: The Drug War's Hidden Economic Agenda." *University of Chicago Law Review*, v.65 (1998).

Clingermayer, J., J. Hecker, and S. Madsen. "Asset Forfeiture and Police Priorities: The Impact of Program Design on Law Enforcement Activities." *Criminal Justice Policy Review*, v.16 (2005).

Ehlers, Scott. *Policy Briefing: Asset Forfeiture.* Washington, DC: Drug Policy Foundation, 1999.

Gardner, Thomas, and Terry Anderson. *Criminal Law.* Belmont, CA: Thomson Wadsworth, 2009.

Greek, Cecil. "A Review of the History of Forfeiture in England and Colonial America." In *Drugs, Crime and Social Policy*, edited by Thomas Mieczkowski. Boston: Allyn and Bacon, 1992.

Hadaway, Brant. "Executive Privateers: A Discussion on Why the Civil Asset forfeiture Reform Act Will Not Significantly Reform the Practice of Forfeiture." *University of Miami Law Review* (October 2000).

Henning, Peter J. "Symposium: Individual Liability for Conduct by Criminal Organizations in the United States." *Wayne Law Review*, v.44 (1998).

Mast, B., B. Benson, and D. Rasmussen. "Entrepreneurial Police and Drug Enforcement Policy." *Public Choice*, v.104/3–4 (2000).

Miller, Mitchell, and Lance Selva. "Drug Enforcement's Double-Edged Sword: An Assessment of Asset Forfeiture Programs." *Justice Quarterly*, v.11/2 (June 1994).

Naylor, R. T. "License to Loot: A Critique of Follow-the-Money Methods in Crime Control Policy." *Social Justice*, v.28/3 (2001).

Newman, J. "Quantifying the Standard of Proof Beyond a Reasonable Doubt: A Comment on Three Comments." *Law, Probability and Risk*, v.9/1 (2006).

Skolnick, Jerome, H. "Policing Should Not Be for Profit." *Criminology and Public Policy*, v.7/2 (2008).

United States Department of Justice, Asset Forfeiture Program. *National Asset Forfeiture Strategic Plan 2008–2012*. Washington, DC: United States Department of Justice, 2008.

Vecchi, Gregory M., and Robert T. Sigler. "Economic Factors in Drug Law Enforcement Decisions." *Policing: An International Journal of Police Strategies and Management*, v.24/3 (2001).

Williams, Howard. *Asset Forfeiture: A Law Enforcement Perspective*. Springfield, IL: Thomas, 2002.

Williams, Marian R. "Civil Asset Forfeiture: Where Does the Money Go?" *Criminal Justice Review*, v.27 (2002).

Worrall, John L. "Addicted to the Drug War: The Role of Civil Asset Forfeiture as a Budgetary Necessity in Contemporary Law Enforcement." *Journal of Criminal Justice*, v.29 (2001).

Worrall, John L. *Asset Forfeiture, Response Guide No. 7*. Madison, WI: Center for Problem-Oriented Policing, 2008.

Worrall, John L. "The Civil Asset Forfeiture Reform Act of 2000: A Sheep in Wolf's Clothing." *Policing: An International Journal of Police Strategies and Management*, v.27/2 (2004).

Worrall, John L., and Tomislav V. Kovandzic. "Is Policing For Profit? Answers From Asset Forfeiture." *Criminology and Public Policy*, v.7/2 (2008).

2

DNA Evidence

Keith Inman
Julie A. Beck
California State University, East Bay

As a new technology in criminal justice, DNA is reforming the criminal justice system, in that it can help solve crimes with unprecedented accuracy. DNA evidence is based on small samples of genetic material from individuals that are collected at the scene of a crime, tested, and stored, and later used as evidence in court. The tremendous value of DNA evidence resides in the confluence of two factors: that violent crime typically results in the shedding of biological material in the form of blood, semen, saliva, small amounts of skin, or hair; and that DNA found in the cells of these samples holds the unique genetic code of the individual to whom it belongs. Once the DNA is analyzed in a crime laboratory, it can be compared to the DNA of any individual, whether a suspect, victim, or witness. If a genetic concordance (the presence of the same trait) is found during this comparison, a strong inference is formed that the person is the donor of the biological material. The term *match* is discouraged, as it is misleading. This evidence aids investigators immeasurably in determining what happened during a violent act, and who was involved in it.

DNA evidence is the most reliable and accurate type of evidence that exists today, far more reliable than other types of evidence such as eyewitness identification and confessions. DNA evidence has helped solve crimes as well as exonerate individuals who have been wrongfully convicted. This last use of DNA is helping to reform the criminal justice system by revealing wrongful convictions due to the unreliability of eyewitness identification, coerced confessions, and other, less discriminating forms of physical evidence. However, using DNA evidence also raises some legal and ethical problems that must be addressed in order to uphold the constitutional rights of both defendants and citizens.

DNA typing in criminal justice emerged from a history of the use of genetic markers as early as 1900; more recently, the admissibility of DNA evidence has created legal and ethic issues, the problem of post-conviction DNA testing, and arguments for and against DNA database expansion as well as the future of DNA research.

History of DNA Typing in Criminal Justice

The value of any genetic-marker system in forensic science is to narrow down the number of potential donors to a biological stain or tissue. The ideal situation is an inference that only one person could be that donor, but no marker—not even DNA—can state with absolute certainty that only one person can be the contributor of a biological material sample.

The use of genetic markers—genetic traits expressed either visibly, such as eye or hair color, or at the molecular level—in forensic science did not begin with DNA; it started with the use of the ABO blood group system as early as 1900 by Karl Landsteiner and Max Richter. Blood groups assisted law enforcement and prosecutors in identifying those involved in violent criminal acts, whether as perpetrators or victims. Finding concordance between a crime scene sample and a particular person's blood type was not particularly discriminating; approximately 50 percent of the population has type O blood, for example. Still, the ability to exclude any number of potential donors by their blood type provided a start to the process of examining biological material in connection with a violent crime.

In the mid-1970s, significant advances were made in developing additional genetic markers that increased the ability to infer the donor of a biological fluid, but the biggest breakthrough came in the mid-1980s, when DNA protocols were developed that excluded almost everyone except the true donor of biological material.

The first DNA technique developed for forensic use, known as RFLP, was highly discriminating; it could narrow down the possible donors of a crime scene stain to just one or a few individuals. However, this method required relatively large amounts of stain or sample for successful typing.

At the same time, researchers were able to perfect a technique that separated sperm DNA from nonsperm DNA, which led to solving sexual assault cases by identifying the semen donor, something that could not previously be achieved. Thus, the first widespread application of DNA typing was used for solving rape and other sexual offenses.

Specialized Processes to Enhance DNA Testing

Subsequent research and validation adapted a Nobel Prize–winning biological technique known as polymerase chain reaction (PCR) to forensic DNA typing. While several genetic marker systems were developed using this method, ultimately, forensic scientists in the United States determined that typing a kind of genetic marker known as a short tandem repeat (STR) provided the best combination of sensitivity, discrimination, and time of analysis. The technique is now capable of successfully typing DNA left from just a few cells, whether from spermatozoa, blood, or skin. This research also resulted in the inclusion of a genetic marker that indicates the gender (male or female) of the individual leaving the sample. Laboratory personnel are now applying DNA typing to a wide variety of problems associated with the successful solution of violent crime, including the typing of weapons, steering wheels, and other items for handler or touch DNA; typing clothing items (such as ski masks used to hide a perpetrator's identity during the commission of a crime) for wearer DNA; along with the more routine typing of blood, semen, and saliva stains left at a crime scene.

In addition to the analysis of normal STR markers, other techniques have been developed that increase the usefulness of DNA typing in special circumstances. In a stain that is a mixture of male and female fluids, some methods can detect DNA only from the male-donated Y chromosome. For example, a male saliva stain mixed with female fluid in an oral copulation case can be typed with this method, known as Y-STR typing. Thus, in cases where the female component would normally mask the male component, Y-STR typing can reveal DNA from just the male donor. Because this type of testing detects DNA from any Y chromosome present, it would not be useful in samples from male-male rapes or assaults that contain mixed fluids from both the victim and perpetrator. There is currently no variation of an STR test that helps detect the female DNA. Because a male has the XY chromosome, he would have the X markers as well, and there would be no similar advantage to having markers on the X chromosome.

For samples that are extremely small or degraded, another type of DNA, inherited only from the mother, can be typed. This DNA is found in the part of a cell known as the mitochondria, and is known as mitochondrial DNA (mtDNA for short). Hair and bones are particularly good candidates for mtDNA analysis, as these biological materials are difficult to type by conventional STR DNA technology. The disadvantage to both Y-STR and mtDNA testing is that they are not as discriminating as normal STR typing, and so are typically used when normal techniques are unlikely to be successful (or have already failed).

Other advances continue in the analysis of old or otherwise limited DNA samples. Improving the STR technology in the aftermath of the September 11, 2001, attacks in New York City allowed for identification of minuscule amounts of badly burned and barely recognizable human remains; this technique has been subsequently used after several natural disasters worldwide to identify human remains.

The Misunderstood Science of DNA Testing

One facet of DNA typing that is frequently overlooked, dismissed, or misunderstood is the population genetics (typically referred to as statistics) aspect of the discipline, in large part because the numerical aspect is intimidating to many people. However, the power and appeal of DNA resides predominately in this area of the field; if every person among millions in the worldwide population had the same DNA, there would be no point in doing the testing, because the likely donor of a sample could not be determined. It is precisely because some statistical significance (or weight) can be applied to the finding of similar types between a crime stain and a specific person that DNA has become such a valuable tool in the administration of criminal justice.

DNA is not capable of indicating that only one individual is the source of a crime sample. Because of that fact, it is critical to use a tool to help determine the significance of the finding of genetic concordance between the crime stain type and the type of the individual (frequently, but not always, the suspect). The statistics given in reports and testimony are provided so that the judge or jury can evaluate the likelihood that the types found in the crime stain are from someone other than the person in question, and that the person has been identified as the donor by chance alone. In other words, what is the probability that the person inferred as the donor of the stain in question is not the true donor, but has been falsely implicated because he (or she) coincidentally has the same type as the actual perpetrator who left the crime scene sample? If the DNA profile in question is very rare, then it is unlikely that someone other than the true donor who has this type would be found, and it is more plausible to accept the inference that the person being typed is indeed the true donor of the crime sample. DNA statistics express this probability in some form or another, and assist in deciding the strength of the proposition that the person being typed is the true donor of the sample.

A significant part of the evolution of DNA typing, in the laboratory as well as in the courts, has involved the development of statistical methods for expressing this probability. Current discussion and development is now centered on understanding the appropriate statistics to use in complex mixtures, low levels of DNA where only partial profiles are found, and what statistics to use when a suspect is identified as the result of the search of a DNA database. One important aspect to understand is that most statistics are given for people who are unrelated; but genetically, the people most likely to share the same types are siblings. Thus, the best alternate suspect in any DNA case is a brother or sister (depending on the gender of the person leaving the crime sample).

DNA Storage

One advantage to typing the DNA present in biological samples is the stability of the DNA molecule. Once dry, the DNA in biological material is stable for decades, if not for hundreds of years. This has allowed the analysis and solution of cold cases that may be 30–50 years old. While technical challenges clearly exist in the analysis of this evidence, and not all such evidence is successfully typed, the payoff in terms of solving cases is worth the extra effort to produce a useful DNA profile. Reviewing and determining whether biological evidence exists in an old case is therefore also a worthwhile effort.

One byproduct of typing evidence in cases predating DNA is the very real possibility of contamination from previous collection and preservation efforts. Prior to DNA analysis, there was little concern of contaminating a crime scene sample with genetic material from scene technicians and detectives, and some samples were handled without the rigorous use of gloves (as they are today). The exquisite sensitivity of DNA requires such careful handling of physical evidence that, not infrequently, DNA profiles developed from old cases turns out to be the profile of a previous technician or analyst.

The standard practice for storing DNA evidence is to ensure that the sample is dry; thereafter, the preferred storage is at freezer temperatures.

Developing Felon Databases of DNA

It was recognized at a very early stage in the development of DNA technology for criminal justice purposes that a repository of DNA types from specific individuals could be compared against DNA developed from crime scenes, providing a new and powerful tool for solving both old and current crimes. This led to federal legislation, as well as statutes passed in every state, enabling such a DNA repository. Known generically as the DNA database, it consists of two equally important parts: a collection of DNA from individuals (typically convicted felons, but in some jurisdictions even those who are merely arrested and charged with a felony), and a collection of DNA produced from crime samples. The DNA from the crime samples is searched against the profiles from the known individuals; if a similarity is found between the sample and a felon, a cold hit is declared, and the individual is then the subject of further investigation for his or her role in the crime. The name of this national database is the National DNA Index System (NDIS), while the overall name for the combined local, state, and federal database is the Combined DNA Index System (CODIS). As of December 2009, it contained over 7,743,329 offender profiles and 298,369 forensic profiles, and has produced over 103,700 hits assisting in more than 101,700 investigations. CODIS's primary means of measuring effectiveness, Investigations Aided, tracks the number of criminal investigations where CODIS has added value to the investigative process.

Over one-third of the crime scene samples submitted to CODIS results in a cold hit. The success is predicated on the observation that relatively few individuals commit the bulk of the crimes. Thus, typing those few individuals should result in the solution of a disproportionate number of crimes, and that seems to be supported by this data.

Conducting a Mass Screening of Ordinary Citizens

Frequently, a search of the database does not result in a cold hit. On rare occasions, when the detective believes that the perpetrator of a crime must be a local citizen or employed at a specific worksite, samples will be requested from these individuals. These samples will be screened and compared to the crime sample; if the true perpetrator has provided a sample, this screening should reveal his identity. Conversely, if an individual refuses to provide a sample, this typically arouses suspicion, and the individual may be investigated anyway.

Such mass screenings of citizens who are not convicted felons or arrestees are unusual in the United States; this process has its origin in the United Kingdom. In fact, the very first use of DNA in a criminal investigation occurred in England, when a mass screening was used by police. The true perpetrator convinced a friend to give a sample in his behalf, but feeling uncomfortable with the request, the friend reported it to the police. A subsequent investigation produced a confession. This was also the first time that DNA was used to exonerate a suspect; another individual had confessed to the crime, but the DNA demonstrated that he was not, in fact, the perpetrator. In addition, in one of Germany's largest mass screenings, 16,400 people were tested in northern Germany for a rape-and-murder case, which resulted in a mechanic being matched with the DNA left behind at the crime scene.

Admissibility of DNA Evidence: History and New Tests

The first few DNA cases in the United States were analyzed by private companies, and little opposition was offered by defense counsel to its admission. That changed when the state of New York prosecuted Joseph Castro for the murder of a young woman and her child. At issue was blood found on Castro's watch. A private firm had performed the analysis and provided a statistic for false inclusion, which the prosecution wanted to present to the jury. The defense objected to its introduction, and a legal admissibility hearing was held. The scientific basis of DNA applied to crime samples, the rigor of the testing by the laboratory, and the statistics offered were challenged by the defense. The judge ruled to exclude the DNA evidence, which set off a series of legal challenges across the country. The scientific basis of DNA testing was rather quickly accepted by most courts, in large part because of the changes in laboratory rigor induced by the Castro ruling, but challenges to the statistical evaluation of DNA evidence persisted for almost a decade. While the statistical evaluation of single-source (one person) samples is accepted in all U.S. courts, challenges are periodically raised for mixed and low-level samples, as well as for the statistic to be used when the suspect is identified through a cold hit in the CODIS database.

Current Legal and Ethical Issues

Problems and questions regarding DNA evidence include individual rights and privacy rights, including those of felons; admissibility of DNA evidence in courts; access to DNA testing post-conviction; use of DNA databases; whose DNA should be in databases; and government surveillance.

Who Should Be in the Database?

Each U.S. state passes legislation enabling the collection of DNA from specific individuals. The criteria for inclusion is typically conviction for a qualifying (serious) felony, but some jurisdictions are expanding the criteria to include those merely arrested and charged with a qualifying felony. In addition, judges sometimes will order an offender included in the DNA database as a condition of probation, even if the underlying conviction is not a qualifying offense.

Other nations around the world are sampling large percentages of their population. England's DNA database contains over five million profiles, which amounts to 10 percent or more of the population. This compares to about 2.5 percent of the U.S. population. The criteria for inclusion is also more lax than in the United States; in England, anyone arrested (and not necessarily charged) is eligible for inclusion in the database.

Ultimately, the decision as to who goes into the database resides with legislative bodies; if elected officials believe that including large percentages of the population in the database will help solve crime, then criteria for inclusion will reflect that belief. Data emerging from research shows, however, that placing more individuals in the database does not solve progressively more crime, and the cost of sampling and typing millions of people may offset the social benefit of crimes solved by cold hits. The debate on this issue may become more heated in the next several years.

Database and Familial Searches

Some statisticians and population geneticists argue that choosing a suspect from a closed population (those in a database) via a cold hit dictates that a different kind of statistic be used to assess the likelihood of a false match. Most, however, believe that no special accommodation is required, since it would be necessary to have similarly excluded millions of other individuals in the same search; the profile did not hit any other felon in the database. This issue has the potential to result in further admissibility hearings, but is unlikely to be successful in challenging the statistics currently offered.

Individuals most likely to share similar (though usually not exact) genetic information are those most closely related, particularly full siblings. Not only does this mean that a sibling is the next best alternate suspect, it also means that if a suspect is not perfectly concordant with the crime sample, but is very close, then it is likely that a relative is the true donor of the sample in question. One case in particular demonstrates this idea. A woman reported being raped by two men. DNA analysis demonstrated not only the presence of two men, but also that they shared a large number of types, suggesting that they were related. Subsequent investigation revealed that the suspect in custody had a brother, and typing of his sample, along with the original suspect, showed that the crime sample contained a composite profile from the brothers.

Extending this concept further to database considerations, it is possible to search a crime sample in the felon database and look not only for perfect matches, but failing that, to look for close matches. If a felon is a close, but not perfect, match to the crime sample, then the odds are high that a close relative is the donor of the sample. Detectives might investigate the family of the convicted felon and determine whether any of them are viable suspects in their case, and perhaps ask for, or apply for a court order demanding, a DNA sample from this new suspect.

The question arises as to what rights both the government and the individual have in this circumstance. If an individual is not in the database, does the government have the right to make him a suspect because his brother is in the database? This is still an emerging issue, not settled either legislatively or by the courts.

Touch/Transfer/Low-Level DNA Samples

With the development of sensitive techniques for the analysis of DNA, analysts have found that while they can examine very low levels of DNA, they are not always successful at obtaining complete results from such an item, leading to partial results. Occasionally some, but not all, of the suspect's types are present in a sample. The best solutions are statistical, but the statistics and required data are complex, still under development, difficult to understand and communicate, and controversial even among analysts.

Another issue concerns relating DNA left by mere touching to the commission of a violent crime. Because humans are constantly leaving behind DNA by a variety of mechanisms, which are still poorly understood, the mere finding of DNA on objects such as knives and guns does not automatically implicate the person whose DNA is found as the perpetrator of the crime. In fact, the small amount of research currently available even suggests that the person last touching an object may not be detectable on the item. Thus, a knife found at a crime scene that was used to stab someone may not contain the DNA of the stabber on the handle of the knife.

Post-Conviction Testing: Access and Timeliness

The first use of DNA to demonstrate that a suspect was wrongly accused occurred in England, but the first post-conviction demonstration of innocence occurred in the United States, when Gary Dodson was shown not to be the semen donor in a rape for which he was convicted. However, the DNA technique used to demonstrate this was so new that neither the judge in the case nor the governor of the state believed the results, and refused to release or pardon Dodson.

This demonstrated the power of DNA to establish the actual innocence of individuals, and the same attorneys who challenged the DNA testing in the Joseph Castro case recognized the value of the technique for excluding individuals as DNA donors in cases where biological evidence existed. Believing that numerous individuals might have been wrongfully convicted, Barry Scheck and Peter Neufeld, founders of the Innocence Project, a national organization offering legal assistance to prisoners who could be exonerated through DNA testing, fought to have such evidence examined to establish the innocence of those individuals. Through a careful screening process, they pursue cases that appear to have wrongful convictions, search for physical evidence in those cases, and where it exists, have that evidence tested for DNA. As of February 2010, over 250 individuals had been exonerated across the country through the application of DNA testing, 17 of whom were on death row.

Most observers within and outside of the criminal justice system continue to be surprised at these numbers. Many point out that these are cases where biological physical evidence exists for testing, and the same wrongful conviction rate cannot extend to those cases for which physical evidence does not exist. Others postulate that the wrongful conviction rate might be as high as 1–3 percent.

Further evaluation of the reasons for wrongful conviction in these cases strongly implicates, singly or in combination, the unreliability of eyewitness identification, false confessions, invalidated or improperly performed forensic examinations, misconduct, informants, and poor representation.

The introduction of DNA testing has provided independent data for evaluating the effectiveness of the administration of criminal justice. One example from among the over 250 individuals exonerated through post-conviction DNA testing is the 1989 case of Christopher Ochoa, who at age 23 was arrested and coerced by police investigators into confessing to a rape and murder he did not commit. Ochoa spent 12 years in prison before he was exonerated with the help of the Innocence Project. Similarly, Beverly Monroe, a scientist and mother, was wrongly convicted of the murder of her longtime boyfriend in 1993. She spent 11 years in jail and prison combined before being exonerated through DNA evidence; it was revealed that her boyfriend had committed suicide.

Despite its successes, significant obstacles to post-conviction testing remain in the criminal justice system, and in some instances the validity of DNA evidence is still challenged in court. While DNA is readily admitted in criminal trials today, and errors in detecting matches using DNA evidence are rare for single-source samples, lawyers and experts may still try to refute the validity of DNA evidence in court for samples with low levels of DNA, mixed samples, and defendants found through a database search. Prosecutors of cases where defendants claimed they were wrongfully convicted sometimes concede upon retrial that while there may not be a DNA match to the defendant, the defendant may still be guilty because he or she may have been present at the crime scene as a codefendant—that is, they claim there may have been two perpetrators at the crime scene, with only one of them leaving their DNA behind. In other cases, the defense may not be given access to DNA evidence because prosecutors may illegally have withheld DNA evidence.

Additionally, although 40 states allow post-conviction DNA testing when requested by an inmate, thousands of convicted felons who claim they are innocent still await DNA testing of their cases. Moreover, many of these laws are limited in scope. Obstacles to testing include requirements in some states that another individual be implicated before access to post-conviction DNA testing is allowed, or not permitting access to DNA testing if the defendant pled guilty at the first trial. In addition, in some states, inmates languish in prison for years, even decades, after they have filed a petition for DNA testing, due to lack of swift or fair proceedings regarding these petitions.

Reforms have been proposed by advocates of post-conviction DNA testing. A national commission on DNA testing has proposed allowing universal access to post-conviction DNA testing where it can establish innocence. Additional reforms proposed by the Innocence Project include eradicating procedural limitations, including ending statutory deadlines for post-conviction testing access, providing adequate funding to facilitate post-conviction DNA testing, and requiring states to better preserve and become more accountable for biological evidence.

A central question in the U.S. debate over DNA databases concerns whether or not, and how far, they should be expanded. Should these databases include, in addition to convicted felons, all arrestees—or even all U.S. citizens? The tension concerns the balance between the benefits for law enforcement that expansion of DNA databases could produce, and the protection of individual rights and privacy. Proponents of expansion seek to solve more violent crime cases more efficiently, while opponents of expansion seek to safeguard constitutional and civil rights. The latter ask how expanding DNA databases might intrude on individual rights and privacy, and potentially expose individuals to new forms of governmental and corporate surveillance and control.

Pro: Support for Expanding DNA Databases

Law enforcement and other advocates of expanding DNA databases, such as citizen and victims' rights groups, argue that expansion of DNA databases will greatly aid law enforcement officials in solving crimes. Currently, felon DNA databases limit so-called matches to only known felons convicted of specific qualifying offenses; the perpetrator of a crime, however, may not have any prior convictions, and thus no match will be found in the felon database. Advocates argue that including DNA samples from an expanded list of qualifying offenses, or from all arrestees, will help to exclude suspects early on, and it would also save money and time.

Advocates of expanding DNA databases also point out that DNA evidence is being used more often in rape cases today than previously, and can solve very old unsolved rape and murder cases. The successful DNA typing of these very old samples has resulted in a change in the statute of limitations in rape cases. Every state has reacted differently to this issue, but for most states, older cases ultimately solved by DNA testing can now be charged and prosecuted. In some cases, the DNA profile itself can be charged with the crime, tolling the statute of limitations. When the profile is subsequently matched to the name of an individual (for example, through a database search) and that individual is apprehended, prosecution can proceed. In addition, long-unsolved cases involving DNA evidence frequently end in pleas or convictions. In one case, two years after a Virginia family's 22-year-old daughter was raped and murdered, the killer was identified from a DNA cold hit made after state law required him to give a DNA sample upon conviction for a subsequent rape and abduction. Some advocates of the expansion of databases also claim that, in general, DNA evidence may lead to longer sentences because of the greater assurance of guilt typically ascribed to DNA evidence.

In Europe as well as the United States, some public health experts and organizations have suggested creating a DNA profile of every infant at birth, and some criminal justice policymakers have supported this idea with the intention of assisting in future criminal identification. Proponents argue that such a database would render DNA as a stronger crime deterrent precisely because it would not be limited to known felons and suspects. Others support expanding DNA databases to include arrestees to reduce the need for post-conviction testing: they claim that including arrestees would narrow down and eliminate suspects early on in the investigative process. Still other proponents claim that DNA databases containing samples from all citizens could eliminate the danger of racial discrimination, as there have been cases in the United States where DNA screenings have focused on certain ethnic groups. Finally, some proponents of expanding DNA databases argue that there would be no real risks of invading an individual's privacy because the innocent should have nothing to hide, while those who are guilty would be quickly identified.

Con: Opposition to Expanding DNA Databases

Those who caution against and oppose the expansion of DNA databases, on the other hand, argue that expansion poses a grave threat to individual rights and privacy. DNA collection has steadily expanded; the first samples included in DNA databases were collected only from convicted sex offenders, not from all convicted felons. Some states, including California, now require police to take DNA samples from all people arrested for a felony (and even some misdemeanors), even though they have not been convicted of any crime. In addition, while mass screening is less common in the United States than in Europe, there have been several larger-scale screenings of ordinary U.S. citizens that have invoked controversy. Civil liberties advocates, such as the American Civil Liberties Union (ACLU), caution that these screening practices go too far and violate citizens' rights to privacy.

Critics argue that certain forms of DNA sampling undermine the presumption of innocence, the basis of the U.S. legal system. Cold hits are random; they do not require that law enforcement officials have any particular suspect in mind. Seeking cold hits in felon databases, and in particular of arrestees, does not necessitate the existence of probable cause to believe that any of the individuals in the database have committed the crime in question. Rather, critics claim, one's mere status as a felon or arrestee becomes the justification for investigating him or her through a cold hit. Running a cold hit on arrestees in particular, argue opponents of expanding DNA databases, undermines the Fourth Amendment protections against unreasonable search and seizure and Fifth Amendment protections against self-incrimination, for arrest does not equal guilt.

DNA Dragnets

Moreover, critics argue that large-scale DNA screenings (sometimes called "DNA dragnets" by critics) also violate Fourth Amendment protections, as they tend to pull many innocent people into its net in search of the guilty few. Mass DNA screenings turn innocent citizens into crime suspects. For example, if a citizen refuses to give a DNA sample, he may experience pressure to nonetheless provide one, lest he engender suspicion and be viewed as a suspect. In Baton Rouge, Louisiana, 1,200 men were asked by police to give saliva for testing in response to the serial murder of four women in 2002. When one citizen refused to give his saliva, claiming that the request was unnecessary because he could prove he was not in the vicinity at the time and the footprint left behind by the suspect was much bigger than his own, he was met with media attention and a court order; the ensuing DNA test resulted in his being excluded as a suspect.

Racial profiling can also enter into mass screening, critics claim. For example, in a 1994 rape case in Michigan where a black man was the suspect in a mostly white community, investigators took 160 samples from African American men. This amounts to a search of their genetic property, and raises the question as to whether such a search is subject to Fourth Amendment protection. An outcry from the black community followed in that African Americans felt they were being randomly singled out. The rapist was only caught when a cab driver noticed blood on his clothes.

Opponents of expanding DNA databases are also concerned with how long the DNA of arrestees who are not convicted or not prosecuted, and those who are acquitted, should be stored. In the Louisiana DNA dragnet case, no matching profiles were found; however, police did not destroy the DNA samples. Instead, they were entered into the state's criminal database, which prompted a lawsuit by citizens.

Other arguments against expanding DNA databases are more pragmatic in nature: Opponents point out that a backlog already exists of hundreds of thousands of DNA samples from crime scenes that have been collected but not yet processed or analyzed. Some research has also indicated the phenomenon of diminishing returns; the cost of entering more individuals into the database does not result in a concomitant escalation in the number of crimes solved.

Finally, civil liberties advocates warn of the potential for expanding DNA databases to include all U.S. citizens at birth. A single sample of DNA contains all of the genetic information about a person, including genes for mental illness, physical disease, and intelligence, among others, and opponents caution that this genetic information could be misused. Significant potential exists, civil liberties advocates claim, for developing and sharing of this biological information, which can lead to "genetic discrimination" by those with power. For example, insurance companies could discriminate regarding health coverage, and employers could discriminate based on information they have about an employee or applicants' character traits, intelligence, or propensity for genetic disease. The potential also exists for increased government surveillance, critics warn: In the wrong hands, genetic information could lead to eugenic state policies such as government-run sterilization programs.

To sum up, the issue of expanding DNA databases raises public safety issues on one hand, and ethical and constitutional questions on the other hand. While proponents of expanding DNA databases claim that it would greatly aid law enforcement in solving violent crime, opponents argue that continued expansion of DNA databases and of screened populations threatens the individual rights and privacy not only of convicted felons and arrestees, but potentially of all citizens.

Future of DNA Evidence and New Scientific Techniques

The reluctance of courts to accept new scientific evidence, coupled with the current capabilities of DNA technology, militates against significant advances in forensic DNA typing. It will soon be possible to sequence a person's entire genome for a very small sum and from a very small sample, and this capability would all but negate arguments that "my brother did it." Nevertheless, the current collection of circumstances will retard the introduction of this testing.

Advances are required in parsing mixtures, and researching the meaning of finding someone's DNA by mere handling. Investigators are submitting items linked to a crime's perpetrator in some way, such as a hat left at a scene or a knife found near a body, and asking that the item be processed for wearer or handler DNA. This frequently results in finding DNA from multiple individuals, and the question arises as to how many contributors are present, whether a specific individual is a potential contributor, and whether all of the DNA types of the wearer/handler are present. These are significant hurdles in assigning the proper weight to give the DNA evidence, which will require much more research than currently exists.

See Also: 6. Exclusionary Rules; 8. Eyewitness Testimony and Accuracy; 11. Jury System.

Further Readings

Akane, A., et al. "Sex Determination of Forensic Samples by Dual PCR Amplification of an X-Y Homologous Gene." *Forensic Science International*, v.52/2 (1992).

Alberts, B. *Molecular Biology of the Cell.* New York: Garland Publishing, 1999.

Anderson, S., et al. "Sequence and Organization of the Human Mitochondrial Genome." *Nature*, v.290 (1981).

Baasner A., et al. "Polymorphic Sites in Human Mitochondrial DNA Control Region Sequences: Population Data and Maternal Inheritance." *Forensic Science International*, v.98/3 (1998).

Bar, W., et al. "DNA Commission of the International Society for Forensic Genetics: Guidelines for Mitochondrial DNA Typing." *International Journal of Legal Medicine*, v.113/2 (2000).

Blake, E., et al. "Polymerase Chain Reaction (PCR) Amplification and Human Leukocyte Antigen (HLA)-DQ Alpha Oligonucleotide Typing on Biological Evidence Samples: Casework Experience." *Journal of Forensic Science*, v.37/3 (1992).

Budowle, B., and Sprecher, C. J. "Concordance Study on Population Database Samples Using the Powerplex™ 16 Kit and Ampflstr® Profiler Plus™ Kit and Ampflstr® Cofiler™ Kit." *Journal of Forensic Science*, v.46/3 (2001).

Culliford, B. J. *The Examination and Typing of Blood Stains in the Crime Laboratory.* Washington, DC: U.S. Government Printing Office, 1971.

DNA Identification Act of 1994 (the Act). Public Law 103-322.

Erlich, H. A., et al. "Recent Advances in the Polymerase Chain Reaction." *Science*, v.252 (1991).

Farnsworth, C. H. "Queensville Journal; Jailed in Killing, He's Guilty Only of Being a Misfit. " *New York Times*, v.144 (April 11,1995).

Federal Bureau of Investigation. "NDIS Standards for the Acceptance of DNA Data." (January 4, 1999). http://www.ncjrs.org/pdffiles1/nij/sl413apb.pdf (Accessed October 2010).

Foderaro, L. W. "DNA Frees Convicted Rapist After 9 Years Behind Bars." *New York Times,* v.140 (August 1, 1991).

Gellman, B. "DNA Test Clears Man Convicted of SE Rape." *Washington Post*, v.113 (March 20, 1990).

Gill, P., et al. "Automated Short Tandem Repeat (STR) Analysis in Forensic Casework—A Strategy for the Future." *Electrophoresis*, v.16/9 (1995).

Glaberson, W. "Rematch for DNA in a Rape Case." *New York Times*, v.145 (April 10, 1996).

Griffiths, A. J. F., J. H. Miller, D. T. Suzuki, R. C. Lewontin, and W. M. Gelbart. *An Introduction to Genetic Analysis.* New York: W. H. Freeman and Co., 1993.

Hartl, D. L., and A. G. Clark. *Principles of Population Genetics.* Sunderland, MA: Sinauer Associates, 1997.

Holland, M. M., et al. "Short Tandem Repeat Loci: Application to Forensic and Human Remains Identification." *Exs*, v.67 (1993).

Hua, Thao, H. G. Reza, and Lee Romney. "New Suspect Charged as Man Held 17 Years Is Freed." *Los Angeles Times,* v.115 (June 22, 1996).

Innocence Project. http://www.innocenceproject.org (Accessed October 2010).

Jeffreys, A. J., et al. "Individual Specific 'Fingerprints' of Human DNA." *Nature*, v.316 (1985).

Kennedy, J. M. "DNA Test Clears Man Convicted of Rape." *Los Angeles Times,* v.113, (January 16, 1994).

Kolata, G. "DNA Tests Are Unlocking Prison Cell Doors." *New York Times*, v.143 (August 5, 1994).

Kunkel, T. "Reasonable Doubt? Witnesses Say Ed Honaker's a Rapist. His Genes Say He's Not. A Forensic Whodunit." *Washington Post*, v.117 (1994).

Lander, E. S., and B. Budowle. "DNA Fingerprinting Dispute Laid to Rest." *Nature*, v.371 (1994).

Lewin, B. *Genes VII*. New York: Oxford University Press, 1999.

Linch, C. A., et al. "Human Hair Histogenesis for the Motochondrial DNA Forensic Scientist." *Journal of Forensic Science*, v.46/4 (2001).

Lodish, H. *Molecular Cell Biology*. New York: W. H. Freeman, 1999.

Montgomery, D. "Prisoners Play the DNA Card for High Stakes." *Washington Post*, v.116 (July 4, 1993).

Mullis, K. B., and F. Faloona. "Specific Synthesis of DNA *In Vitro* Via a Polymerase Catalyzed Chain Reaction." *Methods in Enzymology*, v.155 (1987).

Naito, E., et al. "Sex Typing of Forensic DNA Samples Using Male- And Female-Specific Probes." *Journal of Forensic Science*, v.39/4 (1994).

National Research Council. *DNA Technology in Forensic Science*. Washington, DC: National Academy Press, 1992.

New York Times. "DNA Clears a Man Convicted of Rapes." *New York Times*, v.144 (July 2, 1995).

New York Times. "DNA Testing Frees a Long-Jailed Man." *New York Times*, v.144 (October 22, 1994).

New York Times. "DNA Testing Frees Man Jailed in Rape." *New York Times*, v.142 (April 25, 1993).

New York Times. "Genetic Testing Fails to Prove a Rape Case." *New York Times*, v.137 (April 8, 1988).

Stolberg, S. "DNA Tests Clear Man Charged in Rapes." *Los Angeles Times*, v.111 (1992).

Sullivan, R. "Semen Wasn't Defendants,' FBI Expert Testifies at Jogger Trial." *New York Times*, v.139 (1990).

U.S. Congress, Office of Technology Assessment. *Genetic Witness: Forensic Uses of DNA Tests, OTABA-438*. Washington, DC: U.S. Government Printing Office, 1990.

Valentine, P. W. "Jailed for Murder, Freed by DNA." *Washington Post*, v.116 (June 29, 1993).

Vollen, L., and Eggers, D. *Surviving Justice: America's Wrongfully Convicted and Exonerated*. San Francisco: McSweeney's, 2005.

Watson, J. D., et al. *Molecular Biology of the Gene*. Menlo Park, CA: Benjamin/Cummings, 1987.

3

Double Jeopardy

Paul D. Steele
Morehead State University

The double jeopardy rule prohibits being tried in federal or state court more than once for the same criminal offense. The Double Jeopardy Clause of the Fifth Amendment to the Constitution states that: "… nor shall any person be subject for the same offense to be twice put in jeopardy of life or limb …" In practice, it can be used as a procedural defense in that the defendant may plead that they have previously been acquitted or convicted for the same offense. This is a matter that is usually raised and resolved prior to a trial, a rare exception to the general rule prohibiting appeals from nonfinal orders. If the defendant is able to produce evidence substantiating the assertion of double jeopardy, the court may not allow the trial to proceed.

Double jeopardy is an ancient and seemingly simple doctrine in the law that enjoys widespread public support. Contemporary legal scholars and decision makers consider the protection against double jeopardy to be a fundamental aspect of the relationship between citizens and their government. While the doctrine itself seems straightforward, its interpretation has generated controversy and misunderstanding. Some of this can be attributed to the evolution of the double jeopardy doctrine and to historical shifts in its application. Other disagreements have emerged concerning the application of its cornerstone elements and granting of exceptions to the doctrine. Some legal scholars have concluded that the controversy is grounded in basic differences among members of the U.S. Supreme Court concerning the fundamental intent of the double jeopardy doctrine itself. As a consequence, members of the Court and other legal experts find it difficult to agree in the interpretation and application of key terms such as *acquittal, multiple punishments,* and *same offense.* Even the concept of what constitutes jeopardy is open to interpretation.

History of the Double Jeopardy Rule

The guarantee against double jeopardy can be traced to Greek and Roman times, eventually becoming established in the common law of England. Lord Coke's interpretation of English law in the 17th century served to standardize the definition of double jeopardy as a combination of three common-law pleas: *autrefois acquit, autrefois convict,* and pardon. Any of these pleas were sufficient to bar the retrial of the defendant for the same crime (*United States v. Wilson,* 1975). In his 1772 *Commentaries,* Blackstone originated the use of the term *jeopardy* in describing the principle that one should not be brought into jeopardy of his life more than once for the same offense.

The Massachusetts Colony Constitution was the first colonial charter that guaranteed protection against double jeopardy in its Declaration of Rights. When the U.S. Constitution was ratified in 1787, it did not include a similar declaration. This was rectified by the inclusion of the Bill of Rights in the first 10 amendments to the Constitution. It was James Madison's intention that a constitutional amendment should be included preventing the government from abusing guarantees against double jeopardy. While the final language included in the Fifth Amendment suggests offenses punishable in a corporal manner (i.e., "jeopardy of life or limb"), it has been interpreted to extend protection to all criminal acts. Since the inclusion of the Double Jeopardy Clause in the Constitution, the Supreme Court has attempted to define the specific intentions of those involved in its drafting. At various times, the Court has concluded that its purpose is to prevent the government from wearing down and falsely convicting innocent citizens; prevent the negative financial, emotional, and social consequences of repeated prosecutions; preserve the integrity of final criminal case decisions; restrict prosecutorial discretion in the charging process; and eliminate judicial discretion to impose multiple punishments for the same offense.

When the Bill of Rights was ratified in 1791, double jeopardy guarantees were expressly provided in only two of the 13 states. In fact, for most of the nation's history, the Double Jeopardy Clause has only restricted criminal proceedings in federal courts. As late as 1937, in *Palko v. Con-*

necticut, the Supreme Court rejected an argument that the Fourteenth Amendment extended all of the procedural guarantees found in the first eight amendments to the states. In the majority opinion, Justice Cardozo asserted that while some guarantees in the Bill of Rights formed the basis of liberty, the Double Jeopardy Clause was not counted among these fundamental rights. By 1969, the U.S. Supreme Court reversed its position, concluding in *Benton v. Maryland* that the double jeopardy prohibition is a fundamental right, and therefore extended to criminal proceedings in the states under the Due Process Clause of the Fourteenth Amendment. An unintended consequence of *Benton* was a dramatic increase in the number of U.S. Supreme Court reviews of double jeopardy laws and their application, particularly in the 1970s.

The Attachment of Jeopardy

Central to consideration of the Double Jeopardy Clause is the moment when jeopardy attaches in a criminal proceeding. If jeopardy has been attached, through the final disposition of the case by acquittal or conviction (or in some instances of justified termination without a final order), the government is prohibited from conducting subsequent criminal proceedings. However, if jeopardy has not attached, the government is not barred from starting a new criminal proceeding against the defendant. In practice, jeopardy attaches when a criminal trial has commenced before a competent court. In a jury trial, this occurs when the jury is impaneled and sworn. In a bench trial, jeopardy is attached when the court begins to hear evidence, that is, when the first witness is sworn.

Most states have implemented two-tier trial systems. In these systems, criminal defendants can choose an initial (first-tier) bench trial and, if they are satisfied with the process and outcome, the order of the court is considered final. However, if the defendant is not satisfied with the initial outcome, they can demand a jury trial without claiming that there was an error in the bench trial. The Supreme Court held in *Justices of Boston Municipal Court v. Lydon* (1984) that a retrial after the first-tier trial does not constitute a violation of the Double Jeopardy Clause, even if the second-tier trial results in greater punishment for the defendant, as held in *Colten v. Kentucky* (1972). The Court has acknowledged the significant benefits of the two-tier system for both the state and the defendant, and based their decisions on the concept of continuing jeopardy, that is, where criminal proceedings against the accused have not run their full course. The full course of a criminal proceeding occurs when a defendant is acquitted, accepts their conviction as final, or has exhausted their methods of appeal. Since defendants can make a voluntary choice to participate in a second-tier trial, the jeopardy originally attached in the first-tier trial has not been finalized, but is continued into the second-tier trial, and thus the two-tier system does not violate the Constitution's Double Jeopardy Clause.

Same Offense

The Double Jeopardy Clause expressly prohibits re-prosecution for the same offense. But when can a defendant successfully claim that an offense for which they have been acquitted or convicted is the same? For many years, the Supreme Court followed Blackstone's guideline that two different offenses were the "same" if one is necessarily included in the other. As Blackstone noted in his *Commentaries*, a conviction of manslaughter precludes a later trial for murder because manslaughter is an offense necessarily included in murder. This approach served well into the 20th century, but with the proliferation of overlapping criminal statutes, it has become increasingly difficult to apply Blackstone's guideline. As a remedy for this concern, the Supreme Court constructed a test for same offense in *Blockburger v. United States* (1932). The Court asserted that when the same criminal conduct violates more than one statute, offenses are different if each requires proof of an element (i.e., defendant's mental state, the prohibited action, and/or lack of legal justification) that the other does not. If each requires proof of an element the other does not, then neither can be included within the other.

Using the Blockburger test, there is little controversy about a crime episode that includes the commission of two separate legal offenses involving separate legal elements, such as in the instance of an armed robbery that results in the murder of the victim. Since the armed robbery and murder are not the same prohibited action, a prior conviction for the armed robbery in this crime episode will not bar prosecution in a subsequent murder trial. Also, the Double Jeopardy Clause cannot be invoked if the offender breaks the same law twice; the "same offense" is not defined as a legal category of crime, but rather as the same behavior. The robber, for example, can be tried on multiple occasions for different robberies if they are separate and unrelated.

The question of how closely related the events need to be before the prohibition against double jeopardy can apply is open to discussion, and has been applied inconsistently. For example, in the case of the illegal sale of controlled prescription drugs, the sale of 50 pills is considered a single offense.

The defendant cannot face 50 separate prosecutions for the sale of controlled substances if the sale occurred in a single transaction. On the other hand, if the defendant sold 20 pills in one transaction and then immediately sold an additional 30 pills to the buyer in a separate transaction, prior prosecution on the first transaction may not bar prosecution of the second.

The case of *Ashe v. Swenson* (1970) is helpful in defining "same offense." In this case, six men were playing poker when three or four armed men broke into the room and robbed the poker players. Ashe, one of the men accused of robbery, was charged with robbing Knight, one of the players. While it was clear in court that a robbery occurred, the evidence identifying Ashe as one of the robbers was weak. Ashe was acquitted because of insufficient evidence. Six weeks later, Ashe was again brought to trial for robbing Roberts, another player. Ashe's motion to dismiss the prosecution based on his previous acquittal was denied, and he was convicted after the prosecutor strengthened the identification evidence. The state appellate courts upheld the conviction, but it was overturned in the Supreme Court. The Court made two points in Ashe and similar cases. First, a crime that involves multiple victims can be considered to be a single offense, so trying a suspect for separate violations against each victim is a violation of the Double Jeopardy Clause. Second, since Ashe had been found to not be among the group who robbed Knight in the first trial, he could not possibly have been found guilty of robbing Roberts in the second trial. *Ashe v. Swenson* is a classic example of how the civil law concept of collateral estoppel has been extended into criminal court considerations of double jeopardy.

Exceptions to the Double Jeopardy Clause

There are a number of exceptions to the Double Jeopardy Clause that have emerged through its application and interpretation by the Supreme Court. Some significant examples are related to consideration of separate sovereignties, the termination of cases without acquittal or conviction, and the government's right to appeal final case outcomes.

Separate Sovereignties

A consequence of the federalist style of government is the division of authority between local, tribal, state, and national governments. Each one has its own legal jurisdiction in that each has a legitimate range of power and authority. The individual, however, is subject to the authority of all of these governments. The Constitution recognizes the separate sovereignty of federal and state governments, by indicating that governmental powers are delegated; some exclusively to the federal government, such as the authority to make war, and some concurrently to both federal and states governments, such as the authority to tax citizens and corporations.

Federalist governmental structures present challenges for double jeopardy in same-offense and multiple-punishments considerations. While the Double Jeopardy Clause prohibits being retried for the same offense, it is common for multiple governments to have jurisdiction over the same criminal offense or episode. The Supreme Court has repeatedly held that successive prosecutions involving that same alleged criminal conduct is not a violation of the Double Jeopardy Clause if the cases are brought by separate and distinct sovereignties, each of which have an independent interest in punishing the alleged criminal behavior. The Court has concluded that two offenses have occurred, each under that law of the two government entities, so the prohibition against double jeopardy for the same offense has not been breached.

The separate sovereignties exception is limited to governments that are in fact separate and distinct from each other. So, for example, the Court has determined that states and their subdivisions are distinct from the federal government (*Bartkus v. Illinois, 1959)*, but states and their municipalities are not distinct from each other (*Abbate v. United States,* 1959). Federal and tribal governments have also been determined to be separate and distinct (*Wheeler v. United States,* 1978), as are states from each other (*Heath v. Alabama,* 1985).

Petite Policy

The authority of the federal government is limited by administrative policy in prosecuting cases tried earlier in state courts. Although there is no legal prohibition, Congress has expressly stated that with some offenses, a final order of conviction or acquittal in state court should preclude any subsequent federal prosecution for the same acts. In 1969, the U.S. Attorney General implemented a Justice Department policy of successively prosecuting in federal courts only when the reasons were compelling. This policy ultimately became known as the Petite Policy, after *Petite v. United States* (1969). As stated in the *United States Attorneys' Manual,* this policy precludes successive federal prosecution based on the same acts unless the matter must involve a substantial federal interest, the prior prosecution has left that interest unresolved, and the admissible evidence will probably be sufficient to obtain a conviction for a federal offense. Successive federal prosecutions must be approved by the appropriate assistant attorney general, who should bring the case to the attention of the Attorney General before proceeding.

Government Appeal

An acquittal would seem to present the strongest case for the vigorous application of prohibitions against double jeopardy, barring any government appeal in an effort to retry the accused. However, some exceptions preclude the application of double jeopardy guarantees to some cases that have resulted in acquittal. These exceptions center almost exclusively on the interpretation of what is considered a final and legitimate acquittal. The strongest argument that has been made in favor of placing few, if any, limitations on government appeals was made by Justice Holmes in dissenting to the majority opinion in *Kepner v. United States* (1904). He asserted that defendants were not placed in jeopardy, even after acquittal, as long as all legal actions were part of the same cause. His concept of "continuing jeopardy" was rejected at the time, but the Court has also rejected the opposite; that there should be a prohibition against any appeal by the government against any ruling in favor of the defendant in a criminal case.

The most obvious grounds for granting an appeal filed by the government is when the defendant obtained an acquittal by fraud. If the prosecution can produce evidence beyond a reasonable doubt that the judge or jurors were bribed or otherwise coerced into returning a verdict of not guilty, the acquittal can be set aside upon appeal. The second, and more common, grounds for the exception is when the trial judge acts in error or in an arbitrary manner, with the result of depriving the government of the ability to obtain a legitimate criminal conviction. This is best described by the Court in *United States v. Wilson* (1975). In *Wilson*, the judge granted a final motion to dismiss on the grounds that the trial violated the defendant's rights to a speedy trial. Interestingly, the judge's decision occurred after the jury had returned a verdict of guilty against Wilson. The government appealed the dismissal and the defense countered with a claim of double jeopardy since the final motion of dismissal amounted to an acquittal. The Court rejected the defense's argument, noting that since the government could be granted relief from an erroneous trial decision without holding a second trial, double jeopardy protections were not violated. The dismissal was set aside, and the verdict was reinstated.

The Court's decision in *Wilson* is consistent with that in the case of *Ball v. United States* (1896). In *Ball*, the Supreme Court actually heard the case twice, on two separate matters. First, the Court ruled in favor of the defendants, who appealed their convictions of murder on the grounds of a faulty indictment. The case was remanded to the trial court, where the original flawed indictment was dismissed and the defendants were retried on a new indictment. When they were reconvicted, their case came back to the U.S. Supreme Court, based on the defendant's claim of double jeopardy. This was rejected, since the indictment was not a part of the trial itself, and thus not covered by the double jeopardy prohibition against multiple trials.

Termination Without Acquittal or Conviction

The Double Jeopardy Clause prohibits reprosecution when the case is dismissed without legal cause after the trial has begun, the judge has declared a mistrial and dismissed the jury (without the consent of the defendant), or the charges have been dismissed in return for the defendant becoming a witness for the state. However, this prohibition only applies when the trial phase has begun. As a result, if a defendant's case is dismissed at the preliminary hearing, or if a judge dismisses an indictment (or information) the defendant may be tried for the same offense at a later date.

However, there are exceptions where the trial itself may be terminated without subjecting the defendant to jeopardy for a re-trial. One example is if a jury is discharged for failure to agree on a verdict or some other legal necessity, or due to the illness of a juror, the defendant may be retried. Also, if a mistrial is granted at the defendant's request, the defendant may then be retried for the same offense.

Application in Non-Criminal Proceedings

The Double Jeopardy Clause is specifically intended to apply in the prosecution of criminal cases, and the Supreme Court has repeatedly ruled that civil proceedings do not bar subsequent criminal prosecution and vice versa, as in *Hudson et al.* (1997). Over time, the interpretation of double jeopardy has been broadened to apply in noncriminal court proceedings as well.

The test to determine if double jeopardy is applicable in a civil case is if the judgment awarded is remedial or punitive in intent. In *United States v. Halper* (1989), the Supreme Court held that the general test is if the civil penalty is overwhelmingly disproportionate to compensating the government, thus serving primarily a retributive or deterrent purpose. After Halper was convicted in criminal court for submitting 65 false claims for Medicaid reimbursement, the government sought in civil court to fine him $2,000 for each false claim as well as for additional government legal costs. Since the Supreme Court determined the civil award was far in excess of the real costs or damages for all of the false claims, the Court concluded that the subsequent civil action was punitive in intention, and thus prohibited as a violation of double jeopardy protections. This test formed the basis of the Ninth U.S. Circuit Court's decision in *Montana Department of Revenue v. Kurth Ranch* (1994), where members of the Kurth family were convicted of drug possession in the form of several marijuana plants. In a separate civil action, the state attempted to collect a tax on the marijuana in an amount in excess of eight times the market value of the marijuana. The Court upheld a lower court determination that this constituted a violation of the Kurth's constitutional protection against double jeopardy.

A critical application of double jeopardy in civil proceedings also occurs in the juvenile court. Since *Kent v. United States* (1966) and *in re: Gault* (1967), many rights of due process in criminal proceedings have been extended to juveniles. A significant concern, however, has been the waiver of juveniles into adult criminal court after a juvenile court preceding and judgment, which was allowed in several states for a number of years. Juvenile waiver from civil to criminal court might not constitute a double jeopardy concern if it occurred before jeopardy was attached to the case. For example, in pre-trial proceedings, states such as California held that waiver to adult court for prosecution could occur after a trial has begun in juvenile court, at time of disposition, and even after the child has served time in a juvenile facility. In *Breed v. Jones* (1975), the Supreme Court held that a juvenile who has been exposed to jeopardy in juvenile court adjudication cannot be retried in adult court on the same charge. Underlying this determination is that the final disposition in the juvenile civil court suggests the termination of jeopardy in the first instance, and that the disposition was retributive in intent. Thus, even though the juvenile court is formally civil in nature, the juvenile offender (in this case, Gary Jones), could not be exposed once again to jeopardy in the adult criminal court.

Pro: Arguments in Favor of Double Jeopardy

There is wide consensus in the United States concerning the general principle of protecting against repeated criminal proceedings for the same offense, and the prohibition of double jeopardy is considered to be a fundamental constitutional right guaranteed to citizens. The Double Jeopardy Clause is part of the Bill of Rights, which provides both substantive freedoms (the right of assembly, free speech and press, and to petition) and procedural guarantees (the right of due process of law, jury trial, and legal counsel; and freedom from searches and seizures, self-incrimination, cruel and unusual punishment, and double jeopardy). Both substantive and procedural guarantees are considered to be fundamental to the rule of law in democratic societies because they embody the basic idea of constitutionalism itself: the limitation of government power and a protection of individual liberty.

The importance of the Double Jeopardy Clause is clear in this passage written by Justice Hugo Black in *Green v. United States* (1957):

> The underlying idea, one that is deeply ingrained in at least the Anglo-American system of jurisprudence, is that the State with all its resources and power should not be allowed to make repeated attempts to convict an individual for an alleged offense, thereby subjecting him to embarrassment, expense, and ordeal and compelling him to live in a continuing state of anxiety and insecurity, as well as enhancing the possibility that even though innocent he may be found guilty.

As noted in *Green*, the prohibition of double jeopardy is consistent with common values concerning fairness in society. Given the general grounding of American values in Judeo-Christian religious precepts, it is not surprising to find reference to prohibitions against double jeopardy in the Old Testament. In a more contemporary context, Tom Tyler asserts in *Why People Obey the Law* (2006) that the occurrence of crime is best predicted by the perceived legitimacy of the criminal justice system. A key element of this perception is that justice procedures are fair and unbiased, including the belief that those suspected of a crime are not repeatedly punished, formally or informally, by representatives of the justice system. If the system is perceived as procedurally fair, citizens are more likely to conform to the rules of conduct promoted by that system. Conversely, if the justice system acts in a capricious and procedurally unfair way, citizens feel less bound to adhere to the law.

Con: Arguments Against Double Jeopardy

Given the cultural and historical traditions of our democratic form of government, public opinion and scholarly discussion is consistently supportive of the general concept of protecting citizens from double jeopardy. In practice, however, the interpretation and implementation of the double jeopardy doctrine raises some important questions concerning the degree to which citizens are actually protected and justice is maintained.

First, some justice officials and crime control advocates are concerned that the double jeopardy doctrine might be overly protective in its implementation. One instance where justice might be thwarted is when new information arises after a case has reached a final outcome in the courts. As the Supreme Court held in *Fong Foo v. United States* (1962), even the discovery of new evidence that conclusively proves the guilt of someone previously acquitted is not sufficient to overcome the prohibition against retrial on the same offense. In reviewing the implementation of other procedural rights, the Court has attempted to balance the general concern for public safety and welfare with technical procedures intended to protect the procedural rights of accused persons and have acknowledged the need for some "good faith" exceptions. For example, the Court has held that some violations of the exclusionary rule prohibiting the use of improperly collected evidence in a criminal trial are permissible, as in *United States v. Leon* (1984). At this time, however, no such exception has been implemented to limit the double jeopardy doctrine.

Second, while citizens expect the law to be applied fairly and consistently, this expectation can be difficult to achieve in practice. For example, use of the Petite Rule since its inception has been inconsistent; apparently, the Supreme Court and U.S. Attorney General did not anticipate that the federal government would become much more involved in federalizing crimes and take such an aggressive and outcome-oriented approach in their response to drug and firearm offenses.

Finally, implementation of the double jeopardy doctrine is one of the many arenas in which the larger constitutional concern of balancing the rights of citizens and the government's responsibility to promote the public welfare is played out. Many believe the Supreme Court should take a leadership role in creating such a balance. It seems reasonable that there would be some incremental reinterpretation of the Double Jeopardy Clause since it became part of the Constitution in 1791, but one might expect that repeated application and description would allow the Court not only to keep policies up to date, but also bring clarity and refinement to such an ancient concept. Unfortunately, that has not been the case; the double jeopardy doctrine has become increasingly complex and confusing in interpretation. For example, the Court's position in *Lydon* is grounded upon Justice Holmes's definition of continuing jeopardy in *Kepner v. United States* (1904). By using the continuing jeopardy rational, *Lydon* allows the government, at least in theory, to retry accused persons in a second-tier court even if an acquittal occurred in a first-tier proceeding.

The Court acknowledged in *Burks v. United States* (1978) that their decisions "can hardly be characterized as models of consistency and clarity."

In fact, Burks overruled four other Supreme Court cases from the previous 25 years, and *Scott v. United States*, also resolved in 1978, reversed a major double jeopardy decision (*Jenkins v. United States*) decided only three years earlier that was intended to clarify the double jeopardy doctrine. The confusing state of double jeopardy guarantees is explained in the Fifth Amendment:

> In large part, the re-evaluation of doctrine and principle has not resulted in the development of clear and consistent guidelines because of the differing emphases of the Justices upon the purposes of the clause and the consequent shifting coalition of majorities based on highly technical distinctions and individualistic fact patterns. Thus, some Justices have expressed the belief that the purpose of the clause is only to protect final judgments relating to culpability, either of acquittal or conviction ... in so doing, of course, they are likely to find more prosecutorial discretion in the trial process. Others have expressed the view that the clause not only protects the integrity of final judgments but, more important, that it protects the accused against the strain and burden of multiple trials ... Still other Justices have engaged in a form of balancing of defendants' rights with society's rights to determine when reprosecution should be permitted when a trial ends prior to a final judgment.

See Also: 1. Asset Forfeiture; 11. Jury System.

Further Readings

Abbate v. United States, 359 U.S. 187 (1959).
Ashe v. Swenson, 397 U.S. 436 (1970).
Ball v. United States, 163 U.S. 662 (1896).
Bartkus v. Illinois, 359 U.S. 121 (1959).
Benton v. Maryland, 395 U.S. 784 (1969).
Blackstone, William. *Commentaries on the Laws of England: In Four Books With Appendix.* Clark, NJ: The Lawbook Exchange, 2009.
Blockburger v. United States, 284 U.S. 299 (1932).
Breed v. Jones, 421 U.S. 519 (1975).
Burks v. United States, 437 U.S. 82 (1978).

Colten v. Kentucky, 407 U.S. 104 (1972).

Cornell University Law School, Legal Information Institute. "CRS Annotated Constitution." http://www.law.cornell.edu/anncon/amdt5af rag2_user.html#fnb63#fnb63 (Accessed March 2010).

Ex parte Lange, 85 U.S. 163 (1874).

Felkenes, George T. *Constitutional Law for Criminal Justice.* Englewood Cliffs, NJ: Prentice Hall, 1988.

Fong Foo v. United States, 369 U.S. 141 (1962).

Ganzfried, Jerrold J. "Double Jeopardy and the Waiver of Jurisdiction in California's Juvenile Courts." *Stanford Law Review,* v.24/5 (1972).

Green v. United States, 355 U.S. 184 (1957).

Heath v. Alabama, 474 U.S. 82 (1985).

Hudson, et al. v. United States, 522 U.S. 93 (1997).

In re Gault, 387 U.S. 1 (1967).

Jenkins v. United States, 419 U.S. 522 (1975).

Justices of Boston Municipal Court v. Lydon, 466 U.S. 294 (1984).

Kent v. United States, 383 U.S. 541 (1966).

Kepner v. United States, 195 U.S. 100 (1904).

Miller, Lisa L. *The Perils of Federalism: Race, Poverty, and the Politics of Crime Control.* New York: Oxford University Press, 2008.

Montana Department of Revenue v. Kurth Ranch, 511 U.S. 767 (1994).

Palko v. Connecticut, 302 U.S. 319 (1937).

Petite v. United States, 395 U.S. 784 (1969).

Scott v. United States, 436 U.S. 128 (1978).

Thomas, George C. *Double Jeopardy: The History, the Law.* New York: New York University Press, 1998.

Tyler, Tom R. *Why People Obey the Law.* Princeton, NJ: Princeton University Press, 2006.

United States Attorneys' Manual. www.justice.gov/usao/reading_room/foia manuals.html (Accessed March, 2010).

United States v. Halper, 490 U.S. 435 (1989).

United States v. Leon, 468 U.S. 897 (1984).

United States v. Wilson, 420 U.S. 332 (1975).

Volkert, Adam N. "Fifth Amendment—Double Jeopardy: Two-Tier Trial Systems and the Continuing Jeopardy Principle." *Journal of Criminal Law and Criminology,* v.75/3 (1984).

Westen, P., and Drubel, R. "Toward a General Theory of Double Jeopardy." *The Supreme Court Review,* v.81/169 (1978).

Wheeler v. United States, 435 U.S. 313 (1978).

4

Drug Laws

John Dombrink
University of California, Irvine

During the 37-year history of American drug law creation, the courts and society have wrestled with the contours of racialization, the effects of certain social movement variables, and the stubbornness of the criminal justice system and political system in avoiding meaningful liberalization of drug laws. Sometimes conceptualized as a "victimless crime," drug laws have gone through a slow pace of liberalization. Drug enforcement and punitiveness have been dominant themes in American drug laws and policy.

Drug laws haven't changed much in America over the past 40 years, even as the country has moved away from use of the criminal sanction in the other "victimless crimes," a term used by Edwin Schur in his influential 1965 book, *Crimes Without Victims: Deviant Behavior and Public Policy*. However, the other topics Schur addressed—abortion and homosexuality—have changed dramatically in America and other Western industrialized countries since the time of its publication, and this paradox creates intriguing questions about the effectiveness of drug laws.

From Schur and his contemporary Alfred Lindesmith forward, many scholars, analysts, and activists have critiqued American drug laws and called for their liberalization. Proponents of liberalization present analyses of why changes in traditional American punitive drug laws would be advisable, while opponents of liberalization argue for the status quo.

Drugs: The Stalled Movement for Decriminalization

Some analysts thought that experiments with the decriminalization of heroin and cocaine would follow the path of marijuana decriminalization, and be proposed and adopted in several jurisdictions. Considering the broad sweep of victimless crimes in 1978, it was not difficult to think that, within a few years, legal treatment of these formerly prohibited victimless crimes would be dramatically changed. Marijuana could be purchased at the local drug store, perhaps packaged by tobacco companies under catchy names, as rumors of the time suggested.

Between 1973 and 1978, 11 American states had reduced criminal penalties for possession of small amounts of marijuana. The group included conservative, liberal, rural, and urban states.

Paradoxically, although there is fatigue with the War on Drugs, a declaration made by President Nixon in 1971 to convey the nature of the federalization of drug control policy as the "moral equivalent of war," the cost and futility of drug control—and the racial disparity it created—have not led to wholesale reform.

History: Changing Frames for Drug Laws

There has been a persistent tension in the American treatment of illicit drugs over the last 40 years. The treatment of certain substances has aroused great public interest and fear over the past century. Few legal issues have proven as contested as that of drug policy in the United States.

Many factors have been linked to the emergence of criminal sanctions against the possession and commerce in various drugs. Scholars have noted the racial and other social stigma that became associated with marijuana and contributed to its criminalization during the first part of the 20th century. Race and class issues also have been implicated in the heavy penalization of other drugs, notably crack cocaine in the 1980s. Laws have been formed in times of crises and panic, with social threats associated with race and class often used as triggering events and undercurrents for legislation.

The early decades of the 20th century have been analyzed as a time when the state wrested control of certain narcotic drugs from the still nascent American medical profession. At the beginning of the 20th century, narcotic drugs like morphine were unregulated and used in patent medicines. The federal focus on this perceived social problem culminated in the passage of the Harrison Act in 1914, a federal law that regulated and taxed the production, importation, and distribution of opiates. Within a short time, the typical user of heroin changed from a middle-class female to an urban male of color, as the medical profession ceded control over opiates to the criminal justice system. Marijuana criminalization in 1937 followed along the same lines, and expanded the government criminalization of what were termed *narcotics* and *dangerous drugs*.

In his analysis of American 20th-century drug laws, David Musto argues that the perception of social threat—amplified by the specific racial groups involved (Chinese and opium, blacks and heroin or cocaine, and Mexican Americans with marijuana)—created a situation for the passage of these laws. From passage forward, bureaucratic lawmakers—or "moral entrepreneurs," to use sociologist Howard Becker's term—such as Harry Anslinger, the director of the Federal Bureau of Narcotics, provided aggressive enforcement of these laws, and argued for the expansion of the drug law category.

The recent War on Drugs, in particular the importation, sale, or distribution of heroin, cocaine and crack, and marijuana, has been a feature of the federal government and most state governments. This has coincided with the rise of mandatory prison sentences, increased use of the death penalty, a steep rise in the use of imprisonment; and a reduction in emphasis on the rehabilitative ideal, the use of probation and parole, and attempts to address the root causes of crime. During that time, there has been an active debate among sociological scholars, policymakers, and influencers of liberal, libertarian, and even conservative bents for legalization. Even conservative jurists have called for more emphasis on early intervention, treatment, education, and root causes of drug use.

The 1960s and 1970s: Cultural Strife and Moral Dissonance

With the work of 1960s sociolegal scholars, policy observers, and activists, American drug policy was placed under societal consideration for reform of legal treatment. Marijuana was the first to be singled out, as large numbers of middle-class youth began smoking marijuana in the 1960s, creating greater social awareness of the Draconian nature of American drug laws.

In that era, sociology professor Alfred Lindesmith argued that drug policing was rife with selective enforcement, a theme that has been extended through analysis of racial disparity in drug arrests and prosecutions since then.

The 1960s was a time of cultural contestation regarding drug laws in American society. Marijuana was the locus, and the change in the using population of the drug from minorities to white, middle-class youth and college students caused a reexamination of American policy in this area. Sociologists and legal scholars who studied law creation and law enforcement, such as John Kaplan, argued for the more lenient treatment of marijuana, based on analyses of the drug and its effects. Some showed the change in government frames of marijuana-associated harms from its association with violence to its amotivational encouragement of "dropping out."

These perceived policy misfits—or "moral dissonance"—led to decriminalization. In the 1970s and 1980s, several states decriminalized marijuana possession, so that for instance, in California, possession of less than an ounce of marijuana is treated as a citation offense, with a $100 fine. As part of this reform, growing and distribution of marijuana remained criminalized.

President Nixon energized the federalization of American drug law enforcement, beginning with his pronouncements of a War on Drugs in 1971, following the congressional passage of the Comprehensive Drug Abuse Prevention and Control Act of 1970 (which includes the Controlled Substances Act). Nixon's War on Drugs, as was the Vietnam War, was challenged with resistance, growing drug use, and increased calls for drug law liberalization. The period after that pronouncement, in the second half of the 1970s, witnessed some decriminalization support for at least soft drugs. The articulation of these arguments, couched in language of what would be seen later as the nascent years of America's "culture wars," contributed to a backlash during the Reagan era.

From the Reagan Era Onward

The 1980s was the era of the War on Drugs, and the recriminalization of drugs. The 1980s witnessed a dramatic increase in the American societal consideration of drugs and drug policy. At one level, this was driven by the expansion of the federal government's presence in drug interdiction, which was given a high priority in the border areas of Florida, Texas, and California. The symbolic importance of the topic was significant, and President Reagan used the bully pulpit and the first lady led the Just Say No campaign to wage a cultural war against drugs. The Reagan administration gave voice and preference to antidrug groups, such as parent groups, who were alarmed at increased youth drug use and the liberalization of drug laws in the 1970s.

The federalization of drug control was a major development during this decade. The expansion of the legal net came with passage of the crack provisions in the Anti-Drug Abuse Law of 1986. The brief debate over the wisdom of creating a new category of enhanced penalties for one form of a drug was a result of the moral panic over drugs, often with racial overtones. From this point, the path that had contemplated liberalization diverged radically. Drug arrests grew threefold over 25 years (1982–2007), and contributed greatly to the increase in incarceration during that long period.

Drug arrests grew nationally from 581,000 in 1980 to one million in 1990, and to 1.8 million in 2007. At the same time, the number of state prison inmates incarcerated for drugs rose from 39,000 in 1985, to 202,000 in 1994, to 253,000 in 2005; and in the federal system from 9,500 in 1985, to 95,000 in 2007. According to the Bureau of Justice Statistics, drug offenders accounted for 59 percent of the growth in the federal prison population from 1990 to 2000.

Pro: The Prophylactic Features of Criminalization

In a 2008 op-ed article in the *Wall Street Journal*, former drug czar John Walters (head of the White House Office of National Drug Control Policy, a position created in the 1980s to coordinate the many strands of federal drug law policy and enforcement) points to the reduction in the number of youth using illegal drugs as a measure of the success of the use-reduction strategies of his tenure.

In recent years, he and many other previous drug czars and prohibition supporters have framed the discussion and debates over drug laws as a binary choice between criminalization and legalization. Any alternatives to the current policy are seen as dangerously undercutting societal commitment to reducing illegal drug use, by developing a "drugstore" model of open drug access. Changes would open the Pandora's box of unknown but presumably increased drug use (and abuse). Attending social ills and medical problems would be higher, especially if drug use spread to a younger population.

Those who subscribe to this school of thought believe that use reduction is best attained by supply reduction. Toward that end, the state and federal antidrug laws were passed to sanction drug suppliers, sellers, and users, toward the end of supply reduction.

Those who were focused on supply-side reduction in American drug use heralded the creation and deployment during the 1980s of several innovative laws meant to reduce the wealth and power of drug sellers and traffickers *vis a vis* the criminal justice system. The more timely and invigorated use of the 1970s-era Bank Secrecy Act made the policing of money laundering easier, something that remains a key feature of law enforcement efforts in that field (and other crime areas) nationally and globally. Criminal and civil asset forfeiture remedies in the 1980s were used to incarcerate and tie up the wealth of traffickers. And enhanced penalties for drug kingpins were aimed at disrupting major players in drug trafficking organizations.

Looking beyond interdiction and drug supply enforcement on drug routes and street sales and possession, those supporting these positions also point to ways in which the status quo also allows for greater focus on drug addiction and treatment. To them, the criminal justice system has become the most powerful supporter of addiction treatment. At the same time, such supporters often mention the work of specialized drug courts as providing a therapeutic basis to drug laws. While the use of these courts is widespread in the United States, their costs—and to some, their selectivity—results in a worthy intervention that does not deeply penetrate the breadth of the criminal justice system's processing of drug cases.

Con: Criticism of the War on Drugs

Scholars and activists have criticized the War on Drugs for many reasons, including its often overheated legal formation, its disproportionate effect on persons of color, and its emphasis on crime-control goals at the expense of any conception of drug policy as a public health issue.

There are several strands of arguments either critiquing American punitiveness toward drugs, or proposing alternatives to the emphasis on incarceration. Themes that have propelled arguments and proposals for liberalization include futility, fairness (against a backdrop of racial disparity), and even the right to take drugs for pleasure.

From Schur and Lindesmith forward, there have also been a number of critiques and reform proposals that have emphasized the ineffectiveness and costs of such government sanctioning. Critics of the War on Drugs continue to point to the its failures—an effort which encompasses some $20 billion annually in federal drug expenditures alone (and another estimated $30 billion in state and local expenditures)—and the vitality of alternative measures and approaches. These critics point to the futility of the enterprise, and the racial effect of its most stringent laws.

These proposals would not necessarily include the "drugs are good approach" of some reformers, who have taken an extreme view of British philosopher John Stuart Mill's famous 1859 dictum that personal liberty is a primary goal when harm to others is minimal. Most of the reformers have understood the range of American opinion on these topics over time, and are more pragmatic.

Many of the reform proposals in the last 40 years have focused on decriminalization of drugs, and have usually been very drug-specific. For example, legal scholar John Kaplan, who had argued for the liberalization of marijuana laws in his 1970 book *Marijuana: The New Prohibition*, a decade later explored the thorny issues of addressing a multipronged issue such as heroin addition, with its attendant economic, social, and public health components. "Hard" drugs such as heroin, although primarily analyzed by legal scholars and activists, were also the focus of legal reform efforts. In some countries (although not so much in the United States), they have been decriminalized, such as in Canada, where there are currently heroin injection facilities and heroin maintenance testing facilities.

Even many drug scholars—known more for their incisive scholarship and reasoned analyses than their reformist advocacy—have often remarked about the futility of American drug prohibition regimes. To them, in the face of mass distribution, enforcement has a very hard time controlling their use. To some of them, America's highly punitive version of prohibition is intrusive, divisive, and expensive. This leaves the United States with a drug problem that is worse than that of any other industrialized nation.

By the time that Ethan Nadelman and the drug policy reform group Drug Policy Alliance sponsored its Breaking the Chains: People of Color and the War on Drugs conference in 2002, race was the central fact and metaphor of the drug war, and also attempts to reform it. For although the racial profile of those who used drugs in America wasn't so pronounced, the racial profile of those policed and sanctioned was dramatic.

In further elaborating on the disparity issue, critics also point to the way in which the drug-war net catches persons of low levels across drug networks, often imprisoning the most low-income population, who also have few resources in terms of escaping the full sanctioning power of the criminal justice system. For example, over half of federal crack cocaine offenders and federal powder cocaine offenders are street-level dealers, couriers, lookouts, or those who perform other low-level functions.

Other scholars have depicted the War on Drugs, within the context of a larger war on crime, as efforts and symbols that have transformed the relationship between the state and the individual in modern America. Even conservatives like former U.S. Attorney General Dick Thornburgh—who oversaw some of the expansion of the Justice Department in support of the drug war as U.S. Attorney General under Reagan and George H.W. Bush— have recently come to express their displeasure with overcriminalization by the federal law.

Noted sociolegal scholar Michael Tonry has characterized today's overin-carceration policies that these levels represent—largely directed at drug offenses—as a moral panic, and predicts that Americans 50 years from now will look back at this much in the same way as we look back now at the Salem witch trials.

Hints of a Slowly Shifting Drug Policy

In 2003, the *New York Times* reported that several states had begun to rethink their emphasis on incarceration as the primary response to certain crimes. After two decades of passing ever-tougher sentencing laws and prompting a prison building boom, state legislatures facing budget crises were beginning to rethink their costly approaches to crime control. These states had modified their laws and policies, arguing that instead of being "tough on crime," it is more effective to be "smart on crime." Some states passed laws eliminating portions of the lengthy mandatory minimum sentences so popular in the 1980s and 1990s, restoring early release for parole and offering treatment instead of incarceration for some drug offenders. Perhaps, as Stanford law professor Joan Petersilia has observed, a declining economy (and especially fiscal strains in state budgets) could encourage what reformers and criminologists have struggled to achieve: political support for alternative sanctions.

Challenging the Punitive Approach to Drug Enforcement

In the last 10 years, the monolithic nature of the punitive approach toward drugs in the United States has been challenged incrementally in some locales. The issue of medical marijuana has emerged as one of several fronts where American drug policy has been challenged. Several states have considered policy changes—often through citizen-sponsored referenda—to allow for the merciful use of marijuana to help those with certain medical problems or undergoing chemotherapy for cancer treatment. California led the way, with a treatment-on-demand model from 2000 forward, although a November 2010 proposition to legalize personal marijuana use was defeated. Reformers have been active, in their words, in challenging existing regimes of drug control, drafting ballot initiatives, lobbying for legislation, litigating issues in courts, engaging the media, and shaping public opinion. Efforts to emphasize, as one organization described it, policies that embrace a "just say know" philosophy were promoted to replace the "just say no" emphasis of the Reagan years.

The medical marijuana movement, now in existence in 11 states and the District of Columbia, has been fueled by arguments for compassion, as laws such as California's Compassionate Use Act of 1996 were enacted. Wendy Chapkis and Richard Webb, in their research published in 2008, demonstrate how the claims for compassion for seriously ill individuals, who could benefit from marijuana, helped carve out an exception to large-scale criminalization of marijuana in locales like the ones in their study. These state laws have often been a unique lesson in federalism, as the individual states have crafted state policy aside (or inside) a federal policy that continues to criminalize marijuana. Even counties and cities have differed in their approaches, in a further extension of the localism argument. As states liberalized, the federal policy remained unchanged, differing by Republican and Democratic administrations, until the Obama administration announced its policy not to prosecute medical marijuana cases in states that provided for its availability. Meanwhile, the highest level of public support for complete legalization of marijuana has recently been demonstrated in national polls.

Treatment-on-demand reforms have also proceeded, though not in a widespread manner. In November 2000, by a 60–40 percent vote, California voters passed Proposition 36, the Substance Abuse and Crime Prevention Act of 2000. SACPA is a post-conviction probation and parole program that offers first- and second-time, nonviolent drug offenders treatment instead of incarceration. Instead of jail or prison terms, eligible defendants who met the initial qualifications and who pled guilty could receive forms of drug treatment and social services. It created a new model involving key elements of the criminal justice system in California, including prosecutors, parole, and probation departments, and alcohol and drug agencies and treatment organizations in an innovative manner. Because some of those agencies were opposed to the passage of Proposition 36, implementation was more problematic, as entities could act to further the implementation of the law as the reformers intended, but also to resist or reshape it.

Even before California's 2000 statewide vote, local programs, such as that of San Francisco, were utilizing their discretion in policies to incorporate elements of the harm reduction approach. In New York, after many tries by reformers, the state modified its strict Rockefeller-era drug sanctions, passed in 1972. Some have argued that the reality of costs associated with incarceration has given support to efforts to reduce the reliance upon the criminal sanction, more than philosophical differences.

Attempts to amend the federal Anti-Drug Abuse Act of 1986, with its greater penalties for crack cocaine than for powder cocaine, have gained support, with retriggering taking place in a 2010 congressional bill signed by President Obama. This recalibration, while not at the 1:1 ratio that many drug reformers argued for, nevertheless has narrowed a weight discrepancy that has resulted in the disparity in prosecution and imprisonment for related offenses, with nonwhite crack dealers overrepresented in American courts and prisons. Meanwhile, the federal courts allowed some variety in departures from mandatory sentencing under the relevant laws.

International Parallels

These measures of legal reform and program implementation have paralleled those instituted in several European countries. Notable among these has been the long example of the Netherlands, where a seemingly philosophical bent toward pragmatism has guided the Dutch as they have created a policy that is "hard on drugs, soft on users." Supporters of this approach point to the lower incidence of drug use among youth, and to the lowering of drug-related disease and injury. Not only marijuana, but also "hard" drugs such as heroin have been the focus of the legal reform efforts, as authorities in several European countries embraced the harm-reduction approach. For example, Portugal responded to its high heroin use rate by shifting national drug policy in 2000 to a policy rooted in harm-reduction principles. Its experience has been evaluated by analysts such as Greenwald to be a success, producing lower drug use rates than for other countries in Europe—an important measure of success since it was the high heroin use rate that prompted the legal reform. It has also been a popular reform among the Portuguese, at the same time as it reduced deaths and disease associated with illegal intravenous drug use.

Several European locales, including large Swiss, German, Dutch, and Spanish cities, and Vancouver in Canada, have experimented with "safe injection rooms" or "supervised injection sites." Reports from these entities have described the same decreases in deleterious health consequences that Portugal has seen with its reforms. At the same time, the growth in countries across Europe liberalizing their marijuana laws has made American exceptionalism in this area pointed.

Beginning in the 1990s, the spread of AIDS through the sharing of intravenous needles led to the adoption of needle exchange programs and other measures by several American cities, commonly captured under the policies of harm reduction. In the balance is the assessment of addiction as a disease issue, rather than a moral issue.

Conclusion

It has been over 40 years since Lindesmith analyzed drug policing and prosecutions, and argued that longer sentences and greater expenditure of funds spent on drug law enforcement only insured that the illicit trade would continue and that associated violence would increase. This has been a key argument in proposals of many for drug liberalization since then, but this argument—unlike in other areas of the law—has not gained the traction one might expect, as America embarked on the creation of a series of laws and policies that embraced greater use of incarceration.

In the late 1970s, those who predicted imminent drug decriminalization or legalization in America may have been influenced by the example of gambling legalization, but the emergence of a conservative rebuttal that focused on morality issues changed the political landscape from 1980 onward. While drugs were not a central issue for these largely religious, social conservative groups, the discussion of drug policy shared in a similar backlash to 1970s liberalization, characterized by the parents' groups whose influence was especially felt in First Lady Nancy Reagan's Just Say No campaign on illicit drugs. The emergence of crack, and the powerful effect of racialization on lawmaking, public conceptions, and criminal sentencing, created an unprecedented growth in prison populations that effectively stalled the liberalization impulses of the 1970s. In some ways, the liberalization, which had been based on the growing use of marijuana among white youth, effectively bifurcated the treatment of drugs into those associated with people of color.

A key consideration is thus how to understand American exceptionalism in this area. Why have American lawmakers and policymakers not followed the lead of similarly situated peers in Western industrialized countries who have shifted to a public health model emphasizing harm-reduction goals and reduced reliance on incarceration as the primary response to drug offenses? What explains the lagging pace of drug law modification in America? It appears not to be public sentiment: 20 years after the passage of the crack sentencing laws in 1986, when over 30 percent of Americans identified drugs as the number one problem facing America, that percentage has dwindled to a very minor one percent.

Are we left with what Mark Kleiman of Harvard University has called "a category of grudgingly tolerated vices?" The landscape of contemporary American drug laws and policy is certainly a checkerboard pattern. Recent years have seen the adoption of a series of partial measures and programs that reflected political reality, but also the ambivalence and perceived political costs of changing the situation. In general, the federal government, states, and involved politicians have been slow in addressing perceived inefficacy and inefficiency of punitiveness and criminalization, and reluctant to develop workable and wide-scale alternatives to the use of the criminal sanction.

There was hope that the Carter administration, amid a seeming consensus in 1976 toward the liberalization of marijuana laws, would lead the way in supporting the type of drug liberalization measures that critics and reformers had identified. Any impetus toward this end was derailed by that administration's focus on other pressing national issues, and on the pushback of federal bureaucrats and policymakers toward such a stance. Following that window of opportunity, the confluence of new drugs (crack), widespread focus on drugs as a significant national social problem, and the expanded enforcement views of the Reagan administration put a brake on liberalization proposals, and ushered in an era of increasing criminalization and use of incarceration as a primary goal. The Obama administration has indicated a federal policy shift. Its appointment of a drug czar with an articulation that the War on Drugs is over, and the perception that it has been a war on Americans, indicates some initial movement to modify American federal policies. The majority of Americans support the argument that the War on Drugs has not succeeded. It is unclear as to whether this new policy window will result in a shift in laws and policies that seemed ripe for reform 30 years ago.

See Also: 1. Asset Forfeiture; 12. Mandatory Sentencing; 17. Sentencing Disparities.

Further Readings

Becker, Howard S. *Outsiders: Studies in the Sociology of Deviance.* New York: The Free Press, 1973.

Buckley, William F., Jr. "Free Weeds: The Marijuana Debate." *National Review* (June 12, 1994).

Chambliss, William J. "Another Lost War: The Costs and Consequences of Drug Prohibition." *Social Justice*, v.22 (1995).

Chapkis, Wendy, and Richard J. Webb. *Dying to Get High: Marijuana as Medicine*. New York: NYU Press, 2008.

Currie, Elliott. *Crime and Punishment in America*. New York: Metropolitan Books/Henry Holt, 1998.

DiChiara, Albert, and John F. Galliher. "Dissonance and Contradictions in the Origins of Marihuana Decriminalization." *Law and Society Review*, v.28/1 (1994).

Dombrink, John, and Daniel Hillyard. *Sin No More: From Abortion to Stem Cells, Understanding Crime, Law and Morality in America*. New York: NYU Press, 2007.

Duster, Troy. "Pattern, Purpose and Race in the Drug War." In *Crack in America: Demon Drugs and Social Justice*, edited by Craig Reinarman and Harry G. Levine. Berkeley: University of California Press, 1987.

Goldkamp, John S., Jennifer B. Robinson, and Michael D White. "Do Drug Courts Work? Getting Inside the Drug Court Black Box." *Journal of Drug Issues*, v.31/1 (2001).

Gray, James P. *Why Our Drug Laws Have Failed and What We Can Do About It*. Philadelphia: Temple University Press, 2001.

Greene, Judith, and Vincent Schiraldi. "Cutting Correctly: New Prison Policies for Times of Fiscal Crisis." San Francisco, CA: Center for Juvenile and Criminal Justice, 2002.

Greenwald, Glenn. "Drug Decriminalization in Portugal: Lessons for Creating Fair and Successful Drug Policies." *Cato Institute* (April 2, 2009).

Human Rights Watch. "Race, Drugs and Law Enforcement in the United States." New York: *Human Rights Watch* (March 2, 2009).

Kaplan, John. *The Hardest Drug: Heroin and Public Policy*. Chicago: University of Chicago Press, 1983.

Kaplan, John. *Marijuana: The New Prohibition*. New York: New World Publishing, 1970.

Kelmes, Glenda. "Taking the Initiative: Implementing California's Substance Abuse and Crime Prevention Act of 2000." Masters Thesis. Irvine, CA: University of California—Irvine, March 2003.

Keys, David Patrick, and John F. Galliher. *Confronting the Drug Control Establishment: Alfred Lindesmith as a Public Intellectual*. Albany, NY: SUNY Press, 1999.

Kleiman, Mark A. R. *Against Excess: Drug Policy for Results*. New York: Basic Books, 1992.

Kleiman, Mark A. R. *When Brute Force Fails: How to Have Less Crime and Less Punishment*. Princeton, NJ: Princeton University Press, 2009.

Leuw, Ed, and Ineke Haen Marshall. *Between Prohibition and Legalization: The Dutch Experiment in Drug Policy*. Amsterdam: Kugler, 1994.

Lindesmith, Alfred R. *The Addict and the Law*. Bloomington: Indiana University Press. 1965.

Liptak, Adam. "Right and Left Join Forces on Criminal Justice." *New York Times* (November 23, 2009).

MacCoun, Robert J., and Peter Reuter. *Drug War Heresies: Learning from Other Vices, Times, and Places*. New York: Cambridge University Press, 2001.

Massing, Michael. *The Fix*. New York: Simon and Schuster, 1998.

Mauer, Marc, and Ryan S. King. *A 25-Year Quagmire: The War on Drugs and Its Impact on American Society*. Washington, DC: The Sentencing Project, 2007.

Mill, John Stuart. *On Liberty*. Indianapolis: Bobbs-Merrill, 1956.

Miron, Jeffrey A. "The Budgetary Implications of Drug Prohibition." Unpublished paper. New York: Columbia University, 2008.

Musto, David F. *The American Disease: Origins of Narcotic Control*. New York: Oxford University Press, 1999.

Nadelmann, Ethan. "Let's End Drug Prohibition." *Wall Street Journal* (December 5, 2008).

Petersilia, Joan. "Prisoner Reentry and Criminological Knowledge." *The Criminologist*, v.28/2 (March/April 2003).

Reinarman, Craig, and Harry G. Levine, eds. *Crack in America: Demon Drugs and Social Justice*. Berkeley: University of California Press, 1997.

Reuter, Peter. "Hawks Ascendant: The Punitive Trend of American Drug Policy." *Daedalus*, v.121/3 (1992).

Room, Robin, Benedikt Fischer, Wayne Hall, Simon Lenton, and Peter Reuter. *Trend of American Drug Policy*. Oxford: The Beckley Foundation Global Cannabis Commission, 2009.

Sander, Eli. "The Last Drug Czar." *American Prospect* (June 29, 2009).

Schur, Edwin M. *Crimes Without Victims: Deviant Behavior and Public Policy*. Englewood Cliff, NJ: Prentice-Hall, 1965.

Simon, Jonathan. *Governing Through Crime*. New York: Oxford University Press, 2007.

Skolnick, Jerome H. "Rethinking the Drug Problem." *Daedalus*, v.121/3 (Summer 1992).

Skolnick, Jerome H., and John Dombrink. "The Legalization of Deviance." *Criminology*, v.16/2 (1978).

Sullum, Jacob. *Saying Yes: In Defense of Drug Use*. New York: Tarcher, 2003.

Tonry, Michael H. *Malign Neglect: Race, Crime, and Punishment in America*. New York: Oxford University Press, 1995.

Transform Drug Policy Foundation. *After the War on Drugs: A Blueprint for Regulation*. Executive Summary. Bristol, England: Transform Drug Policy Foundation, 2009.

van het Loo, Miriam, Ineke van Beusekom, and James P. Kahan. "Decriminalization of Drug Use in Portugal: The Development of a Policy." *Annals of the American Academy of Political and Social Sciences*, v.582 (2002).

Walters, John P. "*Our Drug Policy Is a Success*." *Wall Street Journal* (December 5, 2008).

5

DUI Penalties

Wendelin M. Hume
Daryl Kosiak
University of North Dakota

D riving under the influence (DUI) refers to a driver operating a motor vehicle while his driving skills are impaired because of his use of alcohol or other drugs. Most of the focus on this phenomenon has been on the influence of alcohol on someone driving an automobile. More broadly, however, the cause of impairment does not have to be limited to alcohol; the individual does not have to actually be driving, but could be just behind the wheel or in "control" of the vehicle; and the vehicle does not have to be an automobile. A vehicle can refer to just about any type of conveyance, including a bicycle, snowmobile, boat, tractor, airplane, or even a wheelchair. DUI is a crime in most countries, including the United States.

Every week, if not every day, news outlets in most American communities report a fatal automobile accident. In 1980, over 51,000 people became traffic fatality statistics in the United States. Over half of these fatalities involved drivers who had been consuming alcohol. Since the 1980s, the states and federal government have taken steps to reduce the number of alcohol-impaired drivers with the goal of saving lives and improving safety. Some of the mechanisms utilized to reduce DUIs include implementation of laws making it illegal to operate a motor vehicle with blood alcohol content above a certain limit (.10, and later, .08); mandatory sentences for DUI (which can result in jail sentences, evaluation by addiction counselors, and administrative losses of driving privileges); as well as pressure on law enforcement agencies to aggressively enforce impaired-driving statutes.

These efforts have provided seemingly positive results, including contributing to a reduction in the number of traffic fatalities in 2008 to just over 37,000. Of these, almost 14,000 (41 percent) of drivers in such fatal incidents had a blood-alcohol content at or above .01. Of these 14,000 drivers, almost 12,000 had an alcohol content of at least .08, and just over 8,000 of these drivers had an alcohol content of over .15 percent. Statistics collected by the National Highway Traffic Safety Administration (NHTSA) reflect that the median alcohol content for all drivers arrested for DUI is .16, indicating that half of all persons arrested for DUI had an alcohol content at least twice as high as the legal limit. In 2008, the Federal Bureau of Investigations (FBI) noted that law enforcement agencies reported making over 1.5 million impaired-driving arrests. However, those arrested comprise less than one percent of the estimated 159 million persons who self-reported driving after having too much to drink, and represent only a fraction of the approximately 82 million motor vehicle trips where the driver had an alcohol content over the legal driving limit of .08. Despite enforcement efforts, an average of 32 people died each day in 2008 in traffic accidents involving a driver who was under the influence.

Relevant Databases

To study the phenomena of DUI, accurate data is necessary. Since 1982, the Fatality Analysis Reporting System (FARS) has maintained a database of fatal traffic accidents within the United States. The data includes the number of fatal crashes; time of day of the crashes; type of crash (single vehicle, multiple vehicle, or motorcycle); descriptive data on the decedent (driver, passenger, bicyclist, or pedestrian); demographic data on age and sex; and whether alcohol was involved. FARS also provides data on the blood-alcohol content of parties in fatal crashes, ranging from no measurable alcohol, .01 to <.08, .08 to <.15, and .15 and higher. Testing of persons involved in fatal crashes varies by jurisdiction. In 1982, 54 percent of drivers involved in fatal crashes had their blood-alcohol content tested, and this percentage increased to 64 percent in 2004. For analytical purposes, traffic data related to alcohol-impaired driving includes data that is mathematically imputed to fill in the missing data.

The FBI compiles reports from many of the nation's law enforcement agencies on the number of arrests for various offenses, including driving under the influence. Like the FARS data, the FBI information includes demographic information on the age and sex of those arrested.

The U.S. Centers for Disease Control conducts telephone interviews of over 350,000 respondents throughout the United States for a project called the Behavioral Risk Factor Surveillance Survey. This self-report survey has been conducted since the 1980s, and provides current information on a number of health-risk behaviors, including alcohol consumption.

Effects or Influences of Drugs on Driving

When alcoholic beverages are consumed, the body absorbs ethanol from the beverage. Ethanol has a depressant effect on the central nervous system, and even moderate amounts of ethanol can effect perception and reaction time, reduce concentration, and impair vision, especially at night. The absorption of ethanol in the body is dependent upon a number of factors, including the drinker's sex, height and weight, and stomach contents; the type of alcoholic beverage consumed; and general health of internal organs such as the liver. The ingestion of other drugs either in addition to or instead of alcohol can negatively affect driving skills in a similar way, and the extent of the impact can vary by individual and be dependent on the type of substance and dose.

Control of Impaired Drivers

As motorized vehicles became more commonplace in the United States in the early 20th century, most states enacted statutes regulating the operation of motor vehicles while under the influence of alcohol. Limitations on operating vehicles while impaired by alcohol or other drugs have different names in different jurisdictions, with the three most common being Driving Under the Influence (DUI), Driving while Intoxicated (DWI), and Operating a Motor Vehicle while Intoxicated (OWI). Such statutes will be referred to as DUI laws herein.

Prior to the development of modern techniques for measuring the content of alcohol in a driver's system through breath testing, most DUI cases hinged on the testimony of the arresting officer or other witnesses. The opinions of fact finders (judges or juries), using their own experiences, decided whether the behavior evidenced by the arresting officer's testimony constituted driving under the influence. These general factors included the odor of alcohol coming from the driver; the driver's statement as to how much he or she had to drink; whether the vehicle was being operated erratically; the presence of bloodshot eyes, slurred speech, and the outcome of field sobriety tests such as balance (one-leg stand and walk and turn tests); and other testing. In addition to breath testing, more recently, fact finders have had the benefit of videotape from patrol vehicles showing the driving violations and/or the testing that can assist in determining whether a violation of the law has occurred.

Apprehension of impaired drivers usually occurs when erratic driving or another traffic violation is observed by law enforcement, when the driver is involved in an accident, or during sobriety checkpoints. In 1990, the U.S. Supreme Court in *Michigan State Police v. Sitz* ruled that sobriety checkpoints as operated in Michigan did not violate the Fourth Amendment right of drivers to be free from unreasonable search and seizure. The state produced evidence that the average interaction time between driver and law enforcement was 25 seconds, and the checkpoints allowed the officer to briefly examine the driver for signs of intoxication. Some state courts have found greater protection for drivers under their state constitution, and such sobriety checkpoints are not conducted in all jurisdictions.

Measuring Blood Alcohol Content

Jurisdictions have established a measurable legal baseline for legal impairment, which in all 50 states and the District of Columbia is .08. This level can be measured by analysis of the blood, breath, or urine. The generally accepted scientific alcohol content rates are calculated as: (1) the number of grams of alcohol per 100 milliliters of blood, (2) the number of grams of alcohol per 210 liters of breath, or (3) the number of grams of alcohol per 67 milliliters of urine. Due to the immediacy of receiving results via a measurement of breath, most jurisdictions have adopted the use of breath testing as the method of choice.

Possibly the most commonly used breath-testing device is called an Intoxilyzer. Jurisdictions typically approve one or more such testing devices for use within that jurisdiction, and each device is periodically certified to ensure its continued accuracy. Each state is generally responsible for ensuring that persons who operate the testing devices receive appropriate training. In 2009, the Supreme Court decided the case of *Melendez-Diaz v. Massachusetts,* addressing a Sixth Amendment Confrontation Clause issue, which may impact how the federal government establishes the qualifications of breath-testing device operators and the certification of breath-testing equipment.

Implied Consent Laws and Administrative Sanctions

It is popularly believed by judges, prosecutors, and the public that the chances of obtaining a conviction for DUI are greatly improved when the alcohol content of the driver is known. Obtaining a specimen of blood, breath, or urine and testing the sample provides convincing scientific evidence of the level of impairment of a driver, and to establish whether the jurisdiction's *per se* limit (.08 for persons over 21) has been met. Recognizing that not all persons arrested for DUI may consent to providing specimens of blood, breath, or urine, and that using force to obtain such specimens can be dangerous to the driver and others, states began enacting implied-consent laws in the 1950s. Using the state's police power and interest in public safety, all states and the District of Columbia have implied-consent laws, which allow for a person who has been lawfully arrested for DUI to be requested to provide a specimen of blood, breath, or urine, and failure of the person to provide such a specimen will result in the administrative suspension of their driver's license. Some jurisdictions have longer periods of administrative license suspensions for simply refusing to submit to a chemical test than are available if the person is convicted of DUI.

Implied consent laws have been generally upheld as constitutional under both state and federal law. In 1966, the Supreme Court ruled in *Schmerber v. California* that compelling an individual who was arrested for driving while intoxicated to provide a specimen of blood drawn by a physician in a hospital was neither an unreasonable search and seizure under the Fourth Amendment nor violated the driver's Fifth Amendment right against self-incrimination.

Based on *Schmerber*, states could take specimens without the consent of the individual, but most states have opted to avoid increasing public safety risks and imposed sanctions on the individual's driving privileges when a test is refused. In 1979, the Supreme Court in *Mackey v. Montrym* ruled that a state could summarily suspend the driving privileges of a person who refused to submit to a test for driving under the influence pending a prompt, post-suspension hearing. Many states now issue temporary licenses to individuals who refuse alcohol testing, and the burden is on the individual to seek an administrative hearing within the required time frame.

In 1983, the Supreme Court in *South Dakota v. Neville* ruled that the U.S. Constitution allows for admission into evidence at a DUI criminal trial that a person has refused to provide a specimen for testing. Some jurisdictions have enacted statutes making it an additional criminal offense to refuse an alcohol test after being placed under arrest for DUI. Thus, it would be possible to be convicted both for the offense of refusing a chemical test, as well as DUI. While rates of refusal to submit specimens for testing vary among jurisdictions from two to 71 percent, it is estimated that approximately one-fifth of all drivers arrested for DUI refuse to comply with law enforcement requests for alcohol testing.

Forty-one jurisdictions have laws requiring an administrative suspension of driving privileges for testing at or above the .08 level for drivers 21 and over. These suspensions for first-time offenders range from seven days to one year. Thirty-six jurisdictions permit a driver to obtain a restricted driving license during the suspension period upon a showing of hardship, but almost all jurisdictions require some period of suspension. Administrative license suspensions in some jurisdictions can be increased when the driver has previously failed or refused an alcohol test within a set time period, if the driver is under the legal drinking age, or if the alcohol test reflects an alcohol content higher than .15 (.20 in some jurisdictions). Whether license suspension or revocation is the product of administrative action or a criminal sanction, it is estimated that between 25 and 75 percent of drivers with suspended or revoked driving privileges continue to drive. Driving after the privilege has been suspended or revoked carries criminal and administrative sanctions similar to DUI, including additional periods of driving privilege suspension or revocation.

Zero-Tolerance Laws

Ever since Prohibition ended in the 1930s, the states were able to establish legal drinking age laws. In 1971, the Twenty-Sixth Amendment was ratified, giving otherwise qualified persons between 18 and 20 years of age the right to vote. Many states that previously had age 21 legal purchase-and-possess laws lowered the age to 18. Noting an increase in alcohol-related traffic deaths among persons under 21, Congress passed legislation in the 1980s providing economic highway funding incentives to jurisdictions that established a minimum legal age of 21 to purchase and publicly possess alcoholic beverages. In the 1990s, Congress passed additional legislation providing for incentives to jurisdictions to impose a statutory limit of .02 alcohol content for drivers under the minimum legal purchase and public possession age of 21. The number of DUI arrests for the 16–20 age group rose from almost 75,000 (8.4 percent of all DUI arrests) in 1995 to almost 105,000 in 2008 (9.4 percent of all DUI arrests). In 1995, males accounted for 87 percent of all 16–20 age group arrests, and by 2008, that percentage had dropped to 77 percent.

Standard Criminal Penalties for DUI

DUI laws vary among the various jurisdictions, although various pieces of federal legislation have provided states with financially compelling reasons to have some uniformity, including the .08 legal limit for persons legally able to consume alcoholic beverages within the jurisdiction and for lower blood-alcohol content levels for persons under the legal drinking age (.01 or .02). Basic DUI occurs when a person is found to have operated a motor vehicle, at the time of testing or within a set time frame after operating a motor vehicle (usually up two hours), while under the influence of drugs or under the influence of alcohol with a blood alcohol content of .08 or more. First-offense DUI is usually classified as a misdemeanor; however, charges and sanctions may be aggravated in some jurisdictions when the driver is under the legal drinking age for that jurisdiction, when the alcohol content is at .15 or higher, or when there are children in the vehicle. Sanctions for first-offense DUI convictions may include imprisonment, usually not to exceed 30 days. Most jail time is suspended or replaced with community service, fines, and a judicially ordered loss of driving privileges.

Second offenses of DUI within a certain time frame (usually between seven to 10 years), while still classified as a misdemeanor, result in increased sanctions that vary significantly by jurisdiction. Advocates of enhanced penalties for repeat offenders stress that the lighter sanctions imposed for the first offense did not have the desired deterrent effect. Additional DUI offenses within a pre-determined time frame can result in felony DUI charges carrying very severe penalties in terms of incarceration, fines, and loss of driving privileges. Motor vehicle accidents causing death or serious injury to persons or significant property damage can also be prosecuted as felonies.

Nontraditional DUI Penalties

Some jurisdictions have noted that many persons with suspended driving privileges continue to drive during the period of suspension, including those who may qualify for restricted driving privileges and those who do not seek reinstatement after the suspension period has elapsed. This has been related to the economic need to drive to maintain employment coupled with a perceived low probability of apprehension, the cost of driving privilege reinstatement, and increased vehicle insurance cost. Some groups believe the current sanctions for DUI are inadequate and propose adding or enforcing additional sanctions for DUI. These nontraditional sanctions include ignition interlock devices, immobilization, impoundment or confiscation of motor vehicles used in DUI offenses, and license plate impoundment or special markings on license plates to designate persons operating with restricted-privilege operator's licenses to alert the public and law enforcement.

Locking the Ignition

Ignition interlock sanctions have been implemented in 47 jurisdictions, with at least eight jurisdictions mandating ignition interlocks even for first-time offenders with an alcohol content of .08 or higher. An ignition interlock device is a small alcohol detection device connected to the vehicle's ignition. Before the vehicle can be started, the driver must blow into the device, which then measures the alcohol content of the person's breath. The positive limits of the device are low, and if the breath tests at or above the limit, the vehicle cannot be started. The interlock device also requires periodic "rolling" tests of the driver to thwart attempts to circumvent the device, such as having another person provide the initial breath sample or leaving the vehicle running while consuming alcoholic beverages. Improvements in design and technology provide for record-keeping as to when the device was used, the results of each test, and if the device was tampered with. The device may be periodically checked by monitoring officials to assess the driver's compliance with alcohol-consumption restrictions. Violations can result in revocation of suspended portions of any sentence. There are costs to installing and maintaining the device, about $100 per month, which is usually paid by the driver. As this sanction is frequently used as either a condition of probation or a restricted privilege to drive, compliance is monitored by a probation officer or other official.

As of 2004, 13 jurisdictions had statutes that permitted the long-term impoundment of vehicles used in alcohol-impaired driving incidents. The owner of the vehicle is responsible for the costs of the impoundment, including towing and storage. Over one-third of jurisdictions have statutes that allow the government to suspend the registration of a vehicle used in an alcohol-impaired driving incident. This sanction is usually accomplished by confiscation of state-issued license plates, which can be applied to all motor vehicles owned by the violator, not just the vehicle used in the alcohol-related driving incident. This sanction can also be used when a person has been found driving after cancellation of driving privileges.

Over half of all jurisdictions have statutes that permit the government to confiscate a vehicle used in an alcohol-impaired driving incident. When the vehicle is owned by another person, the vehicle may still be confiscated if that person knew or should have known that the driver's use would be contrary to the law and failed to take reasonable steps to prevent the illegal usage. Some jurisdictions have interpreted its confiscation laws to include confiscation of insurance settlements when a vehicle is totaled in an alcohol-related crash.

At least three jurisdictions have statutes that permit the issuance of special distinctive license plates, which permit a re-licensed violator, family member, or other lawfully authorized operator to drive the vehicle. Some jurisdictions permit law enforcement to make investigatory stops of vehicles bearing these special plates to determine if the driver has a valid driver's license. The validity of such stops has been upheld against constitutional challenge in at least two jurisdictions as the courts have construed the application for such special plates to be either an implied consent to an investigatory stop or that the presence of the marked plate establishes the officer's authority to make a limited stop.

Pro: Arguments for Strong Impaired-Driving Laws

A significant amount of time and money has been put into administrative and criminal sanctions for DUI with the belief that such sanctions are necessary and effective. It is also evident that DUIs pose a public safety threat to Americans. In 1982, 43,495 persons were killed in traffic crashes in the United States. It is estimated that alcohol was involved in 57 percent of these fatal crashes, and that drivers with an alcohol level at or above .10 were involved in 20,356 deaths, or 41 percent. In 2008, despite a significant increase in population, licensed drivers, vehicles licensed, and miles traveled, the total number of fatalities was reduced to 37,261, with alcohol involved in 37 percent of fatal crashes; alcohol at a level of .08 or higher was involved in 11,773 deaths, or 32 percent of fatal crashes. At issue is whether the legislation, practices, and policies developed and implemented from the

1980s to today have produced dramatic reductions in alcohol-related traffic deaths and are the most effective way to reduce DUIs.

Most Americans would agree that reducing or eliminating impaired drivers promotes public safety. Many, if not most, traffic safety professionals believe that detecting, apprehending, and adjudicating impaired drivers has important public safety outcomes by reducing crashes, which cause death, injury, or destruction of property. Advocates for strong impaired driving laws believe that to dissuade persons from drinking and driving, the penalties must be perceived as both likely and significant.

While it is difficult to attribute the reduction in alcohol-impaired crashes and fatalities to any one DUI countermeasure, it is difficult to argue that enactment of *per se* statutes, minimum legal drinking age, zero tolerance for underage drinking, administrative license suspensions for exceeding the legal limit or refusal to take requested testing, and the risk of significant fines and incarceration have not had some effect on deterring people from driving under the influence of alcohol or drugs. Administrative license suspensions remove those found to have violated drinking and driving laws from legally operating vehicles, and some studies have found evidence that jail sentences for DUI convictions temporarily reduce recidivism.

Of all drivers involved in traffic fatalities in 2006, 55 percent had an alcohol content of .15 or greater. Continuing emphasis to deter these so-called "hard core" drunk drivers with increased criminal and administrative penalties should lead to a reduction in traffic fatalities. It is estimated that a driver with an alcohol content of .15 or higher is 385 times more likely to be in a single-vehicle crash than a driver with no alcohol in their system.

Nontraditional DUI sanctions such as ignition interlocks, vehicle forfeiture or impoundment, and special license plates to identify vehicles driven by persons with restricted driving privileges are additional disincentives to drinking and driving, and also provide both retributive and specific deterrent emphasis, not only to those persons subject to the sanctions, but also as a general deterrent to the public of the potential consequences for driving under the influence.

Con: Enforcement and Sanctions Are Inadequate

While there have been dramatic declines in alcohol-related traffic deaths from 1982 to 2008, not all the lives saved can be attributed to administrative and criminal sanctions against DUI. During the last 30 years, significant advances have been made in auto and highway safety, including mandatory seatbelt laws and individual vehicle safety devices such as airbags, which have undoubtedly decreased the number of traffic fatalities. Improvements in communications and more and better-trained and equipped emergency response personnel have also contributed to the decline in traffic deaths.

Longitudinal surveys from 1993 to 2002 reflect that self-reported incidents of alcohol-impaired driving varied by less than one half of one percent among respondents, despite significant changes in alcohol-impaired driving control statutes and enforcement practices. Incidents of fatal crashes with an alcohol content of .08 or higher actually increased from 1996 to 2006 for the following age groups: 16–20 (17–19 percent), 21–24 (31–33 percent), 45–54 (18–19 percent) and 55–64 (12–13 percent).

Questionable Deterrence

Deterrence depends upon the belief that the risk of detection, apprehension, and adjudication is greater than the immediate reward of violating the law. Various studies of the risk of detection and apprehension for an alcohol-related driving offense range from a probability of one in 50, to one in 772, to one in 2,000. A number of researchers have concluded that while there was a major decline in alcohol-related traffic deaths from 1982 to 1992, since 1992, the statistics have remained fairly constant at roughly 41 percent of all traffic fatalities.

The prompt administrative suspension of driving privileges has been thought to be a major deterrent to alcohol-impaired driving. The effect of losing one's driving privilege is especially great for those persons without alternate transportation to resources, such as persons in rural areas without access to public transportation. However, various studies have found evidence that between 25 to 75 percent of persons with suspended driving privileges continue to drive, bringing into question the efficacy of suspensions as a deterrent.

Various jurisdictions allow for the impoundment or forfeiture of automobiles as a sanction; however, some of these same jurisdictions have not utilized this sanction, as in some cases the costs related to impoundment or forfeiture of the vehicle exceed its value. So, some persons who drink and drive may to choose to drive a junker vehicle with low market value to mitigate any potential monetary loss. Interlock devices and distinctive license plates have also been thought to be effective, but these devices do not prevent a driver with suspended driving privileges from using a vehicle other than the one with such devices.

Driving under the influence of alcohol or other drugs can be a dangerous practice with potentially fatal consequences for the driver and others. Trying to end this practice has proven difficult, as evidenced by the 1.5 million DUI arrests in 2008. In some states, alcohol-related traffic offenses represent the greatest single offense of arrest, including some with DUI representing 20 percent of all arrests jurisdiction-wide. The emphasis on criminal enforcement and sanctions not only creates a heavy demand on law enforcement assets, but also on the courts and corrections, which then must process those arrested. Despite the enforcement and sanctions known as DUI penalties, recent research has indicated that mandatory fines and jail sentences may not have a statistically significant impact on reducing alcohol-related traffic fatalities.

See Also: 4. Drug Laws; 17. Sentencing Disparities.

Further Readings

Dula, Chris S., William O. Dwyer, and Gilbert LeVerne. "Policing the Drunk Driver: Measuring Law Enforcement Involvement in Reducing Alcohol-Impaired Driving." *Journal of Safety Research*, v. 38/3 (2007).

Fahey, Michael A., and Joel A Watne. "A Brief History of DUI Law in Minnesota and an Overview of the Process." In *Minnesota DWI Desk Book*, edited by the Minnesota State Bar Association. St. Paul, MN: Minnesota State Bar Association, 2006.

Federal Bureau of Investigation, "Uniform Crime Reports." http://www.fbi.gov/ucr.htm (Accessed August 2010).

Insurance Institute for Highway Safety. "Summary of State DUI/DWI Laws." (2009). www.iihs.org/laws/dui.aspx (Accessed August 2010).

King, Pamela A., and Peter D. Magnuson. "Bodily Functions and DWI Law: Scientific Testing of Fluids and Gases for the Presence of Alcohol." In *Minnesota DWI Desk Book*, edited by the Minnesota State Bar Association. St. Paul, MN: Minnesota State Bar Association, 2006.

Kwasnoski, John B, Gerald N. Partridge, and John A. Stephen. *Investigation and Prosecution of DWI and Vehicular Homicide*. Louisville, KY: Lexis Legal Publishing, 1998.

Mackey v. Montrym, 443 U.S. 1 (1979)

Melendez-Diaz v. Massachusetts, 557 U.S. ___, 129 S. Ct. 2527 (2009).

National Highway Traffic Safety Administration. *Digest of Impaired Driving and Selected Beverage Control Laws* Report no. DOT HS 810 827. (2007). http://www-nrd.nhtsa.dot.gov/Cats/listpublications .aspx?Id=F&ShowBy=DocType (Accessed August 2010).

National Highway Traffic Safety Administration. *Refusal of Intoxication Testing: A Report to Congress.* Report no. DOT HS 811 098. Washington, DC: National Highway Traffic Safety Administration, 2008.

National Highway Traffic Safety Administration. *Traffic Safety Facts— 1993: Alcohol.* Washington, DC: National Center for Statistics and Analysis, 1994.

National Highway Traffic Safety Administration. *Update of Vehicle Sanction Laws and their Application.* http://www.nhtsa.gov/DOT/ NHTSA/Traffic%20Injury%20Control/Articles/Associated%20 Files/811028b.pdf (Accessed August 2009).

Nichols, Donald H., and Flem K Whited, III. *Drinking/Driving Litigation.* St. Paul, MN: Thomson-West Publishing, 2006.

Nichols, James L., and H. Laurence Ross. "The Effectiveness of Legal Sanctions in Dealing with Drinking Drivers." *Alcohol, Drugs and Driving,* v.6 (1990).

Quick, Bruce D. *I Only Had Two Beers: A North Dakota Prosecutor's Manual for DUI Cases.* Bismarck, ND: North Dakota Attorney General's Office, 1999.

Quinlan, Kyran P., Robert D. Brewer, Paul Siegel, David A. Sleet, Ali H. Mokdad, Ruth A. Shults, and Nicole Flowers. "Alcohol Impaired Driving Among U.S. Adults, 1993–2002." *American Journal of Preventive Medicine,* v.28/4 (2005).

Schmerber v. California, 384 U.S. 757 (1966).

South Dakota v. Neville, 459 U.S. 553 (1983).

Teigen, Anne, and Melissa Savage. "Last Call: Lawmakers Hope New Technology Could Mean the End to Drunken Driving." *National Conference of State Legislatures* (December 2009).

Voas, Robert B., and David J. DeYoung. "Vehicle Action: Effective Policy for Controlling Drunk and Other High-Risk Drivers." *Accident Analysis and Prevention,* v.34 (2002).

Voas, Robert B., Kenneth O. Blackman, A. Scott Tippetts, and Paul R. Marques. "Evaluation of a Program to Motivate Impaired Driving Offenders to Install Ignition Interlocks." *Accident Analysis and Prevention,* v.34 (2002).

Voas, Robert B., Tara Kelley-Baker, Eduardo Romano, and Radha Vishnuvajjala, "Implied Consent Laws: A Review of the Literature and Examination of Current Problems and Related Statutes." *Journal of Safety Research*, v.40 (2007).

Wagenaar, Alexander C., and Mildred M. Maldonado-Molina. "Effects of Drivers' License Suspensions Policies on Alcohol-Related Crash Involvement: Long-Term Follow-Up in Forty-Six States." *Alcoholism Clinical and Experimental Research*, v.31 (2007).

Wagenaar, Alexander C., Mildred M. Maldonado-Molina, Linan Ma, Amy L. Tobler, and Kelli A Komro. "Effects of Legal BAC Limits on Fatal Crash Involvement: Analyses of 28 States from 1976–2002." *Journal of Safety Research*, v.38 (2007).

Zador, Paul L., Sheila A. Krawchuck, and Robert B. Voas. "Alcohol Related Relative Risks of Driver Fatalities and Driver Involvement in Fatal Crashes in Relation to Driver Age and Gender: An Update Using 1996 Data." *Journal of Studies on Alcohol*, v.61/3 (2000).

6

Exclusionary Rules

James Binnall
University of California, Irvine

For almost a century, the exclusionary rule has been a topic of vigorous debate among legal scholars and practitioners. The exclusionary rule is a judicially recognized legal doctrine that allows the court, in certain situations, to exclude improperly acquired evidence from a criminal trial. Most often, courts invoke the exclusionary rule when suppressing evidence obtained in violation of the Fourth Amendment to the U.S. Constitution. The Fourth Amendment protects citizens from unreasonable search and seizure of their "persons, houses, papers and effects." The exclusionary rule also occasionally operates to exclude evidence that results from violations of the Fifth and Sixth Amendments. The Fifth Amendment prohibits forced self-incrimination and mandates that no person shall be "deprived of life, liberty, or property, without due process of law," and the Sixth Amendment guarantees a criminal defendant the right to counsel in certain circumstances.

Controversy marks the long history of the exclusionary rule. Proponents of the rule argue that the text of the Constitution supports the broad application of the exclusionary rule and that suppression serves as a deterrent to overzealous authorities who occasionally trample on constitutional principles in the quest to prosecute an alleged criminal. Some supporters of the exclusionary rule even advocate for its expansion, noting that over time, the U.S. Supreme Court has narrowed the application of the rule such that it now only applies in select situations. Contrarily, those who criticize the exclusionary rule contend that the framers did not expressly or implicitly authorize the suppression of evidence illegally seized by authorities. Moreover, opponents of the rule allege that it often allows a guilty person to go free, seemingly contradicting principles of justice. Thus, the exclusionary rule remains the topic of a spirited debate that has permeated the American court system at its highest levels.

Building the Exclusionary Rules

Fourth Amendment Context

In 1886, the Supreme Court first recognized the underlying principals of the exclusionary rule in *Boyd v. United States*. In *Boyd*, the government initiated forfeiture proceedings against two brothers who allegedly imported items illegally. During the proceedings, the district judge ordered the Boyds to produce an invoice describing the items the government sought to seize. After producing the requested invoice, the jury held that the Boyd brothers had illegally imported the goods in question and ordered them forfeited to the federal government. The Supreme Court reviewed the *Boyd* decision to determine whether forcing the brothers to produce an invoice violated constitutional principles. The Court held that it did. Specifically, the Court concluded that coercing the brothers into turning over an incriminating invoice violated the Fifth Amendment's prohibition of compelled self-incrimination and the Fourth Amendment's protection against unreasonable search and seizure. Thus, the Court remanded the case back to the district court, noting that the district court judge improperly admitted the invoice evidence in the Boyds' first trial.

Though seemingly promulgating the exclusionary rule in *Boyd*, the Supreme Court did not enunciate the broad proposition that unconstitutionally gathered evidence was inadmissible in a criminal trial. Almost 30 years later, in 1914, the Court expounded upon the exclusionary rule in *Weeks v. United States*. In *Weeks*, the Court assessed the admissibility of evidence obtained by federal authorities during a warrantless search of Weeks's home. Applying the principles of the Fourth Amendment, the Court concluded that the warrantless search of Weeks's home was improper, and that evidence seized during that search was not admissible at any subsequent criminal trial. Hence, the Court overturned Weeks's conviction and began the formal construction of the exclusionary rule. Though scholars routinely point to the *Weeks* decision as the origin of the exclusionary rule, the case reflects an exceedingly narrow version of the rule. In *Weeks,* the Supreme Court held that the exclusionary rule applied only in federal criminal proceedings. The Court also concluded that evidence improperly attained by state officials was not subject to exclusion in federal criminal court. Thus, the exclusionary rule, as outlined by the Court in *Weeks*, permitted states to admit unconstitutionally gathered evidence in state criminal trials.

In 1949, the Supreme Court again faced the question of whether the protections afforded by the Bill of Rights applied to state proceedings. In *Wolf v. Colorado*, the Court reinforced the exclusionary rule's limited scope, holding that states were free to admit improperly seized evidence in state criminal trials. The Court noted that while many states had adopted their own version of the exclusionary rule, and although the facts of *Wolf* amounted to a clear violation of the Fourth Amendment, the rule did not mandate the suppression of the evidence in question because the case involved state criminal proceedings outside of the federal court system. Further, the Court held in *Wolf* that exclusion was not the only effective means of protection from illegal search and seizure, pointing out that civil remedies and internal police disciplinary procedures provided adequate shielding from erroneous investigative procedures.

Contrary to the sentiments of many commentators at the time, the Court's decision in *Wolf* did not wholly authorize unconstitutional search and seizure by state authorities. Following *Wolf*, the Court spurned such contentions and attempted to expand the application of the exclusionary rule. For example, in 1952, in *Rochin v. California*, authorities in California obtained evidence from a man by forcing him to vomit though the use of medication. The Court held that the police's conduct in *Rochin* shocked the conscience, and that evidence acquired as a result of such behavior is inadmissible in any subsequent state or federal criminal prosecution. Eight years later, the Supreme Court, in *Elkins v. United States*, held that the silver platter doctrine was unconstitutional. The silver platter doctrine allowed federal authorities to use evidence obtained by state officials in violation of the Fourth Amendment in federal criminal trials. *Elkins* eliminated this loophole to the exclusionary rule. Thus, in both *Rochin* and *Elkins*, the Court began to expand the purview of the exclusionary rule by carving out exceptions to the *Wolf* holding that hinged on specific factual scenarios.

Yet, in 1961, in *Mapp v. Ohio*, the Supreme Court took a different tact. In *Mapp*, the Supreme Court confronted and overruled *Wolf*, extending the scope of the exclusionary rule. Charged with possession of obscene materials, Ms. Dollree Mapp challenged her conviction and the admissibility of evidence seized during an improper search of her home. Faced with facts similar to those in *Wolf*, the Court held that the Fourth Amendment applied to the states through the Due Process Clause of the Fourteenth Amendment. Accordingly, the Court also concluded that any evidence attained in violation of the Fourth Amendment was inadmissible in state and federal criminal court.

Fifth Amendment Context

Though the Supreme Court initially contemplated the exclusionary rule as a method of protecting citizens against violations of the Fourth Amendment, the Court also extended the reach of the rule to violations of other constitutional provisions. For example, shortly after *Boyd*, the Supreme Court held that the exclusionary rule also applies to the Fifth Amendment prohibition on forced self-incrimination. In 1897, in *Bram v. United States*, the Court concluded that under the Fifth Amendment, coerced confessions are not admissible in federal criminal trials as they are inherently unreliable. Almost 70 years later, in 1964, the Supreme Court extended the Fifth Amendment exclusionary rule to the states in *Malloy v. Hogan*. In *Malloy*, the Court held that evidence acquired in violation of the Fifth Amendment is inadmissible in state criminal proceedings. More recently, the Supreme Court upheld this principle in its now famous decision in *Miranda v. Arizona*, where the Court found a clear violation of the Fifth Amendment and excluded a coerced confession.

Sixth Amendment Context

The Supreme Court has also broadened the exclusionary rule to encompass violations of the Sixth Amendment's right to counsel provision. For instance, in a series of cases decided in the 1960s, the Court undertook the task of determining whether certain factual scenario's surrounding a suspect's admissions or confessions violated the Sixth Amendment and required the exclusion of evidence attained as a result of such constitutional violations. In 1964, the Supreme Court decided *Massiah v. United States*. In *Massiah*, an informant working with federal agents questioned the accused without counsel present. The Court held that the tactics of federal agents in *Massiah* violated the Sixth Amendment right to counsel and excluded the evidence obtained by the informant. Only five weeks later, the Court decided *Illinois v. Escobedo*. In *Escobedo*, like in *Massiah*, the police utilized tactics that violated the accused's Sixth Amendment right to counsel. And, as was the result in *Massiah*, in *Escobedo*, the Supreme Court excluded the improperly garnered evidence, noting that *Gideon v. Wainwright* mandated that the Sixth Amendment's right to counsel applied to the states through the Due Process Clause of the Fourteenth Amendment. Years later, in the 1981 case of *Edwards v. Arizona*, the Court held that evidence acquired without counsel present and after the accused had invoked his desire for the appointment of a lawyer violated the Sixth Amendment and was inadmissible in future criminal proceedings.

In addition, the Supreme Court has concluded that the exclusionary rule will bar the admission of certain identifications made in violation of a suspect's Sixth Amendment right to counsel. For example, on the same day in 1967, the Court held in *United States v. Wade* and *Gilbert v. California* that the identification of a suspect in violation of the Sixth Amendment right to counsel is inadmissible in criminal proceedings. Specifically, in *Wade* and in *Gilbert*, the Court suppressed an improper identification secured by an in-person lineup that circumvented constitutional principals.

Fruit of the Poisonous Tree

Early in the exclusionary rule's history, the Supreme Court recognized that not all improperly acquired evidence was directly related to a constitutional violation. For example, consider a situation in which authorities obtain a constitutionally improper confession and as a result, locate physical evidence that links the suspect to the alleged crime. In such a situation, the exclusionary rule most obviously operates to suppress the illegally attained confession that directly resulted from a violation of the suspect's Fifth and/or Sixth Amendment protections. But, one could argue that the physical evidence seized by authorities was not the direct result of these constitutional violations.

In 1920, the Supreme Court recognized that constitutional violations could not only elicit evidence directly, but could also produce evidence indirectly. In *Silverthorne Lumber Co. v. United States*, authorities illegally searched the premises of a suspected criminal and seized documents improperly. Acknowledging that the search amounted to a violation of the suspect's Fourth Amendment protections, the government then sought to use information contained in the illegally seized documents as support for a subpoena, or a legal order to produce evidence. Laying the foundation of the fruit of the poisonous tree doctrine, the Court held that the government could not use evidence obtained in violation of one's constitutional protections for any purpose. Nineteen years later, in *Nardone v. United States*, the Supreme Court first articulated the fruit of the poisonous tree doctrine. In *Nardone*, the Court held that indirect evidence gathered as a result of illegal wiretapping was inadmissible as fruit of the poisonous tree. The Supreme Court extended this doctrine ever further to include verbal evidence in 1963, in *Wong Sun v. United States*.

Limiting the Exclusionary Rules

Beginning in the 1960s, with few exceptions, the Supreme Court has consistently chipped away at the exclusionary rule's applications. Today, only certain factual scenarios will trigger the suppression of illegally obtained evidence. In fact, the Court's limitations on the exclusionary rule have led some scholars to note that the history of the rule is often easier to write if one outlines its exceptions rather than its applications.

The Supreme Court supported their initial efforts to limit the scope of the exclusionary rule by questioning the justifications for suppressing evidence in criminal trials. When the Court originally recognized and articulated the exclusionary rule, it highlighted its importance as a protective measure that insulated citizens from violations of their constitutional protections. Yet, years later, the Court reassessed the primary purpose of the rule. In 1974, in *Calandra v. United States*, the Court held that the exclusionary rule functioned principally as a deterrent to state or government misconduct. The Court reasoned that if exclusion, in any given situation, does not further the deterrent goal of the rule, suppression is not proper. Simply, the Court articulated a legal balancing test pitting the deterrent benefits of suppression against the social costs of suppression. Thus, in *Calandra*, the Supreme Court definitively concluded that the exclusionary rule does not apply in grand jury proceedings, a decision that marked the beginning of the rule's curtailment.

In 1976, the Supreme Court again ruled that the exclusionary rule was inappropriate in certain situations. Relying on the deterrent rationale for suppression, the Court in *United States v. Janis* concluded that authorities could use improperly seized evidence in forfeiture proceedings. The Court reasoned that in civil proceedings, excluding illegally seized evidence provided no deterrence to investigative authorities. Thus, finding that forfeiture proceedings were civil in nature, the Court held the exclusionary rule inapplicable.

Adhering to its rationale in *Janis*, the Supreme Court later outlined several other instances in which the exclusionary rule does not apply. For example, in 1984, in *I.N.S. v. Lopez-Mendoza*, the Court held that in civil deportation hearings, the suppression of evidence is unnecessary. Again, the Court concluded that because deportation hearings are primarily civil in nature, excluding improperly acquired evidence did little to deter authorities from failing to observe constitutional principals. Similarly, in 1998, in *Pennsylvania Board of Probation and Parole v. Scott*, the Supreme Court held that illegally gathered evidence is admissible in a parole revocation hearing. The Court again noted that a parole revocation hearing, though it implicated incarceration, is primarily an administrative proceeding that does not warrant the exclusion of evidence as a means to deter improper investigative conduct.

The Supreme Court has also limited the breadth of the exclusionary rule by enunciating several unique exceptions to its application in the context of law enforcement procedures. For example, in 1984, in *Nix v. Williams*, the Court established the inevitable discovery exception to the exclusionary rule. The inevitable discovery rule holds that illegally seized evidence is admissible in criminal trials if authorities could have discovered such evidence using methods separate from those the Court deemed unconstitutional. In *Nix*, police violated a suspect's Sixth Amendment right to counsel and as a result, discovered the body of the victim in the case. The Supreme Court concluded that evidence pertaining to the discovery of the body was admissible in the suspect's criminal trial, reasoning that police would have found the body of the victim without the directions provided by the suspect during the period of questioning that violated his Sixth Amendment protections.

Again in 1984, in *United States v. Leon*, the Court created yet another exception to the exclusionary rule that hinged on fact-specific police procedures. In *Leon*, the Court outlined the good faith exception to the exclusionary rule. The good faith exception holds that evidence obtained by law enforcement during the execution of a search warrant unsupported by probable cause is admissible in subsequent criminal proceedings. In *Leon*, an officer conducted a search pursuant to a search warrant, discovered incriminating evidence, and later determined that the search warrant was deficient. The Court held that because a neutral and detached magistrate validated the search warrant in question and the police officer merely relied on the validation provided by the magistrate when executing the warrant, the good faith exception allowed for the admission of the seized evidence. The Court went on to justify its holding by noting that excluding improperly seized evidence from a criminal trial in such a situation does little to deter police misconduct.

Other exceptions to the exclusionary rule dealing directly with police procedure soon followed the inevitable discovery doctrine and the good faith exception. In 1987, in *Illinois v. Krull*, the Supreme Court held that evidence seized in accordance with an unconstitutional statute is admissible in criminal trials, pointing out that suppressing evidence gathered in reliance on current statutes does little to deter authorities from circumventing constitutional protections. In 1995, in *Arizona v. Evans*, the Supreme Court extended such logic by concluding that the exclusionary rule does not apply in situations in which police receive erroneous information from departmental records. Again, the Court hypothesized that suppressing evidence in such circumstances has no deterrent effect.

The Supreme Court has also carved out exceptions to the exclusionary rule that deal directly with evidence obtained by private or foreign parties. For instance, in 1984, in *United States v. Jacobson*, the Court concluded that evidence illegally attained by private parties in the course of a search and turned over to law enforcement personnel is admissible in criminal trials. Also, in 1990, in *United States v. Verdugo-Urquidez*, the Court held that evidence improperly gathered by foreign officials and turned over to domestic authorities does not trigger the exclusionary rule. Yet, the Court's opinion in *Verdugo-Urquidez* stressed that the Fourth Amendment did not fully protect the accused, as he was a foreign citizen facing criminal prosecution in the United States.

Lengthening the list of exceptions to the exclusionary rule are factual scenarios involving third parties. In certain situations, the exclusionary rule will bar the admission of evidence improperly gathered in violation of a third party's rights. For example, in *Brendlin v. California*, the Supreme Court suppressed evidence improperly obtained during an illegal traffic stop. In that case, the passenger, not the driver, challenged the search and won exclusion. Most often, however, the Supreme Court has held that to exclude illegally attained evidence, the party seeking suppression must have suffered the identified constitutional violation. Such situations involve the legal doctrine of standing and have spawned lively debate about the nature of the deterrent justification for the exclusionary rule.

Finally, the Supreme Court has also established a limited exception to the exclusionary rule in the area of impeachment evidence. Generally, impeachment evidence show's the falsity of a person's trial testimony. This exclusionary rule exception allows a court to admit virtually any type of improperly acquired evidence for the sole purpose of impeaching the testimony of the defendant at trial. The Supreme Court announced this broad exception to the exclusionary rule in 1980 in *United States v. Havens,* where the Court upheld the admission of an illegally obtained piece of cloth to rebut the defendant's testimony.

The Current State of the Exclusionary Rule

The exclusionary rule has endured periods of both expansion and contraction, such that its application to any given factual scenario is often difficult to determine. In a recent Supreme Court case, *Hudson v. Michigan,* Justice Scalia outlined the current state of the exclusionary rule, pointing out that the application rule requires the fulfillment of three prerequisite conditions. First, for the exclusionary rule to apply, a constitutional violation must have occurred. Second, the acquisition of the evidence in question must directly result from the constitutional violation. Finally, the deterrent benefits of excluding illegally seized evidence must outweigh the social costs of exclusion. Importantly, while *Hudson* sheds light on the exclusionary rule, the fluid nature of the doctrine and its exceptions make its application largely fact-specific.

Pro: Arguments in Support of the Exclusionary Rule

Proponents of the exclusionary rule contend that the cost-benefit analysis often applied to the rule misconstrues the framers' intentions. Supporters of the rule also contend that suppression is necessary to protect the rights of citizens by deterring overzealous authorities. Accordingly, those exclusionary rule advocates seek to expand the reach of the exclusionary rule, arguing that its exceptions and limitations jeopardize the citizenry by exposing it to potential abuses by law enforcement personnel who occasionally seek to close criminal cases at any cost.

Though some pro-exclusionary rule commentators acknowledge that the framers of the Constitution did not contemplate suppression of evidence, they argue that by virtue of drafting the Bill of Rights, the founding fathers expected adherence to constitutional protections. Supporters also note that identifying instances in which the exclusionary rule deterred police misconduct is a proposition wrought with inaccuracy. Accordingly, advocates allege that the modern cost-benefit analysis that routinely accompanies exclusionary rule issues is misapplied. For example, such a calculation devalues constitutional protections by characterizing adherence to the Fourth, Fifth, and Sixth amendments as costs. Supporters of the rule contend that there is never a cost when authorities dutifully abide by constitutional direction. Thus, any level of deterrence warrants the continued use of the exclusionary rule.

Those in favor of the exclusionary rule also assert that the rule does not favor the guilty or hinder investigative abilities. Advocates of suppression argue that critics concerned that the rule will favor the guilty misconstrue the spirit of constitutional protections. Though suppressing evidence does, in certain instances, exonerate an otherwise guilty person, it also protects society generally against abuses of authority. As some commentators note, the exclusionary rule serves to curb future misconduct rather than rectify past wrongdoing. Thus, as is the case in many other areas of law, the exclusionary rule allows certain guilty parties to go free so as to afford society the protections the Constitution outlines. Proponents of the exclusionary rule also argue that the rule does little to hamper police efforts. Addressing the contention that law enforcement cannot adequately perform their duties with the threat of suppression looming, those in favor of the rule assert that it is the constitutional provisions that rightfully limit police procedure. Therefore, attacks on the exclusionary rule, some claim, are misguided.

Those who believe that the exclusionary rule is fundamental to criminal procedure also maintain that its abolishment could have drastic, negative effects on the criminal justice system. Pro-exclusionary rule scholars note that the issue of suppression calls attention to misconduct and helps clarify constitutional principles. For example, by necessitating judicial review, suppression forces courts to re-examine the contours of investigative procedures and their interaction with constitutional protections. In this way, courts assist police in their efforts to comply with the law while respecting the rights of citizens. Without the rule, some theorize, such review and adaptation will disappear. Many who favor the exclusionary rule also contend that proposed alternatives to suppression would do little to ensure that law enforcement observes constitutional principles. They argue that abolishing or altering the exclusionary rule in ways that narrow its application would grant authorities unchecked power in the course of their duties. In fact, many who support suppression assert that the Supreme Court's increasingly narrow application of the exclusionary rule has already created a criminal justice system that is more accepting of improper police investigative techniques.

Con: Arguments Opposing the Exclusionary Rule

The primary criticism of the exclusionary rule involves its constitutional underpinnings. Some scholars argue that the exclusionary rule is merely a judicially created doctrine not authorized, either explicitly or implicitly, by the language in the Constitution. Additionally, opponents of the exclusionary rule often criticize the doctrine on more general grounds. For instance, some detractors claim that the rule handcuffs law enforcement and that it allows criminals to escape prosecution by suppressing evidence that rightfully condemns their behavior. In addition, those opposed to the exclusionary rule also contend that its deterrent effects are unquantifiable, and that the abolition of the rule would have little to no impact on the criminal justice system.

Yale law professor Akhil Amar is perhaps the most vocal modern critic of the exclusionary rule. In his writings, he echoes the sentiments of many opponents of the exclusionary rule by arguing that the text of the Fourth Amendment, specifically the use of the term *reasonable*, does not warrant the suppression of improperly seized evidence in a criminal trial. He contends that when crafting the Fourth Amendment, the founders merely intended to provide a civil remedy to innocent victims of improper searches and seizures. In such an instance, the aggrieved party could seek monetary compensation from authorities who violated his or her Fourth Amendment rights. But if a jury found an aggrieved party guilty, then civil remedies were not available because authorities' conduct, in such circumstances, would meet the standard of "reasonable" as indicated by a defendant's guilt. In this way, according to Amar, the Fourth Amendment protects the innocent and not the guilty.

Other arguments against the exclusionary rule hypothesize that it limits the freedom with which law enforcement personnel can pursue suspected criminals, and that it rewards those who commit criminal acts. For example, commentators taking this stance argue that the exclusionary rule charges the police with the virtually impossible task of knowing and adhering to all of the legal contours of the duties their position requires. Critics theorize that the threat of suppression forces law enforcement to memorize decades of case-law and legal precedent governing topics like home searches, interrogations, and right to counsel and that such an undertaking is excessively arduous for even the most skilled attorney. Opponents of the rule further contend that the result is the guarantee that the exclusionary rule will assist those who commit crimes. They assert that while law enforcement struggles to avoid illegality, those who consciously deviate from recognized law wait patiently to employ a legal technicality that ensures their freedom.

A final critique of the exclusionary rule is that it fails to actually deter police misconduct. Those who oppose the rule allege that since deterrence is unquantifiable, there is no method for accurately predicting the value of suppression. Supporting this claim, some cite empirical data that suggests police routinely ignore the deterrent impact of the exclusionary rule when criminal prosecution is not an objective of their investigative efforts. For instance, empirical data indicates that police sometimes seize narcotics or weapons simply to remove those items from a high-crime area. In such circumstances, law enforcement is not concerned with subsequent legal proceedings; thus, suppression is not much of a deterrent.

Those opposed to the suppression of evidence as a remedy for constitutional violations propose a host of varied alternatives to the exclusionary rule. The most extreme suggestions center on the idea of eliminating the exclusionary rule entirely. Advocates of this approach argue that civil remedies yielding monetary compensation can ensure that law enforcement complies with constitutional protections. A less drastic alternative suggests that courts assess constitutional violations on a case-by-case basis, choosing when to suppress evidence and when to impose civil liability. And finally, some propose that the law tailor suppression to the severity and egregiousness of the constitutional violation. Such an alteration would presumably demand suppression in serious cases or in cases where police misconduct was particularly outrageous. Conversely, this approach would avoid suppression when constitutional violations occur in minor criminal cases or despite attempts by law enforcement to comply with constitutional principals.

See Also: 11. Jury System.

Further Readings

Alshuler, Albert W. "Studying the Exclusionary Rule: An Empirical Classic." *University of Chicago Law Review,* v.75/1365 (2008).

Arizona v. Evans, 514 U.S. 1 (1995).

Binnall, James M. "Deterrence is Down and Social Costs are Up: A Parolee Revisits *Pennsylvania Board of Probation* and *Parole v. Scott*." *Vermont Law Review,* v.38/199 (2007).

Boyd v. United States, 116 U.S. 616 (1886).

Bram v. United States, 168 U.S. 532 (1897).

Brendlin v. California, 551 U.S 249 (2007).

Calabresi, Guido. "The Exclusionary Rule." *Harvard Journal of Law and Public Policy,* v. 26/11 (2003).

Calandra v. United States, 414 U.S. 338 (1974).

Davies, Thomas Y. "Farther and Farther from the Original Fifth Amendment: The Recharacterization of the Right Against Self-Incrimination as a 'Trial Right' in *Chavez v. Martinez.*" *Tennessee Law Review,* v.70/987 (2003).

Dripps, Donald. "The Case for the Contingent Exclusionary Rule." *American Criminal Law Review,* v.38/1 (2001).

Edwards v. Arizona, 451 U.S. 477 (1981).

Elkins v. United States, 364 U.S. 206 (1960).

Escobedo v. Illinois, 378 U.S. 478 (1964).

Gideon v. Wainwright, 372 U.S. 335 (1963).

Gilbert v. California, 388 U.S. 263 (1967).

Holland, Brooks. "The Exclusionary Rule as Punishment." *Rutgers Law Record,* v. 36/38 (2009).

Illinois v. Krull, 480 U.S. 340 (1987).

I.N.S. v. Lopez-Mendoza, 468 U.S. 1032 (1984).

Kamisar, Yale, Wayne R. LaFave, Jerold H. Israel, and Nancy J. King. *Basic Criminal Procedure: Cases, Comments and Questions.* St. Paul, MN: West Group, 2002.

LaFave, Wayne R. *Search and Seizure: A Treatise on the Fourth Amendment.* St. Paul, MN: Thomson/Reuters, 2010.

LaFave, Wayne R. "The Smell of Herring: A Critique of the Supreme Court's Latest Assault on the Exclusionary Rule." *Journal of Criminal Law and Criminology,* v.99/757 (2009).

Lynch, Timothy. "In Defense of the Exclusionary Rule." *Harvard Journal of Law and Public Policy,* v.23/711 (2000).

Malloy v. Hogan, 378 U.S. 1 (1964).

Mapp v. Ohio, 367 U.S. 643 (1961).

Massiah v. United States, 377 U.S. 201 (1964).

Miranda v. Arizona, 384 U.S. 436 (1966).

Nardone v. United States, 308 U.S. 338 (1939).

Nix v. Williams, 467 U.S. 431 (1984).

Oliver, Wesley M. "Toward a Better Categorical Balance of the Costs and Benefits of the Exclusionary Rule." *Buffalo Criminal Law Review,* v.9/201 (2005).

Pennsylvania Board of Probation and Parole v. Scott, 514 U.S. 357 (1998).

Rochin v. California, 342 U.S. 165 (1952).

Root, Roger. "The Originalist Case for the Fourth Amendment Exclusionary Rule." *Gonzaga Law Review*, v.45/1 (2009–10).

Silverthorne Lumber Co. v. United States, 251 U.S. 385 (1920).

Sklansky, David A. "Is the Exclusionary Rule Obsolete?" *Ohio State Journal of Criminal Law*, v.5/567 (2008).

Tinsley, P., Stephan N. Kinsella, and Walter Block. "In Defense of Evidence and Against the Exclusionary Rule: A Libertarian Approach." *Southern University Law Review*, v.32/63 (2004).

United States v. Havens, 446 U.S. 620 (1980).

United States v. Jacobson, 466 U.S. 109 (1984).

United States v. Janis, 428 U.S. 433 (1976).

United States v. Leon, 468 U.S. 897 (1984).

United States v. Verdugo-Urquidez, 494 U.S 259 (1990).

United States v. Wade, 388 U.S. 218 (1967).

Weeks v. United States, 232 U.S. 383 (1914).

Wolf v. Colorado, 338 U.S. 25 (1949).

Wong Sun v. United States, 371 U.S. 471 (1963).

Yeaton, Dawn. "Civil Forfeiture—Exclusionary Rule—Broadening the Use of Illegally Seized Evidence in Forfeiture Proceedings." In Re Forfeiture of $180, 975, 734 N.W.2D 489 (Mich 2007)." *University of Detroit Mercy Law Review*, v. 86/59 (2008).

7

Expert Witnesses and Hired Guns

Wm. C. Plouffe, Jr.
Independent Scholar

To obtain a conviction of a person for committing a crime, the state, through the prosecutor, must present sufficient evidence to convince the jury of the guilt of the suspect beyond a reasonable doubt. Evidence to support a conviction can take many forms, such as testimonial evidence of witnesses; physical evidence, such as the weapon used in the commission of the crime; and documentary evidence, such as the ransom note employed during a kidnapping. In almost all criminal proceedings, witnesses are the primary source of evidence against the accused. Almost all criminal convictions hinge upon the testimony of the witnesses presented by the prosecution. It is uncommon for criminal convictions to rest solely on physical evidence. The defense can also present its own witnesses.

There are two basic types of witnesses: lay witnesses and expert witnesses. Lay witnesses are those witnesses who can testify to their own personal knowledge, which is usually obtained through the five senses of sight, hearing, smell, taste, and touch. This requirement can be found in Federal Rule of Evidence 602. In other words, if a lay witness saw the suspect shoot the victim, heard the suspect say he or she was going to kill the victim, or smelled the odor of gasoline just prior to the suspect burning down a building, then that witness could testify to those observations. Under Federal Rule of Evidence 701, a lay witness may not present an opinion on an issue except where the opinion is rationally based on the lay witness's perceptions; helpful to a clear understanding of the witness's testimony or the determination of a fact; and not based on scientific, technical, or other specialized knowledge. Thus, a lay witness may not give opinions as to a person's state of emotion, the speed of vehicles, a person's sobriety or intoxication, distances, age or identity of a person, the character of a person, the sanity of a person, or the handwriting of a person.

In contrast, an expert witness may give his or her expert opinion on an issue, but there are certain limitations on expert witnesses, under Federal Rule of Evidence 702. First, the subject of the expert testimony must be based on scientific, technical, or other specialized knowledge, which is beyond the ability of the untrained layman to intelligently determine without specialized understanding. Second, an expert witness will only be allowed to testify to those issues that would assist the jury to understand the evidence. For example, calling an expert witness to testify on the topic of ichthyology would probably not be allowed where the issue to be determined by the jury was whether the victim died of drowning or poisoning, as ichthyology is not germane to the cause of death.

Third, the expert witness must be qualified by knowledge, skill, experience, training, or education. Thus, an expert witness does not have to have a Ph.D. to testify as an expert witness. For example, an auto mechanic who has worked for 30 years could be qualified as an expert witness on the topic of auto repair. Thus, there are numerous ways that a person can be qualified as an expert witness. Fourth, under Federal Rule of Evidence 702, any expert opinion must be based upon sufficient facts or data, a result of reliable principles and methods, and based upon the reliable application by the expert witness of these principles and methods.

Before a person is allowed to testify as an expert witness, that person must be qualified as an expert witness by the court. First, the offering party presents the qualifications of the proposed expert witness to the court. The expert witness will be called to the witness stand and be asked to recite his or her education, experience, training, publications, and previous qualifications as an expert witness. The opposing party will be allowed to cross-examine the proposed expert witness and question his or her qualifications. At that point, the court will make a decision as to whether the proposed expert witness is qualified.

When an expert witness testifies, his or her expert testimony must be based on facts or data, as required by Federal Rule of Evidence 703. It cannot be based on speculation.

Quality of the Science

Any person can claim that his or her opinion is based on scientific principles. However, there are a number of people who are considered to be "quacks" by mainstream scientific authorities, which is why the Federal Rules of Evidence require that all scientific methods and theories be reliable. The U.S. Supreme Court, in the decision of *Daubert v. Merrell Dow Pharmaceuticals* (1993), has clarified how to determine the reliability of science by the employment of the following factors: (1) whether the expert witness's method and theory are objective and can be tested, as opposed to a subjective belief; (2) whether the expert witness's method and theory have been subjected to publication and peer review; (3) the known or potential rate of error of the method or theory; (4) the existence and maintenance of any standards or controls; and (5) whether the method or theory has been generally accepted in the scientific community. By the application of these five factors, trial courts are expected to be the gatekeepers for expert testimony, not permitting expert witnesses to testify unless their methods and theories can meet these five principles. Essentially, it is the duty of the trial courts to prevent "junk science" from being admitted into evidence.

Prior to the *Daubert* test, the courts generally followed the *Frye* test. The *Frye* test was, essentially, the fifth factor in the *Daubert* test: whether the science in question had been generally accepted by the scientific community. The *Frye* test was first formally expressed in 1923 in the decision of *Frye v. United States*. Over the years, many courts adopted the *Frye* test to determine the admissibility of scientific evidence. Although the *Daubert* decision overruled the *Frye* test, at least in federal courts, there are still a number of state jurisdictions that still adhere to the *Frye* test.

One the justifications for the overruling of the *Frye* test was that it did not allow for the admission of new or novel scientific evidence, because many years were required before cutting-edge theories or methods were generally accepted by the scientific community. Under the *Frye* test, new or novel scientific evidence, even if it was extremely accurate and objective and could be repeated with a low rate of error, was inadmissible. Accordingly, the *Daubert* test allows for the admission of new or novel scientific theories or methods if other factors can be met. Thus, even though the old *Frye* test is now one of five factors to be considered when determining the admissibility of scientific evidence, general acceptance by the scientific community is no longer the sole criteria for determining admissibility of scientific evidence, at least in those courts that have adopted the *Daubert* test.

Expert Witnesses in Criminal Cases

Expert witnesses are not uncommon in criminal cases, depending upon the nature and seriousness of the crime charged and the financial resources of the suspect. Many criminal defendants do not have the financial resources to hire their own expert witnesses, and the government will rarely pay for expert witnesses for indigent defendants unless the charges are extremely serious, such as for murder. However, in contrast, the government frequently uses expert witness as a matter of course in many criminal cases, such as traffic accident reconstruction (using specially trained accident reconstruction police officers), drug analysis (using government crime lab technicians), or mental competence (using government-employed or appointed psychiatrists/psychologists).

Psychiatric/Psychological Evaluation

Many years of training are required to become a psychiatrist or psychologist. A psychiatrist holds a medical degree and focuses on the medical aspects of the brain and mental and emotional functioning. A psychologist usually holds a Ph.D. and is not allowed to prescribe medicine. Both are required to be licensed by the state. Some states allow persons who hold an M.A. in counseling or an M.S.W. in social work to become licensed. Each of these professions requires a bachelors degree and at least one additional graduate or professional degree. Thus, they are usually qualified as expert witnesses before courts without any difficulty.

A major defense to the commission of a crime is the insanity defense. A suspect found to be insane at the time of the commission of the crime can be found not guilty by reason of insanity. However, that person will likely have to spend time in a psychiatric hospital. Whenever a suspect raises the insanity defense, the government requires psychiatric/psychological testing. Regardless of the findings of government experts, the suspect will likely hire his or her own psychiatrist or psychologist to provide an expert opinion as to the his or her sanity. Then it is up to the court to determine if the suspect was insane.

The most common test used for the determination of insanity is the M'Naghten test. The M'Naghten test requires that a person is not legally responsible for his or her acts if, due to a defect of the mind, they were unable to understand the difference between right and wrong at the time of the crime. Thus, where the suspect has raised the insanity defense in a criminal trial for murder, the jury would decide between the claims of the government's expert witness that the suspect did understand the difference between right and wrong at the time the act was committed, and the suspect's expert, who claims the opposite.

Another way in which psychiatrists/psychologists are used in criminal cases is to determine whether suspects are sufficiently competent to stand trial. Their employment is similar to that of the insanity defense. Each state usually has psychiatrists/psychologists as employees of the state mental health system, the state corrections system, or the courts to conduct mental health examinations of suspects. If they wish to contest the findings of the state psychiatrists/psychologists, suspects will usually have to hire their own expert. For extremely serious cases such as murder, some courts might appoint a private psychiatrist/psychologist for a suspect if he or she is indigent.

Physical Evidence Evaluation

Physical evidence can provide important support for a criminal conviction. Examples of physical evidence include tire tracks, fingerprints, shoe prints, ballistics, reassembly of glass fragments, fiber analysis, chemical analysis, and paint comparison. Physical evidence is usually processed in two places: at the police station in the detective/crime scene unit or at the police crime lab.

Physical evidence such as tire tracks, shoe prints, and fingerprints are usually handled by a police detective or crime scene specialist. The expert qualifications for these positions include several weeks of specialized police schools for crime scene processing and criminal investigation. Ballistics includes, but is not limited to, the science of comparing bullet cases to firearms to determine a match. Ballistics is usually handled at the crime lab as it involves microscopic comparison of physical objects and chemical comparison of gunpowder residue. Scientific processes such as fiber analysis (to compare recovered thread samples to an original fabric source); chemical analysis (to identify a particular substance, such as cocaine or heroin, and its source); and paint comparison (to determine if paint chips recovered at an accident scene match the paint on a particular car) are also usually handled by a crime lab technician, who is often required to possess a graduate degree in either chemistry or physics. The graduate degree in the hard sciences and the experience in the crime lab are usually sufficient for the crime lab technician to be certified as an expert witness.

Courts generally will not appoint private experts for the evaluation of physical evidence for suspects unless they are indigent, the crime is extremely serious, and the evaluation of such physical evidence was essential to determining guilt or innocence. There are many private experts for such evaluations of physical evidence, such as university professors or retired police officers.

Medical/Biological Evidence Evaluation

Medical evaluations can only be conducted by a degreed medical doctor (M.D.), although in some narrow circumstances, a registered nurse might be allowed to testify. Although an M.D. degree is usually sufficient for most medical expert testimony, on occasion, the court might require the M.D. to have a specialty, such as psychiatry. For homicides, an M.D. is required to perform an autopsy. However, for biological testing, such as the identification of DNA, many crime lab technicians do not hold an M.D. degree and may instead have a Ph.D. in biology or a master of science (M.S).

Coroners are usually M.D.s, although some states do not require the coroner to hold a medical degree. Where there is a dispute as to the cause of death in a criminal case, the defense may want to have their own expert perform an autopsy as well. This is usually quite expensive, and the courts will generally not appoint a private M.D. to perform a second autopsy for an indigent defendant unless significant evidence can be produced showing that a second autopsy is necessary to prevent a miscarriage of justice.

Medical evidence in criminal trials is most commonly used to identify the person suspected of committing a criminal act, where certain biological evidence that did not belong to the victim was found at the crime scene. Prior to the advent of DNA testing, blood type was frequently used. In many cases, blood type could also be obtained from other biological fluids such as semen and saliva. With the advent of DNA testing and its subsequent acceptance in most courts, identification of persons through the use of biological testing has become much more certain.

Documentary and Computer Evidence Evaluation

The identification of documents and handwriting is an important aspect of certain crimes involving documents. While there are no programs that offer college degrees in handwriting analysis, there are courses that involve the technology of paper and ink. Handwriting analysis is a skill that can be learned through technical courses, many of which are offered by law enforcement agencies and are not available to private citizens. Many handwriting analysts learn their trade through working with more experienced analysts. In criminal prosecutions, identification of handwriting can be particularly important, especially in criminal cases that involve threats or extortion.

Another important aspect of documentary evidence subject to expert testimony is that of photography analysis. Through the use of advanced chemical processes and technical instruments, a competent photography technician can determine if and how a photograph has been altered or tampered with. This is also true for a digital photograph, which will have an inconsistent pixel pattern if the file has been altered. Thus, in a criminal proceeding, an expert witness can determine the validity of a photograph and help determine guilt or innocence.

Expert witnesses in the field of computer science are able to retrieve data from computers after the information has been erased, and are able to track communications made over computer networks. These are very technical skills that usually require an advanced education in computer science.

Acoustical Evidence Evaluation

An expert in acoustics, the study of sound, is likely to be trained in physics, even if he or she does not possess a Ph.D. There are a number of technical instruments that can accurately measure, separate, and identify specific sounds that the human ear would not be able to discern or identify. Human voices can also be identified through the use of such technology, even if the voices are muffled through such things as a cloth held over the mouth.

Traffic Accident Reconstruction

One of the more common tasks for police officers is the investigation of traffic accidents. Many police departments have officers specially trained as traffic accident reconstructionists. Usually, these schools last for several weeks and involve training in the various methods for determining the chain of events in traffic accidents by examining such items as vehicle damage, estimated vehicle speed, skid marks, road conditions, weather conditions, and witness statements.

In the event of a major traffic accident, police department accident reconstructionists will be assigned to investigate. Then, at trial, the police officer will serve both as the complaining witness and as the expert witness. However, if the suspect wants to contest the conclusions of the police accident reconstructionist, he or she will have to hire a private accident reconstructionist. Private experts in this field are usually retired police officers and quite expensive. It is frequently not worth the money to hire a private accident reconstructionist unless the accident involved a homicide. It is unheard of for a court to appoint a private accident reconstructionist for a suspect charged with traffic violations due to an accident.

Financial Evaluation

One of the fastest-growing crimes in America is white-collar crime, which usually involves financial crimes and the betrayal of trust. It includes such crimes as embezzlement, securities fraud, bank fraud, and money laundering. Many financial instruments are very complex and difficult even for financial professionals to understand. Accordingly, some large law enforcement agencies have specific units to investigate white-collar crime. These units are usually staffed by accountants and lawyers who understand the financial system and act as expert witnesses in criminal cases.

Private expert witnesses can be obtained by suspects, although the cost can be very high for white-collar crime experts. Highly qualified accountants frequently have master of business administration (M.B.A.) degrees and are certified public accountants, who have usually obtained advanced degrees in accounting. However, many defendants in white-collar criminal cases are highly paid executives who can afford to pay the fees for qualified expert witnesses.

Hired Guns

Hired gun is a derogatory term applied to expert witnesses who will allegedly provide any expert testimony for a fee. The term is usually employed by the opposing party to describe their opponent's expert witness, while upholding their own witness as honest and truthful about the facts of the case (even though the opponent is also paying a fee for their expert witness). Unfortunately, it is extremely rare to find a qualified expert witness who will testify without requiring a fee. Most expert witnesses require the payment of thousands of dollars before they will even review a case. Accordingly, this makes the employment of private expert witnesses by indigent or even working-class or middle-class defendants almost impossible.

Unfortunately, some expert witnesses will give any type of testimony for a price. There have been reports of some expert witnesses taking one position in one case and the opposite position in another case, as long as they are paid their fee. However, despite the reports, such cases are rare, and the opposition can usually gain access to a proposed expert witness's previous testimony and discover such inconsistencies, which would result in their credibility being severely damaged.

As a general rule, the term *hired gun* is more frequently used in civil proceedings where plaintiffs are suing for damages on novel theories of causation and liability. In such cases, the expert witness may be used to advance novel theories or unusual methods of scientific proof in attempt to justify the lawsuit that, under the generally accepted tenets of science, would be considered without merit. Experts such as police officers or crime lab technicians are almost never referred to as hired guns, but expert witnesses hired by criminal suspects are, even though government officials are also being paid for their time and testimony in court.

Pro: Arguments in Favor of Using Expert Witnesses

Juries are selected at random from the residents of a specified geographical area within the court's jurisdiction. Jury lists are usually obtained from voter lists or driver's license records. The strongest argument for the continued use of expert witnesses is the numerous scientific, technical, and/or specialized subjects that simply cannot be understood by the average jury member. It is highly unlikely that any jury would include a person who has the qualifications to address the particular scientific, technical, or specialized issues that arise at trial. Even if the jury did contain such an expert, they would not be eligible for cross examination or presenting a countering point of view. Also, courts tend to frown upon persons on a jury who have specialized knowledge of an issue that is being determined at trial, as juries are supposed to make their decisions based upon the facts presented at trial and not upon their own personal knowledge.

Often in criminal trials, police officers and crime lab personnel are presented as expert witnesses because of the training they receive from law enforcement agencies or the graduate scientific education required for becoming a crime lab technician. Even if police officers and crime lab technicians were not presented as expert witnesses, they would be presenting testimony based upon their own personal knowledge, education, and experience. Many criminal suspects do not possess the college education, advanced training, or specialized scientific education sufficient to counter the testimony presented by the government. As U.S. criminal law is based on due process and as criminal suspects are guaranteed a fair trial by the Bill of Rights, not allowing defendants to present their own expert witnesses violates these basic and fundamental principles of law.

A very important factor in favor of allowing expert testimony in criminal trials is the possibility for any corruption or lack of competence on the part of government officials. There have been numerous examples of crime labs being accused of actually lying about the tests conducted or not conducted on evidence, which occurred in the late 1990s and early 2000s in Oklahoma; and where crime labs have been accused of gross mismanagement resulting in delays, faulty results, and the deterioration of evidence, such as when the Massachusetts State Police crime lab failed to process DNA evidence from a backlog of 16,000 cases, as was discovered in 2007. Further, there are numerous examples of police officials obfuscating or hiding exculpatory evidence.

The ability to present expert testimony is one of the many checks and balances in the American criminal justice system that allow for a fair trial and ensure that innocent people are not wrongfully convicted.

Many innocent people are convicted in the courts of criminal charges they did not commit. The most illuminating proof of this fact is the work of the Innocence Project, where through the use of DNA evidence and expert witnesses, over 200 innocent people have been cleared of charges, many of them removed from death row and saved from execution. The use of expert witnesses is appropriate in criminal trials because the trial judge, under the requirements of the *Daubert* decision, acts as a gatekeeper to prevent poor science from being entered into evidence. This prevents juries from being misled by the false or inaccurate testimony of quacks.

Con: Arguments Opposing the Use of Expert Witnesses

A common criticism of criminal trials is that too many suspects are released on technicalities, thereby defeating justice. Related to this criticism is how criminal defendants use expert witnesses to mislead juries. Police officers, crime lab technicians, and prosecutors are highly trained and cannot hold their positions without the highly specialized training they require. To allow criminal suspects to use expert witnesses to improperly mislead juries against the testimony of government officials risks allowing otherwise guilty criminals to go free.

Criminal trials and sentencing are also accused of taking too much time. Many years can pass before a person convicted of a serious crime, such as murder, and sentenced to death will be executed. Not only do endless appeals delay justice, but the use of expert witnesses can also delay criminal trials. When a criminal defendant presents notice that he or she will be using an expert witness, the trial will be delayed to allow the government to consider the possible testimony of the expert witness.

Cost is another factor. A criminal defendant using expert witnesses increases the time, effort, and resources that the government must expend to counter the defendant's expert witness. When an indigent defendant is allowed to retain expert witnesses, the cost runs into many thousands of dollars, which must be paid by taxpayers. Opponents of expert witnesses uphold that the testimony provided by government experts should be sufficient to provide the jury with a fair evaluation of the physical evidence.

One of the most expensive forms of expert witnesses is used when criminal defendants employ the insanity defense. The basic test for insanity, the M'Naghten test, is vague and the criteria for determining insanity is very subjective. Opponents of the test claim that due to these problematic issues, the decision of insanity should be left to the jury.

Expert witnesses or "quacks" who utilize what is essentially "junk science" are a significant problem with the use of expert witnesses in criminal trials. For example, it was through the use of expert testimony in the 1970s that a new defense of battered woman's syndrome (BWS) was first recognized as a successful defense to crimes, including murder. Junk science can result in juries being mislead into allowing otherwise guilty people to go free when they have committed crimes that should be punished.

The most significant criticism of the use of expert witnesses by criminal suspects is the question of bias. Expert witnesses do not testify for free; they are paid very well for their time and effort, often in the range of tens of thousands of dollars. This introduces the danger of bias, where an expert may favor of the party who is paying for their testimony.

Conclusion

The use of expert witnesses in the American criminal justice system has been criticized, primarily by those who generally wish for swift and inexpensive criminal trials. Conversely, the use of expert witnesses has been allowed by law for many years, and has been supported by many elements of society that support the idea of a fair trial respecting due process. The use of expert witnesses entails certain social costs, which include delay and financial costs. However, not using expert witnesses increases the chances of innocent people being convicted of crimes they did not commit. The challenge is where to strike the balance between efficiency and justice.

See Also: 2. DNA Evidence; 8. Eyewitness Testimony and Accuracy; 10. Insanity Defense; 11. Jury System; 15. Polygraphs.

Further Readings

Bamberger, Phylis Skloot. "Evidence Commentary: The Dangerous Expert Witness." *Brooklyn Law Review,* v.52/55 (1986).

DeWitt, Sonja L. "The Indigent Criminal Defendant, DNA Evidence and the Right to an Expert Witness: A Comparison of the Requirements of Due Process in *State v. Dubose* and *Harris v. State.*" *Boston University Public Interest Law Journal,* v.6/267 (1996).

Estes, Andrea. "Crime Lab Neglected 16,000 Cases: Evidence Was Never Analyzed, Probe Finds." *Boston Globe* (July 15, 2007).

Faigman, David L., and Amy J. Wright. "The Battered Woman Syndrome in the Age of Science." *Arizona Law Review,* v.39 (1997).

Gianelli, Paul C. "Daubert: Interpreting the Federal Rules of Evidence." *Cardozo Law Review,* v.15/1999 (1994).

Golan, Tal. "A Cross-Disciplinary Look at Scientific Truth: What's the Law To Do? Revisiting the History of Scientific Expert Testimony." *Brooklyn Law Review,* v. 71/879 (2008).

Ladd, Mason. "Expert Testimony." *Vanderbilt Law Review,* v.5 (1952).

Oppenheim, Elliott B. "Lessons Learned: The Offensive Use of Medical Evidence in Criminal Defense Cases." *American Health Lawyers Association,* v.19/167 (1010).

Scheck, Barry, Peter Neufeld, and Jim Dwyer. *Actual Innocence.* New York: Random House, 2000.

Vidmar, Neil, and Shari Seidman Diamond. "Juries and Expert Evidence." *Brooklyn Law Review,* v.66/1121 (2001).

8

Eyewitness Testimony and Accuracy

Lisa E. Hasel
University of Florida

An eyewitness is a person who has observed a person commit a crime, or observed a likely suspect immediately before or after a crime was committed. Eyewitness testimony is when an eyewitness testifies in court about the identity of the person who committed the crime. An eyewitness identification is the process by which an eyewitness to a crime claims to recognize someone as being the person who committed the crime in question. Sometimes, the identification is based on what is called a *showup*, which is a one-on-one confrontation between the suspect and the eyewitness, arranged by police. However, this can be an extremely suggestive procedure. Often, the identification is made from confidentially viewing a lineup constructed by police, in which a suspect is embedded among known, innocent persons (fillers). Typically, there are six to eight fillers in a lineup. Sometimes, lineups are conducted in person (live lineups), but often they are conducted using photographs. A witness is said to have made a positive identification if the eyewitness identifies someone from the lineup, regardless of whether or not the eyewitness is accurate.

Eyewitness testimony can be very powerful evidence against a defendant in a court of law, and has been a staple of the criminal investigation and conviction process for centuries. The level of confidence expressed by an eyewitness in an identification is often a strong predictor of juror verdicts. However, mistaken eyewitness identification is the primary cause of the conviction of innocent people. Psychological scientists have accumulated considerable knowledge of the factors contributing to mistaken identification. Particular interest has been directed at police lineups. Errors can occur with surprising frequency, especially when the actual person who committed the crime is not in the lineup. Because they have researched the source of many errors, psychological scientists have been able to create guidelines for law enforcement on how to best construct and administer a lineup to create the best test of an eyewitness's memory of the person who committed a crime. These guidelines have been adopted in many different jurisdictions across the nation, but the movement toward adopting such procedures has been slow.

History of Eyewitness Identification Research

Psychological scientists have conducted thousands of experiments in which unsuspecting people have viewed simulated crimes. German criminologist Franz von Liszt conducted one of the first such documented studies in 1902, when he staged a violent crime in class and asked his students to recall the events. Errors were coded as omissions, additions, and alterations of information, and the students' error rates ranged from 26 to 80 percent. Hugo Munsterberg reported these results in his classic book *On the Witness Stand: Essays on Psychology and Crime* (1908), and became a staunch advocate for the use of psychology to inform the judicial system about the fallibility of memory.

The Research of Loftus and Wells

For a variety of reasons, research by psychological scientists that could be applied to the judicial system waned from World War I until the latter half of the 1970s. However, work by Elizabeth Loftus and Gary Wells sparked a resurgence of interest in the issue of eyewitness identifications and testimony by psychological scientists.

Loftus applied laboratory research on cognitive processes to situations in legal settings. For example, in a study conducted with John Palmer in 1974, Loftus showed participants a slide show depicting a car crash and asked them either "About how fast were the cars going when they hit each other?" or "About how fast were the cars going when they smashed into each other?" Participants who were asked about cars that smashed into each other estimated higher speeds than those who were asked about cars that hit each other, and reported seeing broken glass at the scene of the accident even though there was none. In another study the following year, Loftus found that participants who were questioned about events using the article "the" instead of "a" (e.g., did you see the/a barn?) were more likely to report seeing the item in question, even if the item was not present.

On the other hand, Wells laid a theoretical framework within which eyewitness memory could be studied. For example, in 1978, Wells made the distinction between estimator variables and system variables, a distinction that researchers, legal practitioners, and policymakers still use today. Estimator variables are aspects of a crime that the legal system does not control, and system variables are aspects of a crime controlled by the legal system. An understanding of estimator variables allows for a post-hoc assessment of the chance that a mistaken identification has occurred. Estimator variables are typically sorted into four broad categories: characteristics of the witness (e.g., age, race, or gender); characteristics of the event (e.g., lighting, presence of a weapon, or if the culprit was wearing a disguise); characteristics of the testimony (witness confidence); and the ability of testimony evaluators to discriminate between accurate and inaccurate witness testimony.

An understanding of system variables prevents mistaken identifications from occurring in the first place. System variables can be sorted into four broad categories: instructions (what the lineup administrator tells the witness); content (how fillers are chosen for the lineup); presentation method (how the lineup is presented to the witness); and behavioral influence (how the lineup administrator behaves before, during, and after the lineup). Wells, along with R. C. L. Lindsay, also applied a Bayesian model of information gain to show that nonidentifications (such as an eyewitness saying that the person who committed the crime is not present in the lineup) are more than one and a half times more diagnostic as identifications (such as an eyewitness identifying someone—not necessarily the perpetrator—as the person who committed the crime). However, criminal investigators often discount nonidentifications of a suspect, believing that the eyewitness must be mistaken if he or she did not identify the suspect from the lineup as the person who committed the crime.

DNA Testing and Factors in Eyewitness Error

Although the early eyewitness identification literature published by psychological scientists drew the attention and respect of other psychological scientists, it was not until the mid to late 1990s that the legal system began to take significant notice. This was largely due to the advent of forensic DNA testing, in which claims of innocence by a subset of convicted people could be scientifically tested. In 1996, a U.S. Justice Department report on the first 28 exonerations based on DNA testing revealed that 24 were cases of mistaken eyewitness identification. By 2010, the number of DNA-based exonerations of individuals who were wrongfully convicted stood at more than 250, and over 75 percent of these cases involved at least one mistaken eyewitness identification. These DNA exonerations have resulted in greater communication between the justice system and psychological science on the problem of mistaken identification.

It is impossible to calculate the percentage of eyewitnesses who are accurate or inaccurate in the real world, but eyewitness scientists have found a large number of factors that affect the rate of eyewitness identification errors. Some of these factors are relatively obvious, such as conditions of witnessing that are not conducive to forming a good memory of the facial characteristics of the suspect, like poor lighting, distant viewing, brief exposure to the person's face, and the use of disguises by the person who committed the crime. Other factors might be less obvious, such as nuances in how a lineup administrator instructs the witness or acts immediately following the witness's identification decision, but have the potential to greatly affect eyewitness accuracy and confidence.

The procedure for conducting a lineup has been likened to that of conducting an experiment. Investigators begin with a hypothesis (that the suspect is the person who committed the crime), create a design for testing the hypothesis (either a showup or a lineup), carry out a procedure (provide instructions and present the showup or lineup to an eyewitness), observe and record the eyewitness's behavior (witness decision), and then interpret and revise their hypothesis (whether or not the suspect is the culprit). If criminal investigators treated lineups in this manner, it would be possible to increase the value of information provided by each identification attempt. However, as of 2010, relatively few jurisdictions have adopted procedures that provide adequate experimental control over extraneous influences on eyewitnesses.

Pro: Variables Leading to Accurate Eyewitness Testimony

Just as there are estimator and system variables that decrease accurate identification decisions by eyewitnesses, there are also some that increase accuracy.

Additionally, eyewitness testimony has the potential to be greatly improved if lineup administrators follow certain procedures that have been tested in the laboratory and in the field by psychological scientists. These suggestions were initially only found in the discussion sections of academic papers, but in 1999, the National Institute of Justice brought together psychological scientists, defense attorneys, prosecuting attorneys, and law enforcement agents to create *Eyewitness Evidence: A Guide for Law Enforcement*, which was converted in 2003 into a special report entitled *Eyewitness Evidence: A Trainer's Manuel for Law Enforcement.*

Estimator Variables

In regards to witness characteristics, distinctive faces are much more likely to be accurately recognized than nondistinctive faces, and faces that are highly attractive or highly unattractive are easier to recognize than are faces that are average in attractiveness. And although people are better able to recognize faces from their own race rather than others, Uniform Crime Report data from 2008 reveals that more index crimes are committed within-race than cross-race. Therefore, the decrease in eyewitness testimony accuracy for cross-race identifications may not affect a very large percentage of cases.

There are also event characteristics that lead to enhanced eyewitness accuracy. Although extreme stress inhibits eyewitness ability to encode events for later retrieval, mild to moderate levels of stress can actually enhance eyewitness ability. Additionally, although the presence of a weapon draws attention away from perpetrator's face, it draws attention toward the weapon, leading eyewitnesses to typically be able to recall a large number of details about that weapon.

The confidence-accuracy correlation of 0.37 is the main testimony characteristic that leads to the conclusion that people are unable to accurately calibrate their confidence on their accuracy in an identification decision. However, this correlation is moderated by a number of factors. The overall accuracy of the eyewitness greatly affects the correlation. Accurate eyewitnesses are better at calibrating their confidence than are inaccurate eyewitnesses. The certainty–accuracy correlation is also stronger among choosers (people who make identifications, regardless of whether or not the identification is accurate) than nonchoosers (people who say that the culprit is not in the lineup, regardless of whether or not the culprit is in the lineup). Additionally, a decrease in the extent to which lineup administrators exert influence is accompanied by an increase in the confidence–accuracy correlation.

Another testimony characteristic that has been examined is the speed with which an eyewitness makes an identification. Eyewitnesses who make identifications quickly are more likely to be accurate than eyewitnesses who make identifications slowly. This finding was so robust that eyewitness scientists have called for a 10–12 second rule. Unfortunately, eyewitnesses who are forced to make speedy identifications are not typically more accurate than eyewitnesses who make identifications at their own pace. Therefore, the eyewitnesses who make fast identifications are probably able to do so because of better memories for the witnessed events and the perpetrator.

The ability of testimony evaluators to discriminate between accurate and inaccurate witness testimony appears, at first glance, to be quite poor. However, testimony evaluators do not appear to overbelieve eyewitnesses when witnessing conditions are good. In fact, mock jurors sometimes underbelieve the eyewitnesses who have quite low levels of certainty. Therefore, it is apparent that evaluators of eyewitness testimony are somewhat sensitive to characteristics of the event that may affect testimony accuracy.

System Variables

A pre-lineup instruction explaining that the perpetrator may or may not be present in a lineup has little negative effect on the eyewitness's ability to identify that person if they are in the lineup. However, it does significantly decrease the rate of filler identifications. No empirically determined estimates exist of how often perpetrator-absent lineups are shown to witnesses in actual cases. However, the absence of the perpetrator in the lineup is not necessarily an unusual situation. It simply means that the person of interest (or suspect) is not the person who committed the crime, and that the investigation has focused on the wrong person. It is not likely that the rate of perpetrator-absent lineups in actual cases can be represented by a single base rate or percentage. Instead, the rate of perpetrator-absent lineups is likely to vary in each case and jurisdiction, depending on how much or how little evidence the detectives feel that they need in order to conduct a lineup. Regardless, this instruction decreases mistaken identifications without significantly altering the rate of accurate identifications.

The content of a lineup can also significantly affect eyewitness testimony accuracy. If fillers match an eyewitness's description of the perpetrator instead of matching the suspect, there is an increase in propitious heterogeneity—the extent to which fillers differ from the suspect on features not included in the witness's description. The greater the propitious heterogeneity, the easier an identification task should be for an eyewitness—if the suspect is innocent, he should not look any more like the person who committed the crime than any of the fillers.

The traditional lineup method consists of an eyewitness being shown six photographs simultaneously, but this method fosters a relative judgment-making process. A sequential lineup, however, fosters an absolute judgment-making process. With a sequential lineup, a series of photographs are shown individually to an eyewitness, who makes an identification decision for each photograph. The lineup ends either when the eyewitness reaches the end of the photographs, or immediately following a positive identification. With a sequential lineup, it is important that the eyewitness does not know how many photographs he or she will view, so that the eyewitness does not feel pressured to make an identification solely because he or she is reaching the end of available photographs. Use of a sequential lineup instead of a simultaneous lineup results in a very large decrease in filler identifications, but only a slight decrease in correct identifications in target-present lineups. Because the increased protection for innocent suspects afforded by this procedure is accompanied by a decrease in correct "hits," there has been much debate among legal practitioners about whether or not to implement policies that require sequential lineups.

A lineup administrator's behavior has the potential to influence both eyewitness identification decisions and confidence in identification decisions. Because of this, eyewitness scientists have argued that a lineup administered by the detective in charge of a case creates considerable opportunity for the lineup administrator to influence the eyewitness inadvertently. They have argued that the lineup procedure should instead be conducted using an administrator who does not know which person is the suspect and which are fillers. This is known as the double-blind lineup procedure. When taking the lineup-as-an-experiment analogy, a double-blind lineup procedure seems a rather obvious fix for (typically) unintentional influences from the lineup administrator.

Con: Variables Leading to Mistaken Eyewitness Testimony

Field studies have consistently shown that eyewitnesses will choose a filler from lineups approximately 20 percent of the time. Estimates of correct identification and correct rejection of a lineup are difficult to obtain because this requires the establishment of the truth—knowledge of the true perpetrator of a crime. However, if an investigator puts a suspect in a lineup, then the investigator should have some reason to believe that the suspect is the person who committed the crime. Therefore, once an identification has been made, it may set into motion a variety of cognitive confirmation effects that lead to the suspect appearing to be guilty. This is a positive development if the identification is truly accurate; if not, however, this may lead to an eventual wrongful conviction. The large number of people who have been exonerated based on post-conviction DNA testing, who were mistakenly identified by at least one eyewitness, provides concrete evidence that eyewitnesses can be and often are mistaken, even in high-stakes situations.

Estimator Variables

Witness characteristics such as gender, intelligence, age, and race have been examined to determine whether or not they are indicative of an eyewitness's accuracy. Although gender and intelligence have little effect on eyewitness accuracy, age and race have very strong effects on eyewitness accuracy. People of all ages have similar levels of accuracy if the person who committed the crime is present in the lineup, but if the perpetrator is not in the lineup, very young children and the elderly are more likely to mistakenly identify someone from the lineup than are young adults. Additionally, eyewitnesses are worse at recognizing people of a different race than people of their own race. Although the exact mechanism is unknown, over 25 years of research have supported the finding that it is more difficult to recognize a stranger who was viewed on only one prior occasion if that person was of a different race or ethnicity than the witness.

A disguise worn by the culprit, the length of the event, lighting conditions, the presence of a weapon, and level of stress are examples of event characteristics that have been examined for their influence on eyewitness accuracy. Disguises as simple as covering the hair or wearing sunglasses significantly impair an eyewitness's ability to accurately identify a culprit. The longer a culprit's face is in view and the better the light on the face, the more accurate the eyewitness is at later recognizing the face. Additionally, people who know they are going to witness a crime are better able to identify the person who committed the crime than people who are not aware they are going to witness a crime. The presence of a weapon might signify that a crime is about to take place; however, a weapon decreases the accuracy of subsequent eyewitness testimony. This is because a weapon draws an eyewitness's attention away from the perpetrator's face and toward the weapon, thereby limiting the amount of time spent looking at facial features. A weapon also increases an eyewitness's stress level, which impairs the formation of memories needed for accurate identification decisions from lineups.

The main testimony characteristic that has been examined is the confidence an eyewitness has in an identification. The confidence expressed by the eyewitness is important because identifications that are made with low confidence are usually not considered strong evidence, often do not result in charges, and tend to be unpersuasive at trial. A confident eyewitness, in contrast, is very persuasive. Eyewitness scientists have devoted a great deal of research on the correlation between eyewitness identification confidence and eyewitness identification accuracy. The strength of this relationship varies widely as a function of many different variables across studies. However, a meta-analysis of 30 different studies indicated that the average correlation is approximately 0.37. Eyewitness confidence has the potential to be extremely malleable, and can be greatly affected by the lineup administrator or events that happen after the identification has occurred.

The ability of testimony evaluators to discriminate between accurate and inaccurate witness testimony has been examined using multiple methods. In surveys, subjects are asked the extent to which they believe different factors influence eyewitnesses; in prediction studies, subjects are asked to predict the results of eyewitness identification studies (of which results are already known); and in juror studies, subject-jurors are asked to watch eyewitnesses to real or staged crimes being questioned in order to determine if the witnesses made accurate or mistaken identifications. Overall, people overestimate eyewitness identification accuracy, especially when witnessing conditions are poor. They also typically underestimate the extent to which biasing factors influence eyewitnesses.

System Variables

The failure to use pre-lineup instructions warning the eyewitness that the perpetrator might not be in the lineup, or suggesting that they are in the lineup, leads to high rates of mistaken identification when the person who committed the crime is not in the lineup. Jurisdictions that are quick to assemble a lineup based on mere hunches would be expected to run a higher rate of perpetrator-absent lineups than would jurisdictions that require solid evidence against the suspect before conducting a lineup.

Another factor that contributes to mistaken identifications is the content of a lineup. The use of lineup fillers who fail to fit eyewitness descriptions leads the eyewitnesses to prefer the suspect, even when the suspect is not the person who committed the crime. Consider a case, for instance, in which the eyewitness described the person who committed the crime as a tall male in his 30s with short brown hair and no facial hair. Suppose that the suspect placed in the lineup fit that description, but the fillers had different features—such as short stature, light colored hair, long hair, ages in the 50s, or facial hair. This would make the suspect stand out in the lineup as the person the investigators obviously believe committed the crime.

A technique called the *mock witness procedure* has been developed by eyewitness scientists to assess such biases. Mock witnesses are people who have never previously seen the suspect and are simply given the eyewitness's verbal description of the person who committed the crime. The mock witnesses then view the lineup (or a photo of it) and select the person they believe is the suspect in the case. A fair, six-person lineup should result in only one-sixth of the mock witnesses picking the suspect, and the remainder of the witnesses selecting fillers. The inverse of these ratios (e.g., inverse of 1/6 = 6) is known as the *functional lineup size*. Hence, if one-third of the mock witnesses pick the suspect, the functional size would be three, no matter the number of persons in the lineup. The higher the functional size, the more it is presumed to be protective of mistaken identifications of an innocent suspect. The use of fillers who match the suspect, as opposed to fillers who match the eyewitness description of the person who committed the crime, decreases the functional size of a lineup.

Lineup Presentation Method

The lineup presentation method is another factor that influences identification accuracy. Specifically, the traditional lineup composed of six photographs shown simultaneously to an eyewitness can lead to mistaken identifications. Often, eyewitnesses make a positive identification rather than simply saying "I don't know," even when they have very little basis to make an identification. A common observance among eyewitness scientists is that eyewitnesses are motivated to make an identification (in the interests of justice); if they see all candidates in the lineup at the same time, they will often rely on a relative-judgment process rather than absolute recognition to make the identification decision. A relative judgment is one in which the eyewitness compares each lineup member and decides which one more closely resembles his or her memory relative to the other lineup members. The relative-judgment strategy can be effective if the actual perpetrator is in the lineup, but if not, it will lead to a mistaken identification. Experiments have shown that removing the person who committed the crime from a lineup results in witnesses shifting their identification decision to another lineup member, even though they were warned that the person who committed the crime might not be in the lineup. This phenomenon is especially pronounced when witness memory of the perpetrator is weak.

Administrator's Behavior

Another type of factor that can cause mistaken identifications from lineups is the behavior of the person who administers the lineup. It is common practice for the case detective to administer the lineup, which means that the lineup administrator knows very well which lineup member is the suspect and which are merely fillers. Most initial lineup procedures use photographs, and there is no videotaping of the procedure. And, when photo-lineup procedures are used, there is no right to defense counsel or other neutral parties present to observe the procedure. Experimental simulations have shown that lineup administrators do influence eyewitness identifications in a manner consistent with the administrator's belief about the identity of the suspect. The precise ways in which this occurs are not yet well established, but they appear to be very similar to the experimenter–expectancy effect, in which the results of an experiment are influenced by the expectations of the person who tests the research participants. The lineup administrator might not only influence the identification made by an eyewitness, but also the confidence with which the eyewitness makes an identification.

Therefore, the lineup administrator might induce false confidence in an eyewitness, which refers to a highly confident eyewitness who has nevertheless made a mistaken identification. False confidence can occur for a variety of reasons, including the obvious situation in which an innocent person, who happens to have very high coincidental resemblance to the culprit, is identified. More interesting, however, is the phenomenon of confidence malleability, in which a mistaken eyewitness who was initially low in confidence later becomes highly confident. Confidence malleability is dramatically associated with the post-identification feedback effect. After making mistaken identifications, eyewitnesses who are given feedback suggesting that they identified the right person ("Good, you identified the actual suspect.") undergo a distortion in their memory about their initial uncertainty, and come to believe they were confident all along. The post-identification feedback effect has been demonstrated across a variety of experiments, both in the laboratory and in the field. The result of such feedback is the creation of a confident (yet mistaken) eyewitness.

Conclusion

Eyewitness testimony has been inaccurate in many cases, but it is a staple of the justice system. The recommendations from psychological scientists to legal practitioners who conduct lineups are (1) use a double-blind lineup to prevent the conscious or unconscious biasing of eyewitnesses by a lineup administrator; (2) select fillers who resemble the eyewitness's description of the culprit, not fillers who resemble the suspect, in order to make the task easier for an eyewitness and avoid biasing the witness toward the suspect; (3) provide an instruction that the perpetrator may or may not be present in the lineup, in order to prevent the eyewitness from feeling compelled to make an identification and decrease the tendency to use relative judgment; (4) collect a confidence statement from the eyewitness immediately following the identification, before being given feedback from the lineup administrator to prevent confidence inflation; and (5) record the identification proceedings whenever possible to provide a record of all aspects of the identification.

Jurisdictions such as Suffolk County, Massachusetts; Santa Clara, California; New Jersey; Wisconsin; North Carolina; and Minneapolis have adopted the above-mentioned reforms either as policy or as recommendations for best practices. The list is continually expanding, but it is hard to track where reforms have been made because they can range in size from affecting one police station to affecting an entire state. Another recommendation that many researchers endorse is using a sequential lineup to force eyewitnesses to use an absolute instead of a relative decision-making process. However, because this procedure decreases hits along with mistaken identifications, the choice to adopt sequential lineups depends on what the goal of the lineup is. If the ultimate goal is to have as few mistaken identifications as possible, then a sequential lineup should be used; but if the ultimate goal is to have as many correct identifications as possible, then a simultaneous lineup should be used.

Even as other forensic sciences continue to improve, there will still be little evidence as powerful as an eyewitness pointing at the accused across the courtroom and naming them as the person who committed the crime. If legal practitioners treat eyewitness testimony as trace evidence and take the same precautions with eyewitnesses as they do with other pieces of evidence, then it has the potential to be very accurate.

❖

See Also: 2. DNA Evidence; 7. Expert Witnesses and Hired Guns; 11. Jury System.

Further Readings

Cutler, Brian L., and Steven D. Penrod. *Mistaken Identification: The Eyewitness, Psychology, and the Law.* New York: Cambridge University Press, 1995.

Cutler, Brian L., Steven D. Penrod, and Hedy Red Dexter. "Juror Sensitivity to Eyewitness Identification Evidence." *Law and Human Behavior,* v.14 (1990).

Cutler, Brian L., Steven D. Penrod, and Thomas E. Stuve. "Juror Decision Making in Eyewitness Identification Cases." *Law and Human Behavior,* v.12 (1988).

Douglass, Amy Bradfield, and Nancy Steblay. "Memory Distortion in Eyewitnesses: A Meta-Analysis of the Post-Identification Feedback Effect." *Applied Cognitive Psychology,* v.20 (2006).

Hasel, Lisa E., and Saul M. Kassin. "On the Presumption of Evidentiary Independence: Can Confessions Corrupt Eyewitness Identifications?" *Psychological Science,* v.21 (2009).

Haw, R. M., and R. P. Fisher. "Effects of Administrator-Witness Contact on Eyewitness Identification Accuracy." *Journal of Applied Psychology,* v.21 (2004).

Innocence Project. www.innocenceproject.org (Accessed October 2010).

Kassin, Saul M., V. Anne Tubb, Harmon M. Hosch, and Amina Memon. "On the 'General Acceptance' of Eyewitness Testimony Research." *American Psychologist,* v.56 (2001).

Loftus, Elizabeth F. "Leading Questions and Eyewitness Report." *Cognitive Psychology,* v.7 (1975).

Loftus, Elizabeth F., and John C. Palmer. "Reconstruction of Automobile Destruction: An Example of the Interaction Between Language and Memory." *Journal of Verbal Learning and Verbal Behavior,* v.13 (1974).

Meissner, Christian A., and John C. Brigham. "Thirty Years of Investigating the Own-Race Bias in Memory for Faces: A Meta-Analytic Review." *Psychology, Public Policy, and Law,* v.7 (2001).

Morgan, Charles A., Gary Hazlett, Anthony Doran, Stephan Garrett, Gary Hoyt, Paul Thomas, Madelon Baranoski, and Steven M. Southwick. "Accuracy of Eyewitness Memory for Persons Encountered During

Exposure to Highly Intense Stress." *International Journal of Psychiatry and the Law,* v.27 (2004).

Penrod, Steven D., Solomon M. Fulero, and Brian L. Cutler. "Expert Psychological Testimony on Eyewitness Reliability Before and After *Daubert:* The State of the Law and the Science." *Behavioral Sciences and the Law,* v.13 (1995).

Sporer, Sigfried, Steven Penrod, Don Read, and Brian L. Cutler. "Choosing, Confidence, and Accuracy: A Meta-Analysis of the Confidence-Accuracy Relation in Eyewitness Identification Studies." *Psychological Bulletin,* v.118 (1995).

Steblay, N. "A Meta-Analytic Review of the Weapon Focus Effect." *Law and Human Behavior,* v.16 (1992).

Steblay, N. "Social Influence in Eyewitness Recall: A Meta-Analytic Review of Lineup Instruction Effects." *Law and Human Behavior,* v.21 (1997).

Technical Working Group for Eyewitness Evidence. *Eyewitness Evidence: A Trainer's Manual for Law Enforcement.* Washington, DC: United States Department of Justice, Office of Justice Programs, 2003.

Wells, Gary L. "Applied Eyewitness Testimony Research: System Variables and Estimator Variables." *Journal of Personality and Social Psychology,* v.36 (1978).

Wells, Gary L. *Eyewitness Identification: A System Handbook.* Toronto: Carswell Legal Publications, 1988.

Wells, Gary L. "Eyewitness Identification: Systemic Reforms." *Wisconsin Law Review* (2006).

Wells, Gary L. "The Psychology of Lineup Identifications." *Journal of Applied Social Psychology,* v.14 (1984).

Wells, Gary L., and Amy L. Bradfield. "'Good, You Identified the Suspect': Feedback to Eyewitnesses Distorts Their Reports of the Witnessing Experience." *Journal of Applied Psychology,* v.83 (1998).

Wells, Gary L., and Lisa E. Hasel. "Facial Composite Production By Eyewitnesses." *Current Directions in Psychological Science,* v.16 (2007).

Wells, Gary L., Michael R. Leippe, and Thomas M. Ostrom. "Guidelines for Empirically Assessing the Fairness of a Lineup." *Law and Human Behavior,* v.3 (1979).

Wells, Gary L., and R. C. Lindsay. "On Estimating the Diagnosticity of Eyewitness Nonidentifications." *Psychological Bulletin,* v.88 (1980).

Wells, Gary L., R. C. Lindsay, and Tamara J. Ferguson. "Accuracy, Confidence, and Juror Perceptions in Eyewitness Identification." *Journal of Applied Psychology,* v.64 (1979).

Wells, Gary L., and Elizabeth Olson. "Eyewitness Identification." *Annual Review of Psychology,* v.54 (2003).

Wells, Gary L., Sheila M. Rydell, and Eric P. Seelau. "The Selection of Distractors for Eyewitness Lineups." *Journal of Applied Psychology,* v.78 (1993).

Wells, Gary L., Mark Small, Steven Penrod, Roy S. Malpass, Solomon M. Fulero, and C. A. Elizabeth Brimacombe. "Eyewitness Identification Procedures: Recommendations for Lineups and Photospreads." *Law and Human Behavior,* v.22 (1998).

9

Gun Control Laws

M. Dyan McGuire
Saint Louis University

G un control laws seek to limit the extent to which citizens can keep and own firearms, and often place limits on who can own firearms. For example, gun control laws frequently require that a background check be performed, and those with criminal or mental health records be denied access to guns. In addition, certain types of guns are prohibited. Fully automatic machine guns and other types of guns that are deemed to be especially lethal are often illegal to own under any circumstances. Proponents of these laws argue that gun control laws are necessary to reduce gun-related crime and protect the police and the public from the dangers inherent in the proliferation of guns. Opponents argue that gun control laws impermissibly infringe upon citizens' rights; endanger the existence of democracy by disabling civilian defense capabilities; prevent honest citizens from defending themselves, their families, and their property; and unreasonably restrict gun-related recreational activities like target shooting and hunting.

History of Gun Control and Gun Rights

The battle between government regulation of gun ownership to promote order, public safety, and the consolidation of power, versus the right of the people to keep weapons for purposes of recreation, self-preservation, and as a final bulwark against tyranny has a long and checkered past in American legal history. Although the English crown had previously taken action to limit weapon ownership, the first major attempt to prevent the majority of Englishmen from owning weapons came from an act of the English Parliament in 1671. The Game Act of 1671 imposed such a high property qualification on the right to hunt that it effectively limited hunting to the aristocracy. In addition, it prohibited those not economically qualified to hunt from owning any type of gun or other lethal weapon. It also empowered those who owned lands suitable for hunting to appoint gamekeepers with the authority to search the homes of suspected, unauthorized gun-possessors and to seize any illegal weapons they found. The combined effect of these prohibitions was that only wealthy aristocrats could own and use guns, and everyone else, the vast majority of the population, could be disarmed and thereby neutralized if they were deemed a credible threat to the aristocrats' power and social position.

When the Catholic James II briefly ascended the English throne in 1685, he used the Game Act as a vehicle for disarming his Protestant subjects in an effort to shore up his control of England. This outraged the Protestant ascendancy and helped to galvanize opposition to James II, who was eventually deposed in the Glorious Revolution of 1688. A Protestant, William of Orange, was therefore returned to the throne of England. The new parliament moved to secure some fundamental rights against future changes in the monarchy by passing the Declaration of Rights in 1689, which addressed a number of topics, including the right of Protestants to keep and carry arms. It declared, "the subjects which are Protestants, may have Arms for their Defense suitable to their Condition, and as allowed by Law."

Having inherited this legal tradition, America's founding fathers were well aware of the controversy surrounding gun control. Some of them had actually been on the receiving end of British efforts to disarm suspected patriots in the early days of the American Revolution. One such British attempt formed part of the substance of Paul Revere's warnings on his now famous ride. Had the British been successful in disarming the rebellious colonists, the American Revolution would have ended very differently. Fear of a strong, centralized government having a monopoly on weaponry remained a concern of the founders even after the British had been defeated and the American colonies had gained their independence.

The antifederalists, in particular, feared the accretion of power in the federal government and what that might mean for individual rights and state rights. Concerns specific to the state's right to maintain a militia and the individual's right to keep arms were expressed in the Second Amendment, which went through several iterations. James Madison, the primary drafter of the Second Amendment, finally settled on language that stated, "a well regulated Militia, being necessary to the security of a free State, the right of the people to keep and bear Arms, shall not be infringed." This amendment was meant keep the national government from becoming so powerful it could raise and maintain a standing army capable of subduing the states and the people by force. It also was intended to ensure that a national army, which might not be up to the task of defending the whole nation, would receive help from any militias necessary to protect the states from foreign invaders across the far-flung expanses of the new country. It has also been suggested that southern proponents of the Second Amendment may well have been concerned about the need for the state militia and individual landowners to be armed as a means of controlling and oppressing slaves.

Foreign Examples of Gun Control

Examining more contemporary historical accounts suggests that tyrants and dictators sometimes attempt to shore up their power and position by disarming the citizenry in an effort to ensure that all weapons in the country are in the hands of those loyal to the leader and his or her government. In Germany, for example, the Weimer Republic initiated the disarming of the German people in an effort to "take back the streets" from the politicized, public violence of the 1920s and 1930s. The Nazis extended these laws when they came to power by specifically forbidding Jews from owning guns or other weapons and by exempting Nazi party officials and members of the militarized organizations associated with the Nazis, such as the SS, from the country's restrictive gun control laws. It is frequently argued that these laws, which resulted in the confiscation of weapons not belonging to supporters of the Nazis, rendered the Jews and other disfavored groups like the Gypsies, homosexuals, Poles, and their potential allies defenseless and set the stage for the slaughter of the Holocaust that followed.

Joseph Stalin and Mao Tse-Tung are also reported to have disarmed their political opponents through strict gun control laws and mass confiscations, and then to have slaughtered thousands or even millions of citizens after they had been effectively disarmed. Those who favor gun rights often point to these historical examples and argue that registration of guns leads to confiscation of guns, which leads to restriction of freedom and even the threat of genocide by the government.

While some tyrants have utilized gun control, gun control does not always lead to tyranny, as gun control advocates are quick to note. Those who favor gun control point to the contemporary history of other Western democracies in that gun control does not necessarily result in oppressive government. After American and British legal histories diverged, the English adopted a number of less restrictive gun control laws, including the Gun License Act of 1870, which required people who wanted to carry a gun outside their home to obtain a license from the Post Office; and the Pistols Act of 1903, which prohibited the sale of pistols to those who were not licensed or otherwise entitled to have a gun. While the early acts simply required gun owners to obtain an easily available license and were primarily aimed at generating revenue, a series of progressively more stringent Firearms Acts beginning in 1920 were expressly designed to limit access to guns.

These efforts culminated with the Firearms Act of 1997, which prohibited the ownership of small firearms except for use in humanely killing animals or exterminating vermin, at races associated with athletic events, as trophies of wars, or as guns of historical interest. Notably, and quite contrary to the American model, Britons are expressly forbidden from having guns for purposes of self-defense. Rifles and other sporting guns are also regulated to a much greater extent than they are in America. Subsequent regulation has further restricted gun ownership in England, and today it is very difficult, if not impossible, for the average English citizen to legally obtain a gun. Despite these comparatively stringent gun control laws and the relative lack of guns among the English populace, the English government has arguably not degenerated into tyranny or genocide. Thus, gun control proponents argue that the right to bear arms is not necessarily inherent in or essential for a healthy democracy.

Gun Control Laws and the Constitution

The phrasing of the Second Amendment has engendered significant controversy and given rise to a number of competing interpretations, most of which can be classified as either primarily individualistic or primarily collectivistic in nature.

Those who interpret the Second Amendment as an individual right claim that the right, like most of the other rights contained in the Bill of Rights, belongs to each citizen individually and can be exercised by individuals as they see fit. People who embrace an individualistic interpretation of the Second Amendment tend to be opposed to gun control laws. They argue that the Second Amendment endows every citizen with the right to own guns for a host of legitimate purposes, including recreation, personal protection, and as a bulwark against tyranny. Government interference with that right should be prohibited or at least strictly limited.

Those who embrace a collectivist interpretation of the Second Amendment argue that the amendment was meant to protect the collective right of citizens of a particular state to organize themselves into armed militias for purposes of the common defense. In other words, the collectivist view holds that the Second Amendment was meant to do no more than assure that the federal government did not interfere with the organization and operation of state militias. Those who favor gun control normally favor a collectivist interpretation of the Second Amendment. For them, the right to keep and bear arms should be restricted to those engaged in National Guard duty and similar activities.

The controversy between the individualist school and the collectivist school has raged on for decades, in part because the U.S. Supreme Court has provided little decisive guidance on what the Second Amendment actually means. Although gun rights and gun violence are both prominent features of American life, the Supreme Court has only significantly addressed the meaning of the Second Amendment a few times in the last 100 years. The first case worth examining at some length is *United States v. Miller*, where the defendants were indicted for transporting an unregistered, sawed-off shotgun in interstate commerce in violation of the National Firearms Act. The Court found that the Second Amendment did not provide the defendants with a right to transport such a weapon in interstate commerce. In rendering its decision, the Court appeared to side with the collectivist interpretation of the Second Amendment by noting that such a weapon had no reasonable relation to the preservation or efficiency of a well-regulated militia. Although adherents of the individualist school of thought read the opinion very narrowly, collectivists relied on *Miller* to argue that there was no constitutional barrier to enacting gun control laws that only affected individuals in their private capacity.

After *Miller*, however, the Supreme Court was nearly silent on the subject of the Second Amendment for almost 70 years. During this time, most of the federal circuit courts appear to have assumed that *Miller* called for a collectivist interpretation of the Second Amendment, and were inclined to uphold gun control regulations in the face of Second Amendment challenges that were predicated on an individualistic interpretation of that right. The

Fifth Circuit Court of Appeals in *United States v. Emerson* (2001), however, explicitly embraced an individualistic approach to the Second Amendment in finding that the right to bear arms accrued to the people themselves and not just to the use of arms during or connected to military or National Guard service.

Recent Landmark Cases

With a split among the federal circuit courts, the Supreme Court was eventually called upon to resolve the conflict by clarifying the meaning of the Second Amendment. The Court took that opportunity in 2008 in *District of Columbia v. Heller*. In this case, the Supreme Court squarely confronted the issue of whether a jurisdiction could completely prohibit individuals who were not engaged in militia-related activities from owning any type of handgun and require such individuals to keep all other guns in their possession, like shotguns and rifles, in nonfunctional condition. The Court in *Heller* found both of the District of Columbia's laws unconstitutional, upholding that individuals possessed a constitutional right to bear arms that precluded the government from completely banning the owing of handguns or the keeping of functional guns in the home for defensive purposes. Because *Heller* involved a case arising under the laws of the District of Columbia, it left open the question of whether Second Amendment rights precluded states from totally banning private handgun ownership as well.

Two years later, the Supreme Court answered that question in *McDonald v. Chicago*, which held that ordinances that essentially ban handgun ownership by private citizens infringe upon citizens' rights to keep and bear arms under the Second Amendment. In so doing, the Supreme Court followed the modern trend of incorporating rights contained in the Bill of Rights to the states via the Due Process Clause of the Fourteenth Amendment. Although the *Heller* and *McDonald* decisions create a less favorable legal climate for gun control advocates and guarantees that complete bans preventing citizens from owning guns for self-protection will not be tolerated, it was not a total victory for activists seeking complete abolishment of gun control. The Supreme Court specifically noted that Second Amendment rights were not absolute, and that well-established, long-standing gun control laws like those that preclude felons or mentally ill people from owning guns and those that prevent individuals from carrying concealed weapons are consistent with Second Amendment rights.

Types of Gun Control Laws

An almost endless variety of laws affect guns or gun owners in some way. However, most gun control laws can be seen as attempting to regulate who obtains guns, how they obtain them, and where they can take them afterward.

Keeping Guns out of the Hands of Criminals

The first major type of gun control legislation attempts to keep guns out of the hands of people who will use them for criminal purposes. The chosen mechanism is normally some type of mandatory background check, which must be performed by the seller prior to turning the gun over to the buyer. Typically, people convicted of a felony or a misdemeanor involving violence, such as domestic battery, are ineligible to own a gun. People with a demonstrable history of serious mental illness, such as individuals who have been involuntarily committed, are also usually ineligible for legal gun ownership. While criminal background checks can be accomplished with relative ease, thorough mental health checks are much more difficult to perform, since that information has not historically been collected in a unified and easily accessible form. In order to address this deficit, Congress passed the National Instant Criminal Background Check System (NICS) Improvement Act, which was signed into law by President Bush in January 2008. The purpose of the new law was to augment NICS, which is a Federal Bureau of Investigation (FBI) system used by gun dealers to run required background checks on purchasers with more complete mental health information. The new law gives monetary incentives to states that report people with severe mental illness to NICS and takes money away from states that do not report.

While such laws likely help to limit access to guns for people with an obvious propensity for violence, they are incomplete. It is very unlikely that all people capable of using a gun in a dangerous, illegal, and even lethal way have criminal records or a record of mental health commitment. Cho Seung-Hui, the 2007 Virginia Tech shooter, for example, had been identified as mentally ill but had never been committed or otherwise reported to the state; thus, he was able to buy guns legally because he did not have the type of record that would have alerted a gun dealer that he was ineligible to buy. Also, there is a significant loophole in the federal law requiring background checks on gun purchasers, in that unlicensed gun dealers can sell a gun at a gun show to any individual without performing a background check.

Waiting Periods

Other gun control laws impose a waiting period on buyers. This waiting period not only affords the seller an opportunity to conduct any required background checks, it also provides a cooling-off period for the buyer. In this way, the wait prevents angry people from immediately obtaining guns and seeking retribution before they have had an opportunity to calm down and consider the consequences of killing or maiming the people who enraged them.

Other gun control laws focus on banning particularly dangerous weapons. Fully automatic weapons, which both load and fire automatically, have been illegal for American citizens to own since the 1920s. In the 1990s, efforts to ban semiautomatic weapons, which load but do not fire automatically, also known as assault weapons, were successful. Although the federal government's ban on assault weapons expired in 2004, many states have similar laws that remain in effect. Bans on so-called "cop killers," armor-piercing bullets, are also common. These laws, perhaps in recognition of the inability of government to infallibly identify who can safely own a gun and who may go on a rampage, attempt to prevent anyone from owning weaponry capable of rapid, large-scale carnage.

Safe Storage and Distance

Other gun control laws focus on requiring owners to store their guns in a safe manner. The most stringent of these laws require that guns and ammunition be stored in separate, secure locations. Other safe-storage laws simply require owners to store their guns, which may be kept loaded, in a gun safe. Sometimes, trigger guards and other devices are required as well. The purpose of these laws is to prevent accidental access to guns by incompetent persons such as children who do not know how to safely handle a gun and are likely to injure or kill themselves or others if they fire a weapon. The more these laws erect barriers to accidental access and use by unauthorized persons, the more they inhibit a gun owner's ability to quickly access their gun for emergency self-defense purposes, such as thwarting a home invasion or other crime.

Some gun control measures focus on banning guns from particular locations. Some states, like Georgia, broadly regulate guns and prohibit guns at all public gatherings. Other states rely on more narrowly tailored laws and regulations. Bans on guns in churches or hospitals, for example, are not uncommon. Guns are also banned from most college campuses nationwide, and possession of a firearm in primary and secondary schools is generally not permitted. The idea behind these laws is that certain places should be safe or sacrosanct, and that it is inappropriate or dangerous to bring guns to such places. College campuses encounter frequent drinking and usually have students living in close quarters, which are two factors which might make the eruption of violence more likely. By removing guns from these places, the hope is that the violence can be contained within nonlethal bounds.

Major Federal Gun Control Initiatives

While most gun regulation is the product of a patchwork of state and local laws, the federal government has made a number of notable attempts to create a unified and enforceable nationwide system of gun control. The Gun Control Act of 1968 was enacted in the wake of the assassinations of such prominent public figures as Dr. Martin Luther King Jr. and President John F. Kennedy and his brother Robert. The act prohibited felons, the mentally ill, drug addicts, dishonorably discharged veterans, and illegal aliens from owning guns. It also required dealers to keep permanent sales records and manufacturers to place serial numbers on guns. The Lautenberg Amendment in 1996 expanded the list of undesirables to include people convicted of domestic violence or subject to an order of protection. In 1981, John Hinckley attempted to assassinate President Reagan, and in the process, shot Press Secretary James Brady in the head. Brady was left permanently impaired, and his wife, Sarah, went on to champion the enactment of the Brady Handgun Violence Prevention Act. The Brady Act established a computerized, nationwide background check system that licensed dealers were required to use in checking out perspective buyers to help ensure that the person was legally eligible to own a gun.

Gun Rights Legislation: Conceal and Carry

While advocates of gun control have been somewhat successful in using the political process at both the state and federal level to enact various types of gun control legislation, advocates of gun rights have also been active in using the political process to encourage legislation favorable to their cause. One of the biggest efforts by gun rights proponents to extend and entrench gun rights is evident in their efforts to overturn restrictive or discretionary handgun licensing schemes and replace them with legislation requiring state officials to issue licenses to all qualified applicants.

While there is substantial variation, most states require applicants to have no significant mental health or criminal history and to pass a gun safety class. Some states are more permissive; in Vermont, for example, anyone who can legally own a gun can carry it in a concealed manner without obtaining a permit or license. Other states, like Wisconsin, are far more restrictive and limit the right to carry a concealed weapon for security purposes to particular places such as the individual's home or private place of business. States like Montana have retained some discretion in their licensing laws, allowing the issuing official to deny a license to an otherwise qualified applicant if they can show they have a reasonable basis for believing that the prospective licensee poses a threat to community order or safety. Some states, including Mississippi, include a long list of places where concealed weapons are impermissible even if the person has a conceal-and-carry permit. States like Missouri allow businesses and government buildings to post notices prohibiting even those with a license from entering with a concealed weapon. Still other states, like Alaska, permit local governments to opt-out of some or all of the state's conceal-and-carry legislation.

The conceal-and-carry trend began with the enactment of Florida's conceal-and-carry law in 1987. Many states have followed Florida's example in enacting their own laws. Florida's law provides that the Department of Agriculture and Consumer Services shall issue a license to any applicant so long as he or she is a lawful resident or citizen of the United States; is at least 21 years old; does not suffer from a physical infirmity, which prevents the safe handling of a firearm; has never been convicted of a felony or a misdemeanor involving violence in the last three years and is not the subject of an order of protection; has not been committed for the abuse of a controlled substance or been found guilty of a crime relating to controlled substances within the last three years; does not chronically and habitually use alcoholic beverages or other substances to the extent that his or her normal faculties are impaired; has not been adjudicated an incapacitated person and has not been committed to a mental institution; desires a legal means to carry a concealed weapon or firearm for lawful self-defense; and demonstrates competence with a firearm by taking and successfully completing one of a number of specified firearms safety classes.

Today, the overwhelming majority of states have some form of conceal-and-carry law, either as a result of state law or more rarely, the state supreme court's interpretation of the state's constitution. In addition, states are increasingly enacting reciprocity statutes, which recognize conceal-and-carry licenses issued by their neighboring states and relieve citizens of the burden of obtaining a conceal-and-carry license in states they may visit for short periods of time. Efforts to nationalize the right to carry guns by mandating reciprocity have not yet succeeded, although they have come close. In summer 2009, the U.S. Senate nearly passed a measure that would have allowed people to bring concealed weapons across state lines if they were legally allowed to carry the guns in their home state.

Gun Laws: The Empirical Evidence

Unfortunately, the empirical evidence concerning the impact of firearms legislation is far from conclusive. For example, some studies seem to produce evidence of high rates of defensive use by gun owners, while other studies produce evidence of high rates of suicide and accidental shootings among gun owners. Despite these ambiguities in the available research, both sides in the gun debate cling fiercely to the pieces of evidence that support their side, and ignore or criticize the other side's research.

Pro: Arguments in Favor of Gun Control

Many gun control advocates argue that guns are dangerous instruments, and that as guns become more common in our society, so too will injuries and deaths caused by guns. For them, there is no such thing as a good gun; all guns are potentially lethal and subject to misuse, and should be removed from the general population whenever possible. These people often cite the finding of Dr. Kellermann and his colleagues that gun owners are 43 times more likely to kill a family member or friend with their gun than to kill an intruder. Other gun control advocates, including former President Clinton, focus on the toll gun violence takes on children and frequently cite the statistic that 13 children a day die as a result of gun-related injuries. There are also numerous studies suggesting that when guns are available, rates of suicide, accidental injury, homicide, and domestic violence increase. In addition to the human toll, all of these phenomena also increase the monetary costs of healthcare and criminal justices.

Pointing to tragic mass murders like the 1999 Columbine High School killings or the 1984 massacre at McDonald's in San Ysidro, California, proponents of gun control argue that having guns readily available to the general public makes them available to people who are mentally unstable. Noting that many individuals who "snap" and act out with extreme violence do not have pre-existing records of violence or mental illness sufficient to preclude them from buying guns under existing regulatory schemes, they conclude more stringent laws or even gun bans are necessary to save lives.

And while gun rights advocates point a study done by John Lott and David Mustard, which showed that conceal-and-carry laws tended to cor-related with a reduction in the rates of violent crimes, the researchers also found that property crimes accomplished through stealth tended to increase after conceal-and-carry laws were enacted.

Advocates of gun control also point to other Western democracies that have historically lower violent-crime rates and also lower gun ownership rates than the Unites States, to support the argument that the proliferation of guns in and of itself leads to more gun-related crime. Prestigious orga-nizations like the American Medical Association and the U.S. Centers for Disease Control both support gun control as a public health necessity. For proponents of gun control, evidence of the lethality of America's gun culture justifies tightly controlled access to guns for everyone.

Con: Arguments in Opposition to Gun Control

Advocates of gun rights, on the other hand, look at America's comparatively high violent crime rate and reach a different conclusion. They argue that law-abiding citizens must be able to arm themselves for self-protection. A number of studies support the thesis that American gun owners are suc-cessful in thwarting some crimes. One of the most oft-cited studies was conducted by Gary Kleck and Marc Gertz, which found that Americans use guns defensively between 2.2 and 2.5 times a year. The National Rifle Association currently collects and publishes on its Website newspaper sto-ries from around the country that deal with law-abiding citizens success-fully rebuffing and incapacitating criminals with their handguns. Since data regarding thwarted crimes are not routinely kept in the same manner as data about gun deaths, gun rights advocates argue these saved lives are ignored by researchers and gun control advocates.

Gun rights activists usually support conceal-and-carry laws, arguing that this will enhance the ability of Americans to defend themselves and will deter criminals because they fear that potential victims are armed. A study done by John Lott and David Mustard is often cited in this regard because it found that the enactment of conceal-and-carry laws tended to be correlated with a reduction in the rates for murder and other violent crimes, and con-cluded that conceal-and-carry laws saved lives, even after accidental deaths from handguns were accounted for. While property crimes accomplished through stealth did tend to increase after conceal-and-carry laws were enacted, this prompted the researchers to conclude that criminals switched to property crimes that did not involve interaction with the victim in order to protect themselves from the risks posed by potentially armed victims.

In addition, conceal-and-carry or shall-issue laws replaced more discretionary licensing schemes that purportedly allowed administering state officials to discriminate against applicants based upon race, social class, political affiliation, and even sex, because they were empowered to deny a license for any reason they deemed sufficient. Conceal and carry laws, it is argued, cure this potential for inequity by imposing a nondiscretionary duty on state licensing agencies to issue permits to everyone who applies, as long as they meet the statutorily proscribed qualifications.

Conclusion

The debate over guns is longstanding and has passionate advocates on both sides who are firmly committed to their viewpoint, despite the dearth of definitive evidence either way. Moreover, while the Supreme Court's recent decisions in *Heller* and *McDonald* seem to embrace an individualistic interpretation of the Second Amendment that prohibits total bans on gun ownership by Americans, at least for defensive purposes, the Court nevertheless makes clear that longstanding gun control laws are not necessarily inconsistent with Second Amendment rights. As a consequence, the debate over gun control is here to stay. Both sides will continue to launch legislative initiatives that advance their agenda, but in this political and legal climate, neither side is likely to gain decisive control over the fate of guns in society.

See Also: 1. Asset Forfeiture.

Further Readings

Bogus, Carl T. "The Hidden History of the Second Amendment."
    University of California Davis Law Review, 31/2 (Winter 1998).
Cornell, Saul, and Nathan Dedino. "Historical Perspective: A Well
    Regulated Right: The Early American Origins of Gun Control."
    Fordham Law Review, v.73 (November 2004).

Cramer, Clayton E., and David B. Kopel. "Shall Issue: The New Wave of Concealed Handgun Permit Laws." *Tennessee Law Review*, v.62 (Spring 1995).

Creamer, Robert A. "History Is Not Enough: Using Contemporary Justifications for the Right to Keep and Bear Arms in Interpreting the Second Amendment." *Boston College Law Review*, v.45 (July 2004).

Crooker, Constance E. *Gun Control and Gun Rights*. Westport, CN: Greenwood Press, 2003.

Cummings, P., T. D. Koepsell, D. C. Grossman, J. Savarino, and R. S. Thompson. "The Association Between the Purchase of a Handgun and Homicide or Suicide." *American Journal of Public Health*, v.87/6 (1997).

Dezhbakhsh, Hashem, and Paul H. Rubin. "Lives Saved or Lives Lost? The Effects of Concealed-Handgun Laws on Crime." *The American Economic Review*, v.88/2 (May 1998).

District of Columbia v. Heller, 128 S. Ct. 2783 (2008).

Doherty, Brian. *Gun Control on Trial: Inside the Supreme Court Battle Over the Second Amendment*. Washington, DC: Cato Institute. (2008).

Essig, Phillip C. "Attack on Gun-Death Statistics Distorted the Facts." *Roanoke Times* (May 4, 2000).

Harcourt, B. E. "Cultural Perspective: On Gun Registration, The NRA, Adolf Hitler, and Nazi Gun Laws: Exploding the Gun Culture Wars (A Call to Historians)." *Fordham Law Review*, v.73 (November 2004).

Hepburn, Lisa, and David Hemenway. "Firearm Availability and Homicide: A Review of the Literature." *Aggression and Violent Behavior: A Review Journal*, v.9 (2004).

Kellermann, Arthur L., Frederick P. Rivara, Norman B. Rushforth, Joyce G. Banton, Donald T. Reay, Jerry T. Francisco, Ana B. Locci, Janice Prodzinski, Bela B. Hackman, and Grant Somes. "Gun Ownership as a Risk Factor for Homicide in the Home." *New England Journal of Medicine*, v.329/15 (October 7, 1993).

Kopel, David B. "The Licensing of Concealed Handguns for Lawful Protection: Support From Five State Supreme Courts." *Albany Law Review*, v.68 (2005).

Lindeen, Lance. "Keep Off the Grass! An Alternative Approach to the Gun Control Debate." *Indiana Law Journal*, v.85 (2010).

Lott, John R. *More Guns, Less Crime: Understanding Crime and Gun-Control Laws*. Chicago: University of Chicago Press, 1998.

Lott, John R., and D. B. Mustard. "Crime, Deterrence, and Right-to-Carry Concealed Handguns." *Journal of Legal Studies*, v.26/1 (January 1997).

Malcom, Joyce L. *To Keep and Bear Arms: The Origins of an Anglo-American Right.* Cambridge, MA: Harvard University Press. 1994.

McDonald v. Chicago, 130 S. Ct. 3020; 177 L. Ed. 2d 894 (2010).

Miller, Matthew, Deborah Azrael, and David Hemenway. "State-Level Homicide Victimization Rates in the U.S. in Relation to Survey Measures of Household Firearm Ownership, 2001–2003." *Social Science and Medicine,* v.64 (2007).

Miller, Matthew, and David Hemenway. "Guns and Suicide in the United States." *New England Journal of Medicine,* v.359 (2008).

Narang, Puneet, Anubha Paladugu, Sainath R. Manda, William Smock, Cynthia Gosnay, and Steven Lippmann. "Do Guns Provide Safety? At What Cost?" *Southern Medical Journal,* v.103/2 (2010).

Polsby, Daniel D., and Don B. Kates. "Causes and Correlates of Lethal Violence in America; American Homicide Exceptionalism." *University of Colorado Law Review,* v.69 (Fall 1998).

Roleff, Tamara L., ed. *Gun Control.* Detroit: Greenhaven Press, 2007.

Spitzer, Robert J. *The Politics of Gun Control.* Chatham, NJ: Chatham House, 1995.

United States v. Emerson, 270 F.3d 203 (2001).

United States v. Miller, 307 U.S. 174 (1939).

Wilson, Harry L. *Guns, Gun Control, and Elections: The Politics and Policy of Firearms.* Lanham, MD: Rowman & Littlefield, 2007.

10

Insanity Defense

Frank Butler
La Salle University

Controversy is endemic to the insanity defense. The term *insanity* routinely attracts widespread public attention that is far out of proportion to the defense's impact on criminal justice. Part of this public fascination results from a few truly gruesome and highly bizarre crimes that tend to be sensationalized in the mass media. For example, in the 1990s, the Wisconsin case of Jeffrey Dahmer attracted widespread media and public attention.

Dahmer murdered 17 young men from 1978 to 1991. Commonly, he would drug his victims, sometimes torturing them before killing them, often by strangulation. He dismembered his victims' bodies and attempted to have sexual relations with their corpses. He kept part of the corpses, particularly the skulls, in his apartment. When charged with murder, Dahmer raised the insanity defense, claiming he should be found "not guilty by reason of insanity." His defense was based in necrophilia, a serious mental illness in which a person has urges to have sexual relations with dead persons. Dahmer claimed that he could not control his necrophilia and hence required a regular supply of corpses, which in turn led him to commit the murders. The jury, however, rejected the defense and chose to find Dahmer guilty of murder, for which he was sentenced to life in prison. In 1994, Dahmer was beaten to death by another prisoner.

If the jury had accepted Dahmer's defense, he could have been found not guilty strictly on the basis of insanity at the time of the murders. Public perceptions often question how someone who commits crimes as brutal and inhuman as Dahmer's should even be allowed to raise a defense like insanity. How could a severely depraved person like Dahmer be considered for exoneration of his crimes because of his profound mental illness? If Dahmer wasn't considered too insane to be criminally punished, who should? On the other hand, if a clearly crazed serial killer like Dahmer, who had sexual relations with corpses and even ate some of their body parts, was found not insane, who can possibly qualify as insane?

Procedures Involved in the Defense

The criminal law presumes a defendant is sane at the time of the crime. Thus, insanity is usually an affirmative defense; that is, it is the defendant's obligation to raise it. If successful, a defendant may be found not guilty by reason of insanity (NGRI). This verdict reflects a societal preference for mental-health treatment over criminal punishment for persons whose mental illness was a major factor underlying their crime. The defendant is totally acquitted, even if the prosecution has proved beyond reasonable doubt all the elements of the crime, but the only reason for that acquittal is the jury's or judge's acceptance of the idea that the defendant is not fully culpable for his actions because of the profound effect of his serious mental illness at the time of the crime. Thus, the defense reflects a policy preference that recognizes a need for treatment over punishment, in these particular cases.

Generally, a defendant must give notice prior to trial that he will raise an insanity defense, and he may be required to identify experts who will testify for him in this regard. Often, the court will order a pretrial psychiatric examination by a court-appointed expert, conducted at a mental health facility over a two- to three-month period. If the examination supports insanity, the prosecutor may dismiss charges contingent on the defendant's agreeing to civil commitment at a mental health facility.

Unlike other forms of acquittal, a verdict of NGRI usually does not result in release of the defendant. Rather, he or she is likely to be committed to a mental institution, often for a longer period than a prison sentence for conviction for the same crime. This civil commitment may be automatic upon the finding of NGRI, or it may be discretionary with the trial judge, who generally will require temporary detention for purposes of examination.

A person found NGRI may be detained as long as they remain mentally ill and as long as they continue to be deemed dangerous. Confinement is usually of indefinite length, and is ostensibly for treatment rather than punishment. Generally, in order to be released, the person must prove that he or she is no longer mentally ill or no longer dangerous.

History of the Defense

Early English common law did not recognize an insanity defense. Rather, very serious mental illness could be seen as a reason for the crown to grant pardon. Forms of exculpating the mentally ill for criminal behavior eventually evolved. These were based in the Roman ideas of *no compos mentis* (the accused has "no power of mind") and *furiosus* (the accused is essentially a raging, raving beast). As incorporated into English law, persons who were "mad" were seen as similar to children and brute animals in that they all lacked understanding (*ratio*) and discretion, though the "mad" person could be distinguished in that he could have lucid moments. Initially, for a finding of insanity, a defendant had to prove that he was *furiosus* at the time of the crime. Religious distinctions between man and beast underlaid the idea that a madman lacked complete rationality and hence moral culpability. This is sometimes referred to as the *wild beast test.*

The M'Naghten Test

The *M'Naghten* test for insanity arose in Victorian England in 1843, when Daniel M'Naghten shot the private secretary to the Prime Minister, believing the secretary was the Prime Minister. When the secretary died a few days later, M'Naghten was charged with murder in the first degree. M'Naghten's defense was that he was suffering from a delusion that caused him to believe the Tories were following and persecuting him everywhere he went. Ultimately, M'Naghten was acquitted, but was sent to an asylum for life.

Public outrage at the acquittal led Queen Victoria to demand that the English House of Lords devise a stricter rule. What they devised came to be known as the *M'Naghten* rule, which considers only whether a defendant who was suffering from "disease of the mind" at the time of the crime knew what he was doing or knew that doing it was wrong. The test predates modern psychiatry, with which many of its tenets are in conflict. It takes a strictly cognitive view of insanity, ignoring other legitimate manifestations of mental illness. It also involves a strictly binary decision: either the defendant's cognitive capacity is totally impaired or it is not, and does not recognize that insanity may be a matter of degree. Using the *M'Naghten* test, Daniel M'Naghten himself would likely have been found sane.

As *M'Naghten* is concerned only with cognitive disability and does not consider gradations of incapacity, a person must be completely deficient in cognition to be found insane, a condition rarely found among humans. Also, the test ignores volition, the ability control one's behavior. A person who can distinguish right from wrong, yet is unable to control his or her behavior, is unlikely to be found insane under *M'Naghten*. This test proved highly influential in the United States in the 19th century, and it was the most common test for insanity until the mid-20th century.

Irresistible Impulse

A competing test for insanity, used in a small number of jurisdictions, is called the *irresistible impulse test,* which is somewhat more lenient for defendants. It asks whether mental illness caused the defendant to lack the power to choose between right and wrong, even if he or she did know the difference. Thus, the test allows for volitional impairments, not just the cognitive impairment required by *M'Naghten*. For example, if a person suffers from pathological gambling disorders, they may know that excessive gambling is wrong and perhaps even illegal, but because of biological factors (e.g., low levels of certain neurochemicals such as norepinephrine or serotonin), they may be unsuccessful in trying to reduce the gambling behavior. Though the person likely could not be found insane under *M'Naghten*, they may very well be found insane under irresistible impulse. With this test, a defendant may have planned their behavior, but was unable to control it. A major difficulty with the test is that psychiatrists have no assessment that clearly differentiates levels of impaired capacity for self-control.

The Durham Test

Another variation on insanity was set forth in the District of Columbia in 1954 in the case of *Durham v. United States*. Judge David Bazelon declared the relatively broad rule that insanity exists where the crime was the "product" of mental disease or defect, since those who act in such states are not truly morally blameworthy. But for their mental disease or defect, the defendant's criminal act would not have occurred. The *Durham rule* was used only in the District of Columbia courts and only until 1972.

Durham allowed a wide range of psychiatric testimony with regard to criminal responsibility, including rational, volitional, and emotional components. The testimony was intended, in part, to educate the jury as to what led the defendant to carry out their behavior. The *Durham* rule had the defect of potentially acquitting defendants who knew what they were doing, knew that it was wrong, and could have controlled their behavior. As long as the defendant suffered from some mental disease or defect, without which he would not have committed the criminal act, he could be acquitted, a result contrary to both retributive and utilitarian goals.

American Law Institute Test

The American Law Institute (ALI) developed a test for insanity in 1962, as part of its Model Penal Code. The test specifies that insanity exists when a person's "mental disease or defect" leads them, at the time of the crime, to lack "substantial capacity to appreciate the criminality (wrongfulness) of his conduct or to conform his conduct to the requirement of the law." To the *M'Naghten* test's strictly cognitive (intellectual) approach, the ALI test added a volitional parameter relating to a defendant's inability to choose to follow the law, again rooted in mental illness.

The use of the term *appreciate* made proof of insanity somewhat easier for defendants, though the term is still as vague and lacking definition as the term *know* in the *M'Naghten* test. Additionally, the verb *conform* presumes that psychiatrists can reliably distinguish between those who will not conform and those who cannot conform, a presumption with which many psychiatrists disagree.

Guilty but Mentally Ill

In 1975, Michigan introduced a verdict termed *guilty but mentally ill* (GBMI) for defendants who were not found insane but who were mentally ill at the time the crime was committed. The verdict's appellation conveys that the defendant's guilt is somehow mitigated by mental illness, such that they must receive treatment while incarcerated, though defendants found GBMI may or may not receive treatment. Also, the verdict likely appeals to jurors who are reluctant to declare a defendant not guilty by reason of insanity, fearing they may be released. With GBMI, jurors feel confident about protection (via incarceration) and have their consciences assuaged through the prospect of treatment. Defendants, on the other hand, may receive the worst of both worlds: incarceration as well as involuntary treatment. If a defendant is no longer mentally ill at some point in his detention, he or she must still finish out his sentence of incarceration.

With GBMI, the jury has a choice of four verdicts: guilty, not guilty, NGRI, or GBMI. The last verdict is deemed proper for defendants who are guilty of the crime, were sane at the time of the crime, but were also mentally ill at the time of the crime. The GBMI scheme does not give clear guidance to juries regarding the distinction between mental illness sufficient for GBMI, in contrast to that necessary for NGRI. Also, it indirectly seeks to curtail use of the NGRI verdict, acting as a compromise verdict in which jurors believe they have achieved both safety for society and treatment for the defendant.

A famous case involving GBMI was that of multi-millionaire and philanthropist John Du Pont, who was a major supporter of the U.S. Olympic team. An Olympic wrestler lived with his family on Du Pont's vast estate. In 1996, Du Pont drove to the wrestler's abode on the estate and shot him in the driveway, killing him. The defense and the prosecution agreed that Du Pont was mentally ill, with the defense contending he suffered from paranoid schizophrenia that involved delusions that the wrestler and others were conspiring to murder him. Rather than accept the insanity defense, the jury found Du Pont GBMI, and he was given a sentence of 13 to 30 years in prison.

Insanity Defense Reform Act of 1984

A sea change in the insanity defense occurred in the 1980s. In 1982, John Hinckley Jr. was found NGRI for his attempted assassination of President Ronald Reagan. Hinckley believed the president's death would unite him with his object of infatuation, a Hollywood actress. Similar to events surrounding the *M'Naghten* case, public demands for an end to the perceived leniency of the ALI test resulted in the federal Insanity Defense Reform Act of 1984. This basically paralleled the provisions of the *M'Naghten* test: "severe mental disease or defect" had to lead to inability to "appreciate" either the nature and quality of the defendant's behavior or the "wrongfulness" of the behavior. The act also changed the burden of proof of insanity from the prosecutor's duty to prove sanity beyond reasonable doubt to the defendant's burden to prove his or her insanity by clear and convincing evidence.

The test established by this act is now used in all federal courts. Though modeled closely on *M'Naghten,* the term *appreciate* (in lieu of *know* in *M'Naghten*) somewhat cuts in favor of the defendant, in that it is not solely restricted to examination of the defendant's cognition.

Most states now use some variation of *M'Naghten*. A few (Idaho, Montana, Utah, and Kansas) have abolished the insanity defense and in its stead allow only evidence that tends to negate the *mens rea* (guilty mind) of the crime charged. The defendant must prove that his mental illness prevented him from forming the *mens rea* required for the particular crime. Opponents of this approach question whether it deprives defendants of their right to due process of law by precluding an insanity defense. For defendants who are mentally ill, a guilty verdict (in contrast to an NGRI verdict) affords criminal punishment with no requirement for treatment.

Post-Traumatic Stress Disorder and Postpartum Psychosis

One relatively recent application of the insanity defense involves defendants with post-traumatic stress disorder (PTSD). The disorder, first recognized by the American Psychiatric Association in 1980, refers to a constellation of symptoms consequent on a psychologically traumatic event that is generally outside the realm of normal experience. For example, long after experiencing the traumatic event, a person with PTSD may relive the event in dissociative states; they believe they are experiencing the traumatic event in the present moment. Such events can include military combat, assault, and sexual abuse.

Another fairly new use for the insanity defense relates to postpartum psychosis, when a mother becomes delusional soon after giving birth (e.g., suffering visual or auditory hallucinations), and she views the delusions as reality. Delusions may include thoughts of suicide or infanticide, as well as obsessions about inability to care for the infant or some perceived defect in the infant. Probably the most publicized insanity case of the early 21st century involved postpartum psychosis. The Texas case of Andrea Yates also illustrates some of the controversy surrounding the insanity defense. Yates was a college graduate and registered nurse who married at age 28. In the succeeding seven years she had five children and suffered one miscarriage. In 2001, within approximately one hour, she drowned each of the children in the bathtub.

Yates's fire-and-brimstone religious beliefs fueled obsessions about her being a bad mother. She suffered from delusions that her evilness pervaded her mothering and that she had to kill her children to save them from Satan. She had a history of postpartum psychosis, in addition to two suicide attempts and psychiatric hospitalizations after the births of two of her children. Throughout her marriage, she was almost always either pregnant or breastfeeding, facing regular pressure from her husband to have more children. She also homeschooled all her children.

The major issue at her trial was whether she knew her actions were morally wrong. At her first trial in 2002, the jury found her guilty of first-degree murder, and she was sentenced to life in prison with possibility for parole after 40 years. An appellate court reversed her conviction, due primarily to irregularities in the testimony of the major expert witness for the prosecution. She was granted a new trial in 2006, and this time the jury found her NGRI.

The Supreme Court Gets Involved

While matters of criminal defense are much more commonly resolved by state-level courts, in 2006, the U.S. Supreme Court took the unusual step of deciding a case about the insanity defense. *Eric Clark v. Arizona* involved a 17-year-old boy whose schizophrenia led him to believe his community was infested with hostile space aliens. Ultimately, he concluded that his parents and the police were also aliens, and he shot and killed a police officer who had pulled him over for a minor traffic violation. The defendant's insanity defense was based in the claim that his delusions prevented him from knowing that killing the officer was wrong, since he believed the officer was a space alien who wished to harm him.

Arizona used only half of the traditional *M'Naghten* test, allowing insanity only if the defendant did not know that what he was doing was wrong. The Supreme Court decided that the constitutional right to due process of law does not require a state to use any particular formulation of insanity. Also, the Court held that states may restrict expert testimony on a defendant's mental disease solely to issues of insanity, in light of the presumption of sanity and to avoid misunderstanding and confusion among jurors.

Pro: Arguments in Support of the Insanity Defense

The insanity defense is consistent with retributive theories of criminal punishment. In these views, criminal punishment is earned only when a person freely chooses to commit crime. Much as with children, insane persons lack full mental capacity to truly choose their actions, so they are not nearly as worthy of blame as sane adults. Because they cannot act rationally or truly lack self-control, they are pitied more than they are condemned. Proponents of this view argue that when a person's mental status is considered, criminal punishment violates the retributive principle that punishment must be proportionate to the crime: because these persons are not morally responsible for their actions, they have not earned, or do not morally deserve, criminal punishment. The insanity defense properly reflects the importance of tempering the criminal law with some degree of mercy for those who are not morally culpable. A common perception is that the insanity defense is overused, but in reality, it is used in under one percent of felony cases.

The insanity defense is also consistent with utilitarian theories of criminal punishment. No social good is achieved by punishing persons who cannot be deterred; their actions are irrational because of the profound effects of their mental illness. Also, the insane person is not capable of learning from the punishment of others, so criminal punishment for an insane person is unlikely to deter other insane persons from committing similar crimes. On the other hand, the provision of intensive mental-health treatment may produce societal benefits if the treatment achieves rehabilitation; that is, it allows the person to function in ways in which her mental illness is not determinative of her actions. Incapacitation in the form of imprisonment is counterproductive for these persons, and the isolation and tension inherent in prison environments can easily aggravate mental illness. Thus, incapacitation may paradoxically increase the danger these persons present to society, because imprisonment is apt to worsen their mental illness.

The insanity defense reflects society's moral judgment that those who cannot understand or control their behavior merit treatment rather than criminal punishment. Advocates for the insanity defense claim that it would be cruel and excessive punishment to simply imprison persons whose mental functioning approximates that of very young children. Just as young children cannot be severely punished under the criminal law, adults whose mental illness impairs their ability to understand or control their actions deserve solicitude more so than criminal punishment; although as the courts and society recognize, there usually is a concurrent need to separate them from civil society in order to accomplish treatment.

The insanity defense is necessary as a form of protection for a relatively small set of often-despised persons who lack political power and who are easily demonized in public opinion. In lieu of the politically expedient approach of exaggerating their danger and imposing purely criminal punishment, the insanity defense preserves an opportunity for these often severely stigmatized persons to receive badly needed mental health treatment, even if it is in a secure facility. The insanity defense tempers majoritarian pressures toward extreme—even cruel—punishments for the hapless minority of the insane.

Con: Arguments Against the Insanity Defense

A popular public perception is that the insanity defense is easy to fake. So much of the defense depends on self-reporting of symptoms, and even expert testimony is ultimately rooted in the defendant's own words and behavior. Thus, there is widespread skepticism about excusing what would otherwise be criminal behavior, based largely on information that is provided by a defendant and that may be primarily self-serving.

Although proponents argue that the insanity defense is necessary to protect this small, despised minority who lack political power, in actuality, it is successful only approximately one-fourth of the time. Nevertheless, perceptions strongly influence reality, and it is commonly but erroneously concluded that too many defendants get off easy by using the insanity defense.

Another common attitude militating against the insanity defense involves presumptions about mental illness and dangerousness. Often, the two are conflated, based on popular prejudices about mental illness. Rather than eliciting sympathy or compassion, a defendant who claims they committed a crime because of their mental illness may end up losing their insanity claim because jurors fear him or her, and feel compelled to incarcerate in order to prevent such crimes in the future.

The semantics of various formulations of insanity are problematic in that key terms are often vague. Terms that are rudimentary to the definitions, such as *mental disease, wrong,* and *capacity to conform,* are poorly defined and subject to value judgments on the part of courtroom actors. For example, most American courts interpret the term *wrong* in the *M'Naghten* test to mean morally—rather than legally—wrong. By contrast, England takes the opposite approach. Also, there is no clear demarcation between mental disorder and no mental disorder, though most definitions of insanity posit this as a purely binary decision. Additionally, criteria for release from detention after a finding of NGRI, such as when the person is considered no longer a danger to oneself or others, are so amorphous as to permit indefinite and prolonged detention, contravening a defendant's liberty interests. A major factor contributing to the semantic confusion in insanity is the fact that the defense attempts to marry the sometimes-conflicting languages of psychiatry and law: it is a legal defense, but it is grounded solidly in psychiatric concepts.

The *M'Naghten* version of insanity is generally considered inconsistent with modern psychiatry, particularly in that it disallows many delusions and irrational impulses that often characterize serious mental illness. It simply presumes that everyone can make moral decisions, and it ignores the impact of mental illness upon volitional capacity. Additionally, the test was developed in a politically charged atmosphere; given less politics and more diversity of actors, a very different kind of test may have emerged.

Even a successful insanity defense may not benefit a defendant. Because of societal reservations about the seriously mentally ill, a person who is judged insane often serves significantly more time in detention (albeit not in a prison setting) than a person convicted for a similar crime. John Hinckley Jr. was still institutionalized at a psychiatric hospital 28 years after his NGRI verdict in the attempted assassination of President Reagan.

One popular idea is that insanity is a rich person's defense, based largely on the expensive experts who must be hired to testify for the defense. The perception derives at least in part from selective reporting by the mass media, where sensational journalists laser in on cases involving wealthy celebrities such as Du Pont. However, in reality, the insanity defense is used by defendants from across the socioeconomic spectrum.

A Case in Point

More typical of insanity defendants is Ralph Tortorici, a 26-year-old college student with a long history of serious mental illness, who in 1994 entered a university classroom, barricaded the door, and held the students hostage with the help of his rifle. He demanded to see university and government officials to discuss the computer microchips that he believed had been conspiratorially implanted in his brain and genitals. One of the students rushed Tortorici, whose gun discharged and severely wounded the student. Tortorici was charged with aggravated assault, kidnapping, and attempted murder. Based on his profound paranoid schizophrenia that included depression, delusions, and hallucinations, Tortorici raised the defense of insanity. Consistent with his delusions about a massive conspiracy against him (a conspiracy which included the court), Tortorici refused to be present in the courtroom for his trial in New York. During the usual battle between psychiatrists for both the defense and prosecution at trial, the prosecution successfully discredited the defense psychiatrist in the eyes of the jury, which rejected the insanity defense and found Tortorici guilty after approximately an hour of deliberation. The judge imposed the maximum punishment (20–47 years in prison). Tortorici deteriorated psychologically in prison, and in 1999, he committed suicide by hanging himself with a bedsheet in his cell.

For the crime of homicide, females are appreciably more likely to be found NGRI than males. This may reflect unfairness toward males, who may be seen as more worthy of punishment than treatment. On the other hand, it may reflect gendered stereotypes about females as more mentally unstable, even hysterical, than males. More generally, the defense may be seen as more acceptable in cases involving crimes that are grossly contrary to societal values. For example, only a crazy mother would kill her children; only a crazy person, such as M'Naghten or Hinckley, would try to kill his country's leader.

Finally, from a utilitarian perspective, the insanity defense may convey a wrong message that the mentally ill will not be held responsible for their crimes. Since insanity is exculpatory if it is successful, society may suffer long-term harm because the mentally ill are insufficiently deterred from committing crime.

See Also: 7. Expert Witnesses and Hired Guns; 11. Jury System.

Further Readings

Breheney, Christian, Jennifer Groscup, and Michele Galietta. "Gender Matters in the Insanity Defense." *Law and Psychology Review,* v.31 (2007).

Dressler, Joshua. *Understanding Criminal Law.* New York: Lexis, 2009.

Finkel, Norman J. *Insanity on Trial.* New York: Plenum Press, 1988.

Gerber, Rudolph. *The Insanity Defense.* New York: Associated Faculty Press, 1984.

Leblanc, Stephen M. "Cruelty to the Mentally Ill: An Eighth Amendment Challenge to the Abolition of the Insanity Defense." *American University Law Review,* v.56 (2007).

Maeder, Thomas. *Crime and Madness: The Origins and Evolution of the Insanity Defense.* New York: Harper & Row, 1985.

Manchester, Jessie. "Beyond Accommodation: Reconsidering the Insanity Defense to Provide an Adequate Remedy for Postpartum Psychotic Women." *Journal of Criminal Law and Criminology,* v.93 (2003).

11

Jury System

James Binnall
University of California, Irvine

S ince its inception, the American jury system has elicited praise while inspiring a wealth of criticism. A jury is a panel of citizens chosen by the justice system to adjudicate a criminal or civil matter in a court of law. Jurisdictions select jurors by employing a series of procedures designed to screen out biased or incompetent jurors. Often, this process takes several weeks and involves the cooperation of judges, lawyers, and prospective jurors. If a citizen survives the jury selection process, he or she will participate in trial, becoming an empanelled or seated juror responsible for considering evidence, applying law, and potentially rendering a verdict.

Social science research has reinvigorated the debate surrounding the American jury system. Citing empirical data, critics of the jury system suggest that it is far from the optimal method for settling legal disputes. Specifically, many contend that the jury selection process promotes juror bias by allowing attorneys to engineer juries favorable to their client's position. Moreover, social scientists suggest that jurors have difficulty understanding and applying law in the current trial setting. Finally, others simply note that the jury is an inefficient exercise that causes taxpayers to spend an inordinate amount of money and time on tasks a judge could more competently perform.

Yet, proponents of the jury system respond by noting that the jury is an embodiment of American democracy. Supporters of the jury argue that it infuses the will of the people into the judiciary, providing a constant check on the power of judges and the state. In addition, jury advocates highlight the educational impact of participation in the adjudicative process. In short, the debate surrounding the jury is extensive and polarizing.

Mechanics of the Jury System

The jury selection process starts with the jury summons. A jury summons is a written order, issued by a court, requiring a citizen to appear for jury duty at a specified date and time. Using voter registration roles or driver's license records to construct jury pools or lists, courts randomly select citizens as possible jurors and issue summonses accordingly. Citizens are legally obligated to comply with a jury summons, and failure to do so can result in a fine or other penalty.

The jury selection process next involves establishing juror eligibility. Along with a jury summons, most courts also send citizens a juror questionnaire. A juror questionnaire includes questions designed to verify that a citizen meets juror eligibility requirements. In all jurisdictions, the legislature establishes juror eligibility requirements and codifies these requirements as statutes. Typically, to be eligible for jury service, one must be 18 years of age, a citizen of the United States, a citizen of the summonsing state and county, and able to understand the English language. Moreover, in a majority of states, those who possess a felony conviction are ineligible to serve as jurors.

Unless excused by the court for a personal conflict or condition, those citizens eligible for jury service then take part in voir dire, which is a screening process during which lawyers and judges interview eligible jurors to ascertain whether they are suitable to sit on an empanelled jury. During voir dire, attorneys may challenge a prospective juror for cause or peremptorily. A challenge for cause is an allegation that a juror, by virtue of some characteristic, cannot decide a case impartially. Once an attorney has lodged a challenge for cause with the court, the judge determines whether to excuse the challenged juror. A preemptory challenge is a challenge lodged by an attorney essentially alleging suspicions about a juror's tendency for partiality. Attorneys possess a jurisdictionally predetermined number of preemptory challenges to use during voir dire. Though constitutional safeguards protect against biased or sexist exclusion through preemptory challenges, courts generally afford attorneys wide latitude as to who they may strike from jury service using their preemptory challenges. At the conclusion of voir dire, the jurors that remain make up the empanelled or seated jury and a select number of alternates.

Once empanelled by the court, jurors take part in a trial, considering evidence offered by each party to the litigation. Judges determine the admissibility of each piece of evidence offered by parties to a dispute. Court rules permit jurors to inspect certain forms of evidence, but do not provide jurors the opportunity to pose questions or concerns during trial. At the close of the presentation of evidence, the judge gives jury instructions, informing jurors of the applicable law in the case by reading relevant legal provisions, outlining the elements of the crime or claim at issue. Judges do not provide jurors a copy of the jury instructions.

Next, deliberations begin. Deliberations are private consultations between jurors for the express purpose of determining a victorious party to the dispute. Deliberations take place outside of the presence of the litigants and can last minutes, hours, weeks, or even months. During deliberations, jurors discuss the evidence they heard during trial as well as the law provided to them by the court, and they strive to evaluate each party's claims. Jury deliberations can simultaneously involve heated exchanges and courteous persuasion.

There are two possible outcomes of deliberations. First, a jury may render a verdict. A jury reaches a verdict when it meets the requisite level of juror agreement as to the appropriate outcome of a case. Generally, verdicts in criminal cases require unanimity among jurors, while verdicts in civil cases necessitate merely that a majority of jurors support the final decision. Second, a jury may also declare that it is hopelessly deadlocked or hung. In this situation, jurors cannot reach the requisite level of agreement, even after deliberations. The dispute remains unresolved and the parties have the option of retrying the case to a new jury.

History of the Jury System

The modern American jury system is the product of centuries of evolution, both in England and the United States. In England during the Middle Ages, prior to the jury system, techniques of dispute resolution were rooted in religious beliefs. Specifically, litigants engaged in trial by compurgation, battle, and ordeal as means of settling conflicts. Trial by compurgation mandated that each party to a dispute swear an oath and produce as many compurgators, or oathhelpers, as possible. Compurgators were fellow citizens asked to swear to the validity of a litigant's assertions. Because dishonest testimony amounted to religious impropriety, authorities trusted that the party asserting the rightful claim could produce the greatest number of compurgators.

Trial by battle and trial by ordeal were additional schemes for resolving competing claims in early English history. Trial by battle simply required that parties to a dispute engage in a duel. Authorities regulated the duels, but presumed that God determined the victor and thus, the winning legal claim. Trial by ordeal involved several barbaric tests designed to ascertain the successful party to a legal dispute. For example, one version of trial by ordeal provided the accused in a criminal case the option of proof by boiling water. During this process, authorities required the accused to submerge an arm into a kettle of boiling water to retrieve a submerged stone. Not surprisingly, the accused always suffered instant burns. Three days after the ordeal, authorities removed the bandaged arm to reveal an infected wound if the accused was guilty, or a healing, healthy wound if the accused was innocent. Once again, authorities believed that divine intervention produced accurate legal outcomes.

Perhaps recognizing the logical flaws of these primitive forms of adjudication, English authorities soon outlawed their imposition, turning to the jury as the primary method for solving conflict. Following the Norman conquest of England, to accurately assess taxes, Norman kings relied on the testimony of citizens when determining the ownership of various forms of property. False testimony to the king constituted perjury, and those guilty of such behavior were punished for lying.

Later changes in the English jury system produced other features that still mark today's juries. For instance, early in the jury's history, presentment juries decided whether there was adequate evidence to support criminal charges against a citizen. Today, grand juries operate in a similar fashion, returning an indictment when evidence exists to warrant criminal charges. Early jury systems also utilized petit juries, which determined (as they do today) whether the accused actually committed the crime in question. Moreover, as the English jury system evolved, it prohibited citizens from serving on a presentment jury and a petit jury in the same case, as was customary at the outset of the jury system. This development helped to establish the petit juries as disinterested, fact-finding tribunals, a model to which the modern petit jury still strives to adhere.

Other modifications of the English jury system helped to define the jury's powers. For example, early in the history of the jury, authorities abandoned the practice of punishing jurors who returned a verdict contrary to a judge's opinions. Hence, a jury's verdict was above reproach. This facet of the jury's authority proved instrumental in establishing English legal precedent. In the controversial *Seven Bishop's Trial* in 1688, a jury negated the established legal doctrine of seditious libel, demonstrating the independence of a jury's decision and its ability to change the law.

Settlers imported the English jury system to colonial America as early as 1606, where it was included in the Virginia Company Charter. By the time of the Revolutionary War, all colonies in America used some form of juries in both civil and criminal disputes—though some favored the jury system far more than others. The framers eventually codified the right to trial by jury in the Bill of Rights, ratified on December 15, 1791. The Sixth and the Seventh Amendments to the U.S. Constitution guarantee each citizen the right to a trial by jury in both criminal and civil cases settled in the federal court system. Specifically, the Sixth Amendment provides that "In all criminal prosecutions, the accused shall enjoy the right to a speedy and public trial, by an impartial jury of the State and district wherein the crime shall have been committed," while the Seventh Amendment states that "In Suits at common law, where the value in controversy shall exceed twenty dollars, the right of trial by jury shall be preserved, and no fact tried by a jury, shall be otherwise re-examined in any Court of the United States, than according to the rules of the common law."

The Supreme Court Shapes the American Jury System

Perhaps the legal decision that most influenced the evolution of the American jury system occurred prior to the ratification of the Bill of Rights. In 1735, John Peter Zenger, the editor of the *New York Weekly Journal*, published articles critical of New York Governor William Cosby. Subsequently, the attorney general of New York indicted Zenger for seditious libel. English legal precedent dictated that Zenger was guilty of seditious libel if the jury decided that he, in fact, published the material in question. In such cases, the trial judge, not the jury, assessed the libelous nature of the printed material. But Zenger's attorney, Andrew Hamilton, challenged the jury to use their adjudicative power to recoil against such precedent. Hamilton argued that the use of English legal precedent was inappropriate in the colonies and that the jury ought to determine whether the statements Zenger published were true, and therefore not libelous. In effect, Hamilton attempted to persuade the jury to redefine the law. Shortly after Hamilton's closing argument, the trial judge instructed the jury that they were only to determine if Zenger had published the statements in question. Nevertheless, the jury responded to Hamilton's prompts and returned a verdict of not guilty, effectively defining the power of the jury and its role as a facilitator of legal change in the United States.

Over a century later, the Supreme Court undertook the most daunting task facing the American jury system. Though *Zenger* firmly established the jury as a powerful democratic institution, the composition of the jury remained a point of contention in the United States. Following the Civil War, the Fifteenth Amendment gave African Americans the right to vote. Yet, the Fifteenth Amendment did not address an African American's right to sit on a jury. In 1880, the Supreme Court decided *Strauder v. Virginia*, a case involving a Virginia statute that limited jury participation to only white males. Reviewing the statute, the Court held that while states were free to define juror eligibility requirements, such requirements are constitutionally impermissible if they deny citizens the opportunity to serve on a jury because of their race or color.

Though seemingly rectifying the problem of juror discrimination, the *Strauder* decision addressed only one form of exclusion. In *Strauder*, the Supreme Court failed to expand jury pools to include women. In 1920, while the Nineteenth Amendment to the Constitution granted women the right to vote, almost all states and the federal government denied women the opportunity to serve on a jury. Jurisdictional preclusion of women jurors endured until the Supreme Court detailed the fair cross section requirement of the Sixth Amendment in a series of landmark cases.

In 1946, the Supreme Court decided *Thiel v. Southern Pacific Co.*, a civil case involving the practice of barring blue-collar workers from the jury pool. In that case, the jury commissioner and the clerk of court testified that they regularly left wage laborers off of jury lists. The Court held that the practice of precluding day laborers from jury pools unconstitutional because the Sixth Amendment required that a federal jury pool represent a fair cross-section of the community. Thus, in *Thiel*, the Court first enunciated the fair cross-section requirement.

Months after *Thiel*, the Supreme Court heard *United States v. Ballard*. In *Ballard*, the Court assessed the constitutionality of excluding women from federal jury pools in the southern district of California. The Court held, as it did in *Thiel*, that the fair cross-section requirement of the Sixth Amendment prohibited the exclusion of women, as such a practice would result in a federal jury pool different than the community. *Ballard* marked the first instance in which the Supreme Court failed to authorize the systematic exclusion of women from juries. Nevertheless, because the Sixth Amendment only applied to the federal court system, *Ballard* had little impact on the sexist state juror eligibility requirements that pervaded the nation.

Yet, in 1968, the Supreme Court applied the Sixth Amendment to the states through the Due Process Clause of the Fourteenth Amendment. Specifically, the Court's decision in *Duncan v. Louisiana* ensured that the fair cross-section requirement of the Sixth Amendment governed state juries. Soon after, the Court again addressed the preclusion of women from juries, but in light of their holding in *Duncan*. In *Taylor v. Louisiana*, the Court invalidated a Louisiana statute that kept women out of state jury pools. Because states use the same juror lists to choose prospective jurors for both civil and criminal juries, *Taylor* provided women the opportunity to serve on juries without restriction.

Fair Cross-Section Requirement

In 1979, over 10 years after the Supreme Court decided *Duncan*, the Court clarified the fair cross-section requirement of the Sixth Amendment. In *Duren v. Missouri*, the Court held that a state or the federal government violates the fair cross-section standard if (1) they exclude from the jury pool a group that is distinctive in the community; (2) such that the jury pool fails to reasonably and fairly represent that group; and (3) the jury pool inadequately represents that distinctive group because of systematic exclusionary policies. In 1990, in *Holland v. Illinois*, the Court further explained that the purpose of the fair cross-section requirement, in accordance with the Sixth Amendment, was not to construct representative juries, but to promote impartial juries. Today, this principle still guides Supreme Court opinions regarding other aspects of juries.

Along with a jury's composition, its size has also been the subject of litigation. In 1970, in *Williams v. Florida*, the Supreme Court held that although most states required that a jury consist of 12 jurors, that number was largely the result of tradition and had no practical justification. Assessing the constitutionality of juries smaller than 12 jurors, the Court concluded that a Florida jury of six jurors was constitutionally permissible. Nevertheless, almost all jurisdictions still require 12-member juries in criminal trials, but a majority of states and the federal government allow juries as small as six members to decide civil matters.

The Supreme Court has also weighed in on the issue on the unanimity requirement of the jury process. While a jury verdict traditionally required that jurors unanimously agree on a trial outcome, in 1972, the Supreme

Court held in *Apodaca v. Oregon* that the Constitution does not require unanimous verdicts. The Court's decision, however, had little impact on criminal juries. In the United States, all except two states require unanimous verdicts in felony criminal cases. Yet, a vast majority of states do not require juror unanimity in civil matters. Six years after *Apodaca*, in *Burch v. Louisiana*, the Supreme Court clarified its position on the size and unanimity of juries, noting that a verdict rendered by a six-person jury was only constitutional if it was unanimous.

In the 1980s and 1990s, the Supreme Court once again found itself forced to address juror selection practices that excluded both minorities and women from juries. In 1986, the Supreme Court held in *Batson v. Kentucky* that using preemptory challenges to exclude racial minorities from juries violated the Equal Protection Clause of the Fourteenth Amendment. Then in 1995, in *Purkett v. Elem*, the Court readdressed the discriminatory use of preemptory challenges when it held that excluding women solely on the basis of their sex violates the Equal Protection Clause and is unconstitutional.

Constitutional safeguards prevent discriminatory jury selection procedures in two ways. First, as was the case in *Duren*, the fair cross-section requirement of the Sixth Amendment prohibits systematic exclusion of distinctive groups from jury lists or pools. Second, though the fair cross-section requirement does not apply to empaneled juries, the Equal Protection Clause of the Fourteenth Amendment forbids the federal government or states from allowing the preemptive dismissal of prospective jurors solely on the basis of race or sex.

The same year that the Supreme Court decided *Batson*, it also considered the jury's role in death penalty cases. In capitol cases, along with determining guilt or innocence, the jury also determines whether a criminal defendant deserves to die at the hands of the state if convicted. When selecting death-qualified juries, the court excludes for cause jurors who indicate that they could never impose a sentence of death. In *Lockhart v. McCree*, a criminal defendant argued that by eliminating jurors who could not condemn a convicted criminal to die, courts create juries that are prone to convict. Yet, the Supreme Court found this argument unpersuasive, noting the inefficiency of seating two juries, one during the guilt phase and one during the penalty phase. The Court also concluded that death-qualified juries did not violate the fair cross-section requirement, as the issue dealt with empanelled juries, not jury pools. Finally, because a proper voir dire also detects and removes jurors who would automatically impose the death penalty, the Court supported constitutional measures that remove jurors who could never order death.

Pro: Arguments in Support of the American Jury System

Supporters of the current jury system contend that its detractors overestimate the jury's shortcomings while underestimating its benefits. Specifically, jury proponents argue that juror bias does not detract from the neutrality of the tribunal, but actually enhances the objectivity of the adjudicative process. Moreover, those who favor the current jury system point out that the primary value of the jury is not its judicial function. Instead, they assert that the jury process is principally an educative experience, through which citizens learn democratic ideals by participating in the administration of justice.

In *We, the Jury*, law professor Jeffrey Abramson challenges critics of the current jury system who argue that juror bias threatens the integrity of the adjudicative process. He argues that traditional conceptualizations of the jury miss the mark and that the fair cross-section requirement stands for the principle that embracing juror bias promotes impartiality. Specifically, Abramson hypothesizes that when courting a host of viewpoints, the jury selection process enhances deliberations by promoting rich exchanges of ideas and experiences. This dynamic, Abramson and others assert, is the essence of the decision-making process. Scholars taking this view bolster their claim by noting the Court's propensity to favor inclusivity when assessing the constitutionality of jury selection processes. Hence, while those skeptical of the jury process often describe juror biases as negative attributes of the adjudicative system, some characterize a juror's preconceived attitudes quite differently, viewing them as an asset to the jury.

Some advocates of the American jury system argue that the jury embodies democratic ideals. In 1835, Alexis de Tocqueville, a French political scientist and sociologist, published *Democracy in America*, a work chronicling his travels through America during the nation's infancy. In *Democracy in America*, Tocqueville discusses several prominent features of democracy, including the jury. Analyzing the jury system as an impartial observer, Tocqueville praised America's adjudicative process as a method for placing power in the hands of ordinary citizens and thereby protecting society from rulers who may attempt to wrestle control from the populace. Tocqueville hypothesized that juries provide citizens the opportunity to partake in judicial functions, promoting respect for the justice system and democracy generally. He further notes that because juries and judges perform similar functions in America's justice system, citizens who serve on juries possess an increased admiration for the judiciary. Today, proponents of the jury system often cite Tocqueville's insightful commentary on the American justice system, arguing that while juries may exhibit flaws, they are a crucial component of a thriving democracy.

More recently, Supreme Court Justice Stephen Breyer echoed Tocqueville's sentiments regarding participation in democracy. Justice Breyer's concept of active liberty reflects a desire for citizens take part in governance. Active liberty, Justice Breyer argues, occurs when a nation shares its sovereignty with its people. Much like Toqueville, Justice Breyer asserts that the sharing of authority legitimizes the rule of law. He goes on to contend that participation in government educates the citizenry, and that such an education is most meaningful when it is direct. Proponents of the jury system often note that the jury is the most direct form of civic participation. Hence, many view the jury system as an indispensible educative force that promotes democracy by legitimizing the law in the eyes of the governed.

Con: Criticisms of the American Jury System

Critics of the American jury system contend that flaws in the jury process jeopardize the justice system. Among these critics are legal scholars, psychologists, and social scientists, many of whom suggest that changes in the structure of the jury system are necessary to ensure both the efficiency and accuracy of the adjudicative process. The jury system requires that jurors consider only trial evidence and accurately apply the law to such evidence. Implicitly, the jury system also mandates that jurors harbor no preconceived attitudes or biases about a case and can understand legal standards. But social science research raises questions as to whether the jury system, as presently constituted, promotes juror impartiality or juror comprehension. Additionally, those who question the jury's utility support their contentions by noting the diminishing rate at which conflicts actually result in litigation, asserting that the jury's functional flaws, in part, lead a majority of litigants to resolve both criminal and civil disputes prior to trial.

Noted jury researchers Saul M. Kassin and Laurence Wrightsman point out that to achieve juror impartiality through the current jury selection process, it is necessary that lawyers and judges actually strive, through the use of voir dire, to select a neutral tribunal, and that they employ proven methods for achieving juror objectivity. But, lawyers frequently use voir dire to construct a jury favorable to their client's position by utilizing preemptive strikes to remove jurors that appear to be favorable to the opposing party. Moreover, the methods of questioning used by judges and lawyers during voir dire often amounts to intuition or pseudo-psychology. Kassin and

Wrightsman assert that scientifically selecting juries with the help of proven psychological techniques greatly increases the chances that the questioners will achieve their desired results—whatever they may be. Hence, those who allege that juror bias plagues the current jury selection process suggest that eliminating or limiting preemptory challenges, shortening voir dire, and employing scientific methods of questioning will reduce the risk of empanelling juries that are partial.

Other research tends to show that jurors cannot understand, interpret, or apply the law. In *The American Jury*, Harry Kalven Jr. and Hans Zeisel report the findings of the first large-scale, empirical jury study. The study surveyed the verdicts of 3,576 criminal trials and 4,000 civil trials to determine the number of cases in which the judge's verdict differed from that of the jury. The data revealed that in both criminal and civil trials, jurors and judges disagreed on the verdict in 22 percent of the assessed cases. Critics of the jury system argue that the discrepancies in verdict outcomes stem from jurors' inability to comprehend jury instructions, though Kalven and Zeisel maintain that a host of factors could have led to verdict differences. Nevertheless, later studies tested jurors' knowledge of the law immediately following jury instructions. The results indicate that jurors have trouble answering basic questions about legal principles as instructed by judges, lending support to the theory that jurors and judges decide litigated matter distinctly based on their incongruent understanding of the law. Accordingly, those who seek to improve juror competence have provided alternatives to traditional jury instructions, which include educating jurors about the law prior to trial, allowing jurors to take notes or ask questions during trial, helping jurors with structuring deliberations, and providing a form of jury instruction that is case-specific.

A final criticism of the current jury system centers on its time-consuming and costly structure. Some who question the jury system's efficiency argue that spending even minimal resources to question jurors is unnecessary, because jury selection can never predict the verdict propensities of a given juror. Because situational factors are the primary predictors of human behavior, even extended interrogation during a lengthy voir dire fails to ascertain juror tendencies. Such critics contend that voir dire is simply a superfluous exercise ripe for elimination. Less drastic reformers point out that policymakers can make juries more efficient by streamlining certain aspects of the jury process. For example, legislative measures requiring smaller juries and verdicts that are not unanimous would save time and money. Although constitutional protections would limit the extent of such reform, legal precedent does allow for a departure from 12-person juries and unanimous verdicts, making alterations of the current system possible.

See Also: 3. Double Jeopardy; 6. Exclusionary Rules; 7. Expert Witnesses and Hired Guns; 8. Eyewitness Testimony and Accuracy; 17. Sentencing Disparities.

Further Readings

Abbott, Walter F., Flora Hall, and Elizabeth Linville. *Jury Research: A Review and Bibliography*. Philadelphia: American Law Institute–American Bar Association, 1993.

Abramson, Jeffrey. *We, the Jury: The Jury System and the Ideal of Democracy*. Cambridge: Harvard University Press, 1994.

Adler, Stephen. *The Jury: Trial and Error in the American Courtroom*. New York: Times Books, 1994.

Apodaca v. Oregon, 406 U.S. 404 (1972).

Batson v. Kentucky, 476 U.S. 79 (1986).

Binnall, James M. "Sixteen Million Angry Men: Reviving a Dead Doctrine to Challenge the Constitutionality of Excluding Felons From Jury Service." *Virginia Journal of Social Policy and the Law,* v. 17/1 (2009).

Breyer, Stephen. *Active Liberty: Interpreting Our Democratic Constitution*. New York: Alfred A. Knopf, 2005.

Burch v. Louisiana, 441 U.S. 130 (1978).

Dufraimont, Lisa. "Evidence Law and the Jury: A Reassessment." *McGill University Law Journal*, v.53/199 (2008).

Duncan v. Louisiana, 391 U.S. 145 (1968).

Duren v. Missouri, 439 U.S. 357 (1979).

Ellsworth, Phoebe C., and Alan Reifman. "Juror Comprehension and Public Policy: Perceived Problems and Proposed Solutions." *Psychology, Public Policy and Law*, v.6/788 (2000).

Haddon, Phoebe A. "Rethinking the Jury." *William and Mary Bill of Rights Journal*, v. 3/29 (1994).

Hans, Valerie P., and Neil Vidmar. *Judging the Jury*. Cambridge: Basic Books, 1986.

Hastie, Reid, ed. *Inside the Juror: The Psychology of Juror Decision Making*. Cambridge, UK: Cambridge University Press, 1993.

Hastie, Reid, Steven D. Penrod, and Nancy Pennington. *Inside the Jury.* Cambridge: Harvard University Press, 1983.

Holland v. Illinois, 493 U.S. 474 (1990).

Jonakait, Randolph N. *The American Jury System.* New Haven: Yale University Press, 2003.

Kalt, Brian C. "The Exclusion of Felons from Jury Service." *American University Law Review,* v. 53/65 (2003).

Kalven, Harry, Jr., and Hans Zeisel. *The American Jury.* Boston: Little, Brown, 1966.

Kassin, Saul M., and Lawrence S. Wrightsman. *The American Jury on Trial: Psychological Perspectives.* New York: Hemisphere Publishing Corp., 1988.

Kleinig, John, and James P. Levine, eds. *Jury Ethics: Juror Conduct and Jury Dynamics.* Boulder, CO: Paradigm Publishers, 2006.

Levy, Leonard W. *The Palladium of Justice: Origins of Trial by Jury.* Chicago: Ivan R. Dee, 1999.

Lief, Michael S., Mitchell H. Caldwell, and Ben Bycel. *Ladies and Gentlemen of the Jury: Greatest Closing Arguments in Modern Law.* New York: Scribner, 1998.

Lockhart v. McCree, 476 U.S. 162 (1986).

Oldham, James. *Trial by Jury: The Seventh Amendment and Anglo-American Special Juries.* New York: New York University Press, 2006.

Purkett v. Elem, 514 U.S. 765 (1995).

Shuy, Roger. "How a Judge's *Voir Dire* Can Teach a Jury What to Say." *Discourse and Society,* v.6/207 (1995).

Strauder v. Virginia, 100 U.S. 303 (1880).

Taylor v. Louisiana, 419 U.S. 522 (1975).

Thiel v. Southern Pacific, 328 U.S. 217 (1946).

Tocqueville, Alexis de. *Democracy in America.* Garden City, NY: Anchor Books, 1969.

United States v. Ballard, 329 U.S. 187 (1946).

Vidmar, Neil, and Valerie P. Hans. *American Juries: The Verdict.* Amherst: Prometheus Books, 2007.

Williams v. Florida, 399 U.S. 78 (1970).

Wrightsman, Lawrence S., Saul M. Kassin, and Cynthia E. Willis, eds. *In the Jury Box: Controversies in the Courtroom.* Thousand Oaks, CA: Sage, 1987.

Young, William G. "Vanishing Trials, Vanishing Juries, Vanishing Constitution." *Suffolk University Law Review,* v.40/67 (2006).

12

Mandatory Sentencing

Noelle E. Fearn
Saint Louis University

M andatory sentencing policies are legislative efforts that enhance the sentencing provisions for convicted criminal defendants. Sentencing enhancement is achieved by either requiring a sentence of imprisonment, denying the possibility of probation or other community sanction, or by lengthening the actual time served in prison for particular types of criminal offenses. There are a variety of mandatory sentencing policies, but the two primary models of these policies are three-strikes statutes and truth-in-sentencing statutes (TIS). However, other mandatory sentencing provisions, such as violent offender incarceration, are also becoming more popular. Mandatory sentencing policies of all kinds have become quite common in the United States. In fact, by the mid-1990s, all 50 states and the federal government had enacted at least one, and typically several, mandatory sentencing provisions.

The expressed purpose of mandatory sentencing policies is twofold: deterrence and incapacitation. General deterrence is the process whereby potential criminal offenders are dissuaded or prevented from engaging in criminal activities because they fear the harsh punishment that will (likely) result, due to these mandatory sentencing policies. Specific deterrence is the process whereby actual offenders are dissuaded or prevented from further engagement in additional criminal behaviors because they fear suffering again from the harsh punishment that followed their previous criminal activity. Incapacitation, the other main goal of mandatory sentencing policies, focuses on protecting society from victimization through the removal of certain kinds of repeat, violent, or otherwise dangerous criminal offenders from society through the use of long prison sentences.

There is, however, widespread debate regarding the value and effectiveness of these mandatory sentencing policies. On the one hand, mandatory sentencing provisions are viewed as beneficial, as they serve three major functions. First, they limit judicial discretion in the imprisonment decision, which is especially important because many believe judges' sentencing decisions are not objective or neutral, but may instead be biased, resulting in disparate sentences for convicted criminal offenders. Second, they act as both a specific and general deterrent to actual and potential criminal offenders, respectively. Third, they serve to incapacitate dangerous and/or violent criminal offenders in prison so they cannot engage in further criminal activity that harms individuals and society.

On the other hand, mandatory sentencing policies have been criticized for their negative impacts on society, the criminal justice system, and the offender, for several reasons. First, they do not actually eliminate sentencing discretion, but instead simply move it from the judge to the police and/or prosecutors, so that discretion is not gone but rather displaced. Second, they do not reduce criminal activity, attributed often to the fact that criminal justice officials may and do circumvent the application of these policies in cases where they believe the outcomes to be inappropriately harsh. Finally, they contribute to the skyrocketing prison population in the United States and the significant increases in the economic and social costs associated with imprisoning more individuals, and doing so for longer periods of time.

Other issues surrounding mandatory sentencing policies include: the symbolic nature of these policies, public opinion on these policies, and potential disparate effects on criminal defendants from racial or ethnic minority groups. Thus, any discussion of mandatory sentencing guidelines and issues includes an examination of the history and description of mandatory sentencing policies along with the rationale for these policies, an investigation of the research on the effectiveness of mandatory sentencing, the pros and cons of these policies, and a discussion of the role of mandatory sentencing policies in the future of the U.S. criminal justice system.

A Brief History of Mandatory Sentencing

Mandatory punishment for criminal behavior is not a recent idea; it can be traced back to the colonial period. There is evidence that the legislatures of colonial America created predetermined punishments for most crimes, and the colonial courts were given very little, if any, leeway when imposing sentences on individuals convicted of these crimes. These legislated criminal punishments included both monetary and corporal punishments such as fines, death, forced labor, the pillory, and whipping. Gradually, however, the presence and use of the sentencing policies that prescribed these kinds of punishments faded, so that by the early 1800s, they were virtually nonexistent. By this time, most states' legislatures had rewritten their sentencing statutes to provide more discretion to the judge in making sentencing decisions and to reduce not only the requirement of corporal and capital punishments, but also the availability of these punishments for many kinds of criminal offenses—effectively making imprisonment the primary method of criminal punishment.

Mandatory sentencing policies next appeared in the United States with the enactment of a 1926 New York criminal statute. This statute mandated life in prison for offenders convicted of a felony crime, provided that they had two prior convictions for felony offenses. Over the next 10 to 15 years, most U.S. states followed suit and passed similar laws mandating life in prison for habitual, chronic, or career offenders. Many of these statutes specified that life-in-prison sanctions were appropriate and required upon offenders' third or fourth convictions in felony cases. In the 1950s, California passed a law requiring a consecutive 5–10 year prison sentence for offenders who possessed firearms during the commission of any felony offense (this enhancement was in addition to any punishment imposed for the original felony). The U.S. Congress also set out mandatory minimum prison sentences for offenders convicted of specific kinds of drug importation and drug distribution crimes in its 1956 passage of the Narcotic Control Act. For the most part, the federal drug crime law and the recidivist-focused statutes of the 1920s and 1950s were the only mandatory sentencing policies enacted until the 1970s.

Describing Mandatory Sentencing Today

Contemporary mandatory sentencing provisions are somewhat different than those found earlier in American history. Today's statutes tend to focus less on establishing mandatory minimum sentences for particular criminal offenses, or groups of offenses, and more on mandating significantly harsher (longer) sentences for crimes in which particular, aggravating circumstances are present. Further, today's mandatory sentencing enhancement provisions are set up to accomplish two interrelated goals in response to these aggravated criminal cases: to significantly increase the length of time that convicted offenders serve in prison; and to completely eliminate the availability of suspended sentences, probation, and other community-based sanctions.

The most common aggravated circumstances highlighted in states' mandatory sentencing policies are: weapon possession or use, repeat or habitual offender status, drug-related offenses, sex-related offenses, and drunk driving. By the mid-1990s, all 50 states self-reported at least one kind of state-legislated mandatory minimum sentence provision corresponding to one or more of the categories listed above. Five states—Colorado, Illinois, Pennsylvania, Rhode Island, and Wisconsin—reported the use of mandatory minimum sentences for all five of these aggravated circumstances categories, as well as using mandatory minimum sentences in criminal cases characterized by other aggravating circumstances. Further, the type of drug-related mandatory minimum sentencing provisions vary greatly across states that have these policies, especially in regard to the kinds and amounts of drugs required that trigger the mandatory minimum sentence. Approximately 32 states report some kind of drug-related mandatory minimum provision, 41 states report a repeat offender mandatory minimum sentence policy, 42 states report the presence of a weapons-related mandatory minimum provision, 27 states report provision of a drunk-driving mandatory minimum sentence, and 17 states report a sex offense mandatory minimum sentence provision. Other behaviors for which mandatory minimum sentences are reported include: crimes against persons from vulnerable populations (e.g., the elderly and children); offenses committed by individuals while under the control of the courts or corrections; and offenses committed in or around certain locations (e.g., day care facilities, school grounds, and public transportation facilities).

Rationale for Mandatory Sentencing

Legislatures pass mandatory sentencing statutes to achieve several interrelated goals that are utilitarian in nature. A utilitarian framework is used here to denote that these goals work to produce or depend on changing individual offenders' mindsets when choosing whether or not to engage in behaviors that would trigger a mandatory sentencing response from the criminal justice system. These goals, as stated in the U.S. Sentencing Commission's report, include: deterrence, retribution, incapacitation, elimination of disparity, inducement of pleas, and inducement of cooperation.

The present discussion on rationale focuses on the other goals for mandatory sentencing policies as stated in the U.S. Sentencing Commission's report. Retribution is typically seen as the oldest reason for punishment, and is often simply defined as "an eye for an eye." This punishment philosophy sees punishment as responsive to and necessary for the crime committed. The inducement of pleas and inducement of cooperation are intertwined, although the outcome in criminal cases may be different if only one of these goals comes into play. More specifically, the inducement of a plea (especially to a lesser charge, or without a mandatory sentencing provision attached) results in reduced use of the court's time and resources, regardless of the sentencing outcome for the offender. However, the inducement of cooperation may not result in this time or resource savings, but rather in the offender sharing information with the prosecutor that may lead to additional criminal charges against other individuals or groups, but may or may not lead to a mandatory sentence for the offender in question.

There are many reasons given for the presence of mandatory sentencing provisions in the federal and states' penal codes. The examination and evaluation of these provisions, however, tends to focus on the degree to which they actually deter or prevent crime, whether or not they result in the effective incapacitation of dangerous, violent, and/or threatening offenders through the use of long imprisonment sentences; analyses of the costs and benefits associated with mandatory sentencing policies; and the impact of these policies on the criminal justice system.

Effectiveness of Mandatory Sentencing

Research examining the effectiveness of mandatory sentencing policies on crime and crime rates has typically focused on weapons-related and drug-related policies, the two offenses most commonly targeted by both state and federal legislation. Some of these studies reported modest reductions in gun-related crimes, at least in the short term. Other studies, however, reported no evidence of the prevention of gun-related crime associated with the presence of weapons-related mandatory sentencing provisions. A six-city study on sentencing enhancements for gun use found a deterrent effect for homicides, but not for other crimes of violence. An assessment of mandatory sentencing drug laws in New York City failed to find a deterrent effect of the laws on subsequent drug crime in the city.

Evaluations of the incapacitation effect of mandatory sentencing policies focus primarily on whether these policies affect the level of imprisonment or the length of the prison term for violent or otherwise dangerous offenders. Overall, the results from these studies suggest that the likelihood of imprisonment is not changed, and thus neither is the overall level of incarceration, with the implementation of these kinds of provisions. Depending on the study and the location, there is some evidence indicative of an increase in the length of prison sentences for those offenders who are incarcerated. However, additional studies suggest that it is not dangerous, violent, or threatening offenders who feel the brunt of mandatory sentencing policies, but rather drug-related offenders, who are likely disproportionately affected—particularly minority drug offenders—by increasing not only the likelihood of a prison sentence, but also the length of that sentence.

Cost/benefit analyses of mandatory sentencing policies generally indicate that these policies are quite expensive. The most thoroughly examined of these policies is California's "three-strikes-and you're-out" provision. Policymakers and researchers assumed that California's three-strikes laws would have a great incapacitative effect, but not a deterrent effect on crime. The general results of the cost/benefit analysis indicated that California's three-strikes laws, over the next 25 years, would (1) triple the prison population; (2) add about $5.5 billion more each year for a total additional cost of $137.5 billion; and (3) produce a 28 percent reduction in serious crime, resulting in a cost of about $16,300 for each prevented crime. Although not on the same large scale as California, other cost/benefit analyses of mandatory sentencing policies indicate relatively high costs for relatively low benefits.

There have been numerous studies conducted on the impact of mandatory sentencing provisions on the criminal justice system, particularly the impact of these policies on federal and state corrections. These studies, taken together, suggest that mandatory minimum sentencing policies significantly affect the workings of the criminal justice system. Michael Tonry summarized the impacts of a variety of sentencing reforms, including mandatory sentencing laws, on the criminal justice system and reported that (1) arrest rates for offenses targeted by mandatory minimum sentences decrease; (2) criminal justice officials tend to exercise greater discretion when deciding when to apply and when to avoid the application of these harsher sentencing directives; (3) case dismissals and diversions increase; (4) plea negotiations decrease, trial rates increase, and sentencing delays increase; and (5) sentences become longer.

The body of research on mandatory sentencing provisions has contributed to the widespread debate on the efficacy these policies. Moreover, the results of various research studies have been used to support both sides of the debate on this issue.

Pro: Arguments for Mandatory Minimum Sentencing

Individuals and groups in favor of mandatory minimum sentencing cite several reasons for their support of this kind of legislation. The primary reasons are deterrence, incapacitation, limiting judicial discretion, symbolic (and actual) retribution, and equitable sentencing outcomes. These arguments are related both to sending a message to the public (particularly potential offenders) and to responding effectively and proportionally when people choose to disobey the law, and especially when offenders recidivate (continue to engage in criminal activities), disregarding both the messages attached to these policies as well as the specific application of these policies to their past behaviors. Moreover, advocates of mandatory sentencing policies applaud the fact that these provisions restrain judges' abilities to tinker with sentencing outcomes for individuals, particularly when judges utilize their discretion in order to reduce sentence lengths or otherwise impose more lenient sentences on offenders convicted of dangerous or threatening offenses (e.g., violent crimes, drug crimes, and sex crimes). Additionally, proponents of these policies assert that the reduction or elimination of judicial discretion also results in more fair and equitable sentences for offenders charged with and convicted of similar crimes.

Protecting the Public

Legislators, policymakers, scholars, and others in favor of mandatory sentencing policies have cited public fear of criminal victimization and the public's call for harsher sentencing of violent and dangerous offenders as the impetus for and justification of these provisions. Further, they argue that identifying these kinds of high-risk and threatening offenders and then removing them from society and isolating them in prisons for longer periods of time (or even life sentences) results in increased public safety along with a message sent to offenders that this kind of behavior will not be tolerated and strict punishments will be imposed. At the same time, proponents of these policies suggest that the implementation and use of these policies also send a symbolic (and actual) message to the public that their safety is critically important and that every effort will be made to identify, punish, and isolate those offenders who pose a risk to individual and public safety.

For example, in 1993, the highly publicized abduction and murder of 12-year-old Polly Klaas, by Richard Allen Davis, a chronic criminal offender who had been released early from his prison sentence, resulted in California's passage of their present three-strikes law. This response by the California legislature signaled to the public as well as the entire criminal justice system that the state legislature had decided that the identification of dangerous offenders at high risk for recidivating was possible and that the identification and subsequent mandatory sentencing of these offenders would result in increased community safety. This response also signaled to potential and actual violent, chronic offenders that a concerted effort would be made to identify them, investigate their criminal behaviors, and subject them to lengthy, mandatory prison sentences.

Additionally, proponents of mandatory sentencing argue that overall, these policies increase the likelihood of a prison sentence as well as the length of these custodial sentences. Related to this increased certainty and severity, proponents suggest that actual and potential offenders will be both deterred and incapacitated. More specifically, the idea is that individuals who contemplate engaging in offenses that are governed by mandatory sentencing policies will be less likely to take part in these activities because they are subject to such severe sanctions (evidencing a general deterrent effect). Along the same line, offenders who have previously been subject to the control and punishment of the criminal justice system will be significantly less likely to continue partaking in illegal activities subject to mandatory sentencing policies (evidencing a specific deterrent effect). However, offenders who continue engaging in criminal behaviors in spite of these threats will then be charged under mandatory sentencing provisions and (if convicted) be given much longer prison sentences (e.g., 25 years to life in prison). This evidences the incapacitation effect associated with mandatory sentencing provisions; individuals imprisoned under these policies will spend significant periods of time behind bars, making it impossible for them to continue committing crimes against individuals and society, further increasing public and community safety.

Sentencing Equity

Proponents of mandatory sentencing policies argue also that these policies enhance sentencing equity as they remove significant discretion from sentencing judges. For several decades, researchers have examined sentencing outcomes from a variety of perspectives, and have produced a large body of literature on sentencing decisions. Researchers have been interested in, among other things, examining how and why sentencing decisions differ for offenders who have similar criminal histories and are convicted of similar offenses. Much of this research has focused on the racial or ethnic group membership of offenders along with other extralegal factors such as age, sex, socioeconomic status, marital status, and employment status. Since mandatory sentencing policies focus primarily on the presence of specific aggravating circumstances (such as the presence of a weapon, harm to children or the elderly, or dangerous location of the offense such as a daycare or school) and specify the particular prison sentence to be imposed (i.e., ineligibility of a community-based sanction), they significantly reduce the ability of sentencing judges to take into consideration other, perhaps mitigating factors and to impose different (or more lenient) sentences. Thus, proponents of mandatory sentencing provisions suggest that they increase the equity of sentences imposed on criminal offenders in America's courts so that offenders who commit the same types of crimes end up with the same type of punishment.

While deterrence, incapacitation, retribution, limits on judicial discretion, and increased sentencing equity have been provided as arguments supportive of mandatory sentencing policies by those in favor of these legislated initiatives, there are also a variety of corresponding arguments against mandatory sentencing by critics of these laws.

Con: Arguments Against Mandatory Minimum Sentencing

Individuals and groups that oppose mandatory minimum sentencing also cite several reasons for their disagreement with these policies. Many of the arguments used to support mandatory sentencing are the same arguments used by opponents of these policies and those who call for a reconsideration of the use of mandatory sentencing. More specifically, critics of mandatory sentencing point to many of the published evaluations on these policies and argue that they have not resulted in increased levels of general or specific deterrence, do not provide significant incapacitation or increased public safety, have not increased sentencing equity or fairness, have displaced (not removed) discretion from the judge to the police and prosecutors, may disproportionately negatively impact minority or otherwise marginal offenders, are too rigid (inflexible), and are quite expensive.

Opponents of mandatory sentencing argue that these policies have not effectively produced the reduction in crime that was promised through their deterrent message. Instead, research indicates that there is wide variability in the application of criminal charges that carry mandatory sentence penalties; differences have even been found between jurisdictions within the same state, such as California. Opponents suggest that a widespread reduction in crime has not been realized, at least in part, because criminal justice decision makers (police and prosecutors) utilize their discretion more carefully when deciding whether to arrest and/or to prosecute individuals in cases that trigger mandatory sentencing penalties, especially when these decision makers perceive the likely outcome as much too harsh given the case or individual circumstances. This is related to a second argument: the displacement of discretion from the sentencing judge to earlier points in the criminal justice system, specifically to more discretionary decision making by the police and prosecutors.

Discretion and Bias

Critics argue that evaluation research on the application of mandatory sentencing policies indicate that police use significant discretion in decisions to arrest offenders, as arrests for offenses governed by mandatory penalties go down almost immediately after these laws go into effect. Further, they argue that prosecutors also use their discretion to dismiss or divert these kinds of cases out of the formal criminal justice system, which leads to increased trial rates for individuals who remain in the system and are formally prosecuted, along with corresponding reductions in plea negotiations. Additionally, critics argue that individual liberties and the ability of criminal defendants to exercise their constitutionally protected due process rights are infringed upon by pressure to plead guilty to an offense not governed under mandatory sentencing penalties or take the chance of receiving a lengthy mandatory prison sanction if they choose to exercise their right to a jury trial. Prosecutors, then, retain significant discretionary power; thus, opponents of mandatory sentencing suggest that there is still vast discretion used in the application of these policies, only this discretion has been removed from the sentencing judge and instead now resides primarily with the prosecutors in the courtroom, and with the police on the streets when deciding whether or not to make formal arrests.

Related to the remaining presence of discretion is the criticism that inequity remains a problematic issue in sentencing decisions. Particularly important are the inequities related to minority or marginal status. This concern primarily involves the apparent, disparate, negative impact these sentencing provisions seem to have had on offenders from certain racial and ethnic minorities and lower socioeconomic strata. For example, the focus on certain kinds of drug crimes (particularly those typically associated with certain groups of people or social classes) in some mandatory sentencing policies has been criticized for being both class- and racially or ethnically biased. The federal drug law, which lays out a 100:1 differential ratio for the amount of powder versus crack cocaine possession needed to trigger a mandatory five-year prison sentence, is one example that critics use to illustrate their charges of the racial and economic bias in mandatory sentencing provisions. Opponents of these policies further argue that because certain criminal justice decision makers still retain discretion with regard to choosing whether to apply mandatory sentencing provisions, these provisions may not be made in a racially objective way; decisions may, in fact, end up being influenced by extralegal factors anyway. Further, critics of these policies who call into question the neutral application of the mandatory sentencing laws suggest that they further aggravate and expand the already overwhelming, disproportionate representation of minorities (especially African Americans and Hispanics) and the poor in U.S. prisons.

Rigid and Expensive

Contemporary mandatory sentencing policies have also been criticized for being too rigid and inflexible. Opponents of these policies point to the importance of individualizing criminal sentences in order to take into account both aggravating and mitigating circumstances. They argue that providing a one-size-fits-all mandatory sentence for offenders is inappropriate, and that true deterrent and incapacitative responses to criminal behavior must take into consideration both individual and situational factors that may have contributed to the criminal activity. Further, they question the use of scarce, costly prison space for whom it is likely unnecessary.

Related to the misuse of scarce, expensive resources, critics of mandatory sentencing point to the ever-increasing costs associated with the imprisonment mandated by these policies. Not only do these mandatory sentencing provisions aim to increase the numbers of offenders in prisons and the length of time these offenders have to serve (thus increasing the overhead costs associated with imprisonment), but they have also been charged with contributing to increased costs within the court system. More specifically, mandatory sentencing policies that lead to increased trials and reduced plea bargaining certainly produce increased costs related to the formal processing of these cases, from the initial court hearing through sentencing and any appeals.

Moreover, the cost of prison is exponentially increased for any additional offenders who might otherwise have been sentenced to a community-based sanction, such as probation, intensive probation supervision, house arrest, or electronic monitoring, as imprisonment is much more costly than any of the alternatives. For example, depending on location, imprisonment for one year costs about $20,000–$30,000, whereas traditional probation costs roughly one-tenth as much. The cost of imprisonment is further exacerbated by increasing the prison sentences, by a number of years, for those convicted under mandatory sentencing provisions. Critics of mandatory sentencing point out that many of the offenders sentenced to significantly long prison terms (25 years to life) inevitably age and grow ill in prison, thus further contributing to escalating imprisonment costs, which now must include health care costs.

Future Issues in Mandatory Sentencing

Due primarily to the message of public safety, the mandatory sentencing provisions implemented across the country over the past 30–40 years are likely to persist. However, as prison populations have skyrocketed over the past 30 years or so, the widespread debate regarding mandatory sentencing will almost certainly continue, and in all probability become even more hotly contested. The United States incarcerates over two million people in its prisons, jails, and juvenile facilities, and the U.S. incarceration rate is higher than in any other developed country in the world. These facts alone should facilitate continued interest in sentencing policies and outcomes by researchers, policymakers, criminal justice decision makers, and the public.

See Also: 4. Drug Laws; 14. Plea Bargaining; 17. Sentencing Disparities; 19. Three-Strikes Laws.

Further Readings

Alschuler, Albert W. "Sentencing Reform and Prosecutorial Power: A Critique of Recent Proposals for 'Fixed' and Presumptive Sentencing." *University of Pennsylvania Law Review*, v.126 (1978).
Barkow, Rachel E. "Recharging the Jury: The Criminal Jury's Constitutional Role in an Era of Mandatory Sentencing." *University of Pennsylvania Law Review*, v.152/1 (2003).

Bessant, Judith. "Australia's Mandatory Sentencing Laws, Ethnicity, and Human Rights." *International Journal on Minority and Group Rights*, v.8 (2001).

Bureau of Justice Assistance. *National Assessment of Structured Sentencing*. Washington, DC: U.S. Department of Justice, Office of Justice Programs, Bureau of Justice Assistance, NCJ 153853, 1996.

Chen, Elsa Y. "The Liberation Hypothesis and Racial and Ethnic Disparities in the Application of California's Three Strikes Law." *Journal of Ethnicity in Criminal Justice*, v.6/2 (2008).

Coleman, Belinda. "Driving While Disqualified or Suspended under s 30 of the *Road Safety Act 1986 (Vic)*: Abolition of the Mandatory Sentencing Provision?" *Deakin Law Review*, v.11/2 (2006).

Denton, David. "Squaring the Circle: Reconciling Clear Statutory Text with Contradictory Statutory Purpose in *United States v. Whitley*, 529 F.3d 150 (2d Cir. 2008)." *Harvard Journal of Law and Public Policy*, v.32/3 (2009).

Irwin, John, and James Austin. *It's About Time: America's Imprisonment Binge*. Belmont, CA: Wadsworth Publishing, 2010.

Lowenthal, Gary T. "Mandatory Sentencing Laws: Undermining the Effectiveness of Determinate Sentencing Reform." *California Law Review*, v.81 (1993).

Mazza, Carl. "A Pound of Flesh: The Psychological, Familial, and Social Consequences of Mandatory Long-Term Sentencing Laws for Drug Offenses." *Journal of Social Work Practice in the Addictions*, v.4/3 (2004).

McPheters, Lee R., Robert Mann, and Don Schlagenhauf. "Economic Response to a Crime Deterrence Program: Mandatory Sentencing for Robbery with a Firearm." *Economic Inquiry*, v.22/4 (1984).

Merritt, Nancy, Terry Fain, and Susan Turner. "Oregon's Get Tough Sentencing Reform: A Lesson in Justice System Adaptation." *Criminology and Public Policy*, v.5/1 (2006).

Nienstedt, Barbara Cole. "The Use of Mandatory Sentencing Legislation as Symbolic Statements." *Policy Studies Review*, v.6/1 (1986).

Parent, Dale, Terence Dunworth, Douglas McDonald, and William Rhodes. *Key Legislative Issues in Criminal Justice: Mandatory Sentencing*. Washington, DC: U.S. Department of Justice, Office of Justice Programs, National Institute of Justice, NCJ 161839, 1997.

Pratt, Travis C. *Addicted to Incarceration: Corrections Policy and the Politics of Misinformation in the United States*. Thousand Oaks, CA: Sage, 2009.

Roberts, Julian V., Nicole Crutcher, and Paul Verbrugge. "Public Attitudes to Sentencing in Canada: Exploring Recent Findings." *Canadian Journal of Criminology and Criminal Justice* (January 2007).

Sorenson, Jon, and Don Stemen. "The Effect of State Sentencing Policies on Incarceration Rates." *Crime and Delinquency*, v.48/3 (2002).

Stith, Kate. "The Arc of the Pendulum: Judges, Prosecutors, and the Exercise of Discretion." *The Yale Law Journal*, v.117 (2008).

Terblanche, Stephan, and Geraldine Mackenzie. "Mandatory Sentences in South Africa: Lessons for Australia?" *The Australian and New Zealand Journal of Criminology*, v.41/3 (2008).

Tonry, Michael. "Criminology, Mandatory Minimums, and Public Policy." *Criminology and Public Policy*, v.5/1 (2006).

Tonry, Michael. "Mandatory Penalties." *Crime and Justice: A Review of Research*, v.16 (1992).

Tonry, Michael. *Sentencing Matters*. Oxford, England: Oxford University Press, 1995.

Tonry, Michael. *Sentencing Reform Impacts*. Washington, DC: U.S. Department of Justice, National Institute of Justice, 1987.

White, Rob. "10 Arguments Against Mandatory Sentencing." *Youth Studies Australia*, v.19/2 (2000).

13

Miranda Rights

Kimberlee Candela
California State University, Chico

In 1966, the U.S. Supreme Court issued one of its most important criminal procedure rulings: *Miranda v. Arizona*, which addresses an individual's Fifth Amendment rights within a custodial interrogation. The Fifth Amendment to the U.S. Constitution provides that "[n]o person shall ... be compelled in any criminal case to be a witness against himself." This is commonly referred to as the "privilege against self-incrimination:" one has a constitutional right not to incriminate one's self. Traditionally, this right has been interpreted to protect a criminal defendant from being called to testify at his own trial. It also applies to grand jury proceedings, where one has a Fifth Amendment right to refuse to answer questions for which the answer may be incriminatory. However, in *Miranda*, the Court was examining circumstances far earlier in the criminal case timeline. At issue was whether the protections of the Fifth Amendment apply when the police are interrogating a criminal suspect in custody. The *Miranda* opinion, authored by Chief Justice Earl Warren, concluded the protections do apply, for custodial interrogation is inherently coercive, thus "compelling." To allow the protection of a criminal suspect's Fifth Amendment rights during custodial interrogation, then, the police must advise him of his right to remain silent, as well as the right to counsel. If the police fail to so advise the suspect, any ensuing statement is inadmissible in court as evidence.

The decision divided both the Supreme Court (5–4) and the nation. Critics of the decision argued it would hobble law enforcement in procuring confessions, resulting in valuable evidence being lost and criminals going free. Proponents of the ruling hailed it as a critical and necessary safeguard of a key constitutional right in an era where police brutality was not uncommon. Congress responded to the critics' outcry by passing the Omnibus Crime Control and Safe Street Acts of 1968, which purported to overrule the *Miranda* ruling. However, both federal and state prosecutors deferred to the *Miranda* ruling and did not choose to invoke the federal law for decades. Thus, its constitutionality went unchallenged until the Court granted certiorari in *Dickerson v. United States* (2000). In *Dickerson*, the Rehnquist court (a more conservative court than the Warren court) upheld *Miranda*, declaring it to be a constitutional decision that could not be legislatively superseded. Nor, the Court concluded, should *Miranda* be overruled by the Court itself, for under the legal doctrine of *stare decisis* (deference to previously decided matters), *Miranda* had become so "embedded in routine police practice" that "the warnings have become part of our national culture." *Miranda*, however, does not remain untouched: Court rulings have chipped away at its tenets over the years. Examples include the decision of *Harris v. New York* (1971) that statements obtained in violation of *Miranda* could be used to impeach a testifying defendant, as well as the ruling of *New York v. Quarles* (1984) that instituted a public safety exception. Still, it is clear that after the key ruling in *Dickerson* and the passage of over four decades, the primary principles of *Miranda* are an integral part of police procedure, popular culture, and American jurisprudence.

The Law Prior to *Miranda*

The Fifth Amendment privilege against self-incrimination traces its lineage to protests against inquisitorial methods of interrogation in England. When the United States was formed, the founders included this privilege in the Bill of Rights (the first 10 amendments to the Constitution), thus proclaiming it to be one of the fundamental protections of the individual citizen against the possible tyranny of the federal government. An early decision of the Court addressing this right, *Twining v. New Jersey* (1908), concluded that the states need not honor an accused's Fifth Amendment privilege against self-incrimination—thus reflecting the judicial philosophy of the time that the rights and protections contained in the amendments were applicable only against the federal government. This jurisprudence began to change in the 1930s, as the Court selectively incorporated certain fundamental rights from the Bill of Rights into the Due Process Clause of the Fourteenth Amendment. The effect of this selective incorporation is that, over several decades and on a case-by-case basis, the Court ruled that the states could not violate certain fundamental individual rights. Many of the rulings occurred during the civil rights movement of the 1960s, and by the end of the Warren court (1969), the states were required to afford their people the rights (save just a few) that were enumerated in the Bill of Rights.

So, in 1964, the privilege against self-incrimination became safeguarded against state action via the Fourteenth Amendment's Due Process Clause. That ruling, *Malloy v. Hogan,* and another that same year, *Escobedo v. Illinois,* set the stage for the issues that the Court would need to address in *Miranda. Escobedo* responded to questions posed about the Sixth Amendment right to counsel during interrogation. In that case, Mr. Escobedo was held and questioned at police headquarters; his retained attorney was also present, but precluded from seeing his client. Mr. Escobedo asked repeatedly to consult with his attorney and that request was repeatedly denied. Interrogation continued and, eventually, Mr. Escobedo made inculpatory statements that were used at his trial.

When reversing that conviction, the *Escobedo* court expressed concern about the nature of police investigations, emphasizing that a criminal justice system that comes to depend on confessions is "less reliable and more subject to abuses than a system which depends on extrinsic evidence independently secured through skillful investigation." The Court explained that the Sixth Amendment right to counsel would be a "very hollow thing" if it were not extended to interrogation, for without that right, the trial would be reduced to an "appeal from the interrogation." *Escobedo,* forging new territory, raised questions about the state of the law, as well as differing interpretations by various state and federal courts. The Court granted certiorari in *Miranda* (and three related cases) to resolve some of those questions.

Prior to *Miranda,* grounds to exclude a defendant's statement from trial evidence were limited to the issue of voluntariness. Confessions can still be challenged on this basis. Under a defense challenge, the prosecution is charged with establishing the voluntariness of the statement, which is determined by analyzing the "totality of the circumstances" surrounding the statement. Generally, for a confession to be ruled involuntary, there must be some police action involving coercion, either physical (sleep or food deprivation or beating) or psychological (threats or promises of leniency). While this standard lives on, the law of interrogations and admissibility of statements and confessions changed radically with the advent of the *Miranda* ruling.

Ernesto Miranda

In 1963, Ernesto Miranda was convicted in Maricopa County, Arizona, of kidnapping and rape. The evidence established that Mr. Miranda had confessed to these crimes orally and then in a signed written statement. Under cross-examination by defense counsel, the police officers admitted they did not advise Mr. Miranda that he had a right to consult with an attorney and to have one present during the interrogation. However, at the top of his signed statement, there was a typed paragraph stating that the confession was made voluntarily, without threats or promises of immunity and "with full knowledge of my legal rights, understanding any statement I make may be used against me." An officer testified that he read this paragraph to Mr. Miranda, apparently after the oral confession.

After his convictions, Mr. Miranda, through his attorney, appealed to the Arizona Supreme Court, which affirmed his conviction. The U.S. Supreme Court reversed, concluding that there was a failure to "effectively protect" Mr. Miranda's "right not to be compelled to incriminate himself." Furthermore, the "mere fact that he signed a statement which contained a typed-in clause stating that he had full knowledge of his legal rights does not approach the knowing and intelligent waiver required to relinquish constitutional rights."

Miranda v. Arizona is the lead case in this opinion, which is actually a combination of four separate court cases. In addition to *Miranda*, there were two other state cases: *Vignera v. New York* and *California v. Stewart*, as well as a federal prosecution, *Westover v. United States*. In each case, the Court concluded that the police had not effectively protected the individual's privilege against self-incrimination during interrogation. *Miranda*, *Vignera*, and *Westover* were all reversed, for in each, the lower courts had affirmed convictions that were based in part on confessions that should have been excluded. The California Supreme Court's ruling in the *Stewart* case was affirmed, for there, the state court had concluded this failure to advise was reversible error under *Escobedo*.

Following the Supreme Court's reversal of Ernesto Miranda's convictions, his matter was remanded to the trial court, where he was tried again in 1967 without the confession as evidence. He was once again convicted and sentenced to state prison. Released in 1972, he capitalized on his name recognition by selling *Miranda* warning cards that he autographed for $1.50. After serving another stint in prison for parole violations, he died in 1976 within a month of his release, stabbed to death in a bar fight.

The *Miranda* Ruling

The case opens with the Court's recognition of the significance of this decision, for the case raises questions that go to the "roots of American criminal jurisprudence: the restraints society must observe consistent with the Federal Constitution in prosecuting individuals for crime." The Court announces that it is critical to protect the constitutional rights of the individual against "overzealous police practices" and so pledges to provide "concrete constitutional guidelines for law enforcement agencies and courts to follow."

The lengthy case opinion (over 60 pages) is scholarly and eloquent, with evocative, often passionate, language. The first section of the substance of the opinion begins with an examination of the interrogation process, recounting that in each of the four cases, salient features were shared: specifically, "incommunicado interrogation of individuals in a police-dominated atmosphere, resulting in self-incriminating statements without full warnings of constitutional rights." The Court instructs that examples of police physical brutality are "sufficiently widespread to be the object of concern" and would not be eradicated unless there were proper limitations placed upon custodial interrogation.

Further, elaborate psychological tactics are very common and places the suspect being interrogated at a distinct disadvantage. Those tactics include isolating the suspect from any outside support; lying to the suspect about the nature of the evidence; making an interrogation private, with just the suspect and the investigator present; and the Mutt and Jeff method. Even in the absence of physical brutality or such psychological strategies, "the very fact of custodial interrogation exacts a heavy toll on individual liberty, and trades on the weakness of individuals." Thus, the *Miranda* decision does not focus on statements that are traditionally involuntary, but rather on the "interrogation atmosphere and the evils it can bring." The Court observes that the "potentiality for compulsion is forcefully apparent," and therefore a statement obtained from a defendant cannot truly be the product of his free choice "unless adequate protective devices are employed to dispel the compulsion inherent in custodial surroundings." Unless the defendant is aware of his constitutional rights and makes a "voluntary, knowing and intelligent" waiver of his right to counsel and right to remain silent, the statement will not be allowed as evidence against him.

In the second section of the *Miranda* opinion, the Court summarizes the history of the privilege against self-incrimination and stresses its central importance in the country's criminal justice system. Noting its origins in "ancient times" and referencing the Star Chamber, the Court explains that the privilege reflects the respect the government must accord to the "dignity and integrity of its citizens." This privilege is "the essential mainstay of our adversary system," for the structure of our criminal justice system requires that the government "produce the evidence against him by its own independent labors, rather than by the cruel, simple expedient of compelling it from his own mouth." Thus, the privilege can only be fulfilled when a person is truly guaranteed the right to remain silent "unless he chooses to speak in the unfettered exercise of his own will." For this privilege to have meaning, it must apply not only at trial, but also at the time of custodial interrogation.

Miranda's third section sets out the requirements: what must be done to ensure an accused will be "adequately and effectively apprised of his rights" and that the exercise of those rights will be "fully honored." The Court observes that while these safeguards do not create a "constitutional straitjacket," they must be observed unless there is some other equally effective procedure to protect these rights. Moreover, because the privilege is "so fundamental" to our system and the giving of an adequate warning "so simple," this bright-line rule requires the advisements in all cases. In the absence of such warnings, a court will not examine individual circumstances to divine, for instance, whether a particularly well-educated suspect might be independently aware of his rights.

Court Specifies the Language of the Warnings

Thus, in language now well known to American adults and children alike (made famous by depictions on television and films), the Court specifies the warnings. Prior to custodial interrogation, an individual must be warned that "you have the right to remain silent, that anything you say can be used against you in a court of law, that you have the right to the presence of an attorney, and that, if you cannot afford an attorney, one will be appointed for you." The Court expounds on each of these advisements. First, the warning of the right to remain silent functions to make one aware of this right, as well as to help "overcome the inherent pressures of the interrogation atmosphere." Second, warning the individual that anything he does say "can and will be used against you in court" informs him that he is "not in the presence of persons acting solely in his interest." Third, advising the individual of his right to counsel, both to consult with and to have present in any ensuing interrogation, is "indispensable to the protection of the Fifth Amendment privilege," for it reduces the likelihood of coercion significantly. Finally, given the abundance of indigent people in the criminal justice system, and because "the financial ability of the individual has no relationship to the scope of the rights," the warning must also include one's right to appointed counsel if he is indigent.

These advisements of rights must be given prior to custodial interrogation. Later cases clarified these terms. One is in custody if under formal arrest or its functional equivalent; that is, when law enforcement officials have deprived the individual of his "freedom of action" in "any significant way." Put another way, would a reasonable person in those circumstances feel free to leave? Interrogation refers not only to express questioning, but also to any "words or actions on the part of the police" that the police should know are "reasonably likely to elicit an incriminating response."

As for the application of this new procedure, in a decision issued shortly after the *Miranda* opinion, the Court explained that both the *Miranda* and the *Escobedo* decisions would only apply prospectively to trials that began after the issuance of the relevant case opinion. Among other considerations, retroactive application of the new law would "seriously disrupt" the administration of justice.

The Aftermath

The final section of the *Miranda* opinion is the majority response both to these dissenting justices, as well as to the expected outcries from prosecutors, law enforcement, and the general public. This section begins with the acknowledgment of a "recurrent argument" that "society's need for interrogation outweighs the privilege." However, the Court suggests that the limitations now placed on the interrogation process "should not constitute an undue interference with a proper system of law enforcement." Furthermore, the Federal Bureau of Investigations' practices provided a foundation for the advisements adopted in *Miranda*. As part of their best practices, they had for years employed just those sorts of advisements. The Court remarked that providing these admonishments had not unduly burdened the work of the Federal Bureau of Investigation. Other countries also employ such cautionary warnings, and their experience indicates that "the danger to law enforcement in curbs on interrogation is overplayed." The Court rejects Harlan's urging of a deferral to the legislature, for "[w]here rights secured by the Constitution are involved, there can be no rulemaking or legislation which would abrogate them."

Outside the Court, law enforcement, prosecutors, and politicians proclaimed that the *Miranda* ruling went beyond constitutional requirements and was just the sort of ruling that had the potential to hinder law enforcement in its ability to fight crime. Scenarios were envisioned and publically discussed, wherein criminals guilty of heinous crimes would be set free on this technicality, only to re-offend. The sentiment was so strong and the concern so great that Richard M. Nixon focused on the *Miranda* ruling as a part of his U.S. presidential campaign platform in 1968, when he spoke repeatedly of examples of murderers set free by *Miranda*. He posited that the *Miranda* ruling, in combination with some of the other Warren-era criminal procedure decisions, had significantly weakened law enforcement; legislation was needed to attempt to restore the balance between the police and criminals. After his election, Nixon addressed the "liberalism" of the Warren court by appointing the conservative Warren E. Burger as chief justice to replace Earl Warren and filling two other slots with justices he believed to be politically and legally conservative.

Congress, the Court, and the Problem of Miranda

However, even before Nixon took office, Congress had already addressed the "problem of *Miranda*" by passing legislation that attempted to overrule *Miranda*: 18 U.S.C. Section 3501, part of the Omnibus Crime Control and Safe Street Acts of 1968. Because it was such a blatant attempt to overrule the Court's ruling, a ruling purportedly grounded in the Constitution, neither state nor federal prosecutors invoked the law. The statute decreed that a confession that would otherwise be inadmissible under *Miranda* "shall be admissible in evidence if it was voluntarily given," as determined by the court using a "totality of the circumstances" test. This statute thus set out to restore the law to its pre-*Miranda* state.

When no head-to-head confrontation between statute and court ruling came about, the question simmered: Were the requirements of *Miranda* advisements of constitutional status? Some opponents of *Miranda*, including politicians and academics, as well as law enforcement officers, prosecutors, and victim rights groups, continued to challenge the ruling as illegal policymaking by an activist, overreaching Court, and poor policy-making at that, for it interfered with the gathering of valuable and reliable evidence.

Did this 1968 law overrule *Miranda*? The question was finally resolved some 34 years after *Miranda* was decided in the case of *Dickerson v. U.S.* (2000), which determined that the law did not overrule *Miranda*. *Dickerson*, by a 7–2 decision, was authored by the conservative Chief Justice Rehnquist and declared that, despite some previous case language inferring that *Miranda* rules were merely prophylactic, the holding was of constitutional status. "In sum, we conclude that *Miranda* announced a constitutional rule that Congress may not supersede legislatively." Further, the Court, citing *stare decisis*, declined to overrule it: "*Miranda* has become embedded in routine police practice to the point where the warnings have become part of our national culture." While precedent may be overruled when "subsequent cases have undermined their doctrinal underpinnings," that has not happened in the *Miranda* line of cases. Some academics who study and write about *Miranda* continue to question the propriety of declaring *Miranda* of constitutional stature. While *Dickerson* did not completely quiet the critics, most Court observers believe it retired the question of whether a more conservative Court might overrule *Miranda* some day.

Subsequent Caselaw

Over the years, there have been numerous Court decisions addressing and explaining *Miranda*. Some of those decisions have limited *Miranda*, to the dismay of its supporters and the relief of its opponents. For example, in *Harris v. New York* (1971), the Burger court held that statements obtained in violation of *Miranda*, while not admissible in the prosecution's case-in-chief, could be used to impeach a defendant who chose to testify at his trial. This was so because the "shield provided by *Miranda* cannot be perverted into a license" to commit perjury. The Court carved another exception, for the exigency of public safety, in *New York v. Quarles* (1984), where statements could be obtained from the suspect without the giving of *Miranda* warnings. The Court declared this exception both narrow and necessary, for the threat to the public safety "outweighed" the need for the *Miranda* rules. In *Davis v. United States* (1994) the Court rejected some lower courts' holdings that any mention of counsel was sufficient to invoke, ruling "[m]aybe I should talk to a lawyer" is not a clear and unambiguous invocation, therefore not a request for counsel. In the "cat-out-of-the-bag" ruling of *Oregon v. Elstad* (1985), the Court held that an initial accidental failure to give *Miranda* warnings did not taint a later, *Mirandized* statement, thus allowing the second statement to be admissible into evidence. However, in *Missouri v. Seibert* (2004), the Court disapproved of a police department policy in which the police would intentionally withhold the *Miranda* warnings, hoping to gain a confession. Upon the success of that strategy, a short break would be given and then another confession taken with the proper warnings. The Court announced this was a violation of *Miranda*, opining this law enforcement practice "disfigured" the holding of *Elstad*.

Other rulings directly strengthened and supported the *Miranda* ruling. The Court concluded that the burden to establish a knowing and intelligent waiver of rights rests upon the state, and must be established by a preponderance of the evidence, thus clarifying that the defendant only need raise the issue and does not have to prove the lack of waiver. Other protections were established in *Doyle v. Ohio* (1976) and *Edwards v. Arizona* (1981). *Doyle* prohibited prosecutors from referring in a trial to a criminal defendant's silence after receiving *Miranda* warnings. The protections afforded by *Miranda* would be circumvented if a suspect could be punished by invoking his rights. *Edwards* expounded on the meaning and consequences of an individual invoking his rights under *Miranda*. Specifically, if a suspect has invoked his right to counsel, then interrogation must cease, and will not resume unless the suspect initiates it. A contact initiated by law enforcement after an invocation does not lead to a valid waiver of the right to counsel. Some three decades later, via *Maryland v. Shatzer* (2010), the Court explained that the ruling was limited to situations where the suspect remained in "investigative custody." Thus, if the suspect has left that custody and returned to his normal life, police may re-initiate contact after 14 days. This is so even where, as in *Shatzer*, the "normal life" the suspect returned to was prison, where he was already serving a sentence for an unrelated crime.

In addition to *Shatzer*, the Court decided two other cases in the 2009–10 term, both of which also contracted the boundaries of *Miranda*. In *Florida v. Powell* (2010), the Court concluded that an admonition on the right to counsel is sufficient if it advises of one's right to consult with an attorney before questioning, but does not expressly state that an individual has the right to have counsel present during the interrogation.

Berghuis v. Thompkins: *A Critical Change*

More dramatically, in *Berghuis v. Thompkins* (2010), a deeply divided Court (5–4) addressed a suspect's ambiguous response to the *Miranda* warnings. The majority decision was authored by frequent-swing-vote Justice Kennedy, who joined the four conservative members of the Court. The ruling announced that the police are not required to obtain a waiver of an accused's right to remain silent before beginning interrogation, so long as the suspect has been properly admonished. Mr. Thompkins neither expressly invoked nor waived his right to remain silent, but sat almost entirely silent through a nearly three-hour interrogation. Toward the end, he affirmatively answered three inculpatory questions. The Court declared an invocation of the right to remain silent must be made unambiguously; merely remaining silent is insufficient. Thus, a suspect such as Mr. Thompkins, who received and understood the *Miranda* warnings, did not clearly invoke his right to remain silent, and then gave a subsequent statement to the police, waiving that right. The Court instructed that the "main purpose" of *Miranda* is to ensure that a suspect is advised and understands his right to remain silent and right to counsel. To require law enforcement to end interrogation on the basis of anything less than an unambiguous invocation of the right to remain silent would place a "significant burden on society's interest in prosecuting criminal activity."

A passionate dissent protested this "substantial retreat" from the protections against compelled self-incrimination that *Miranda* prescribed. The four liberal justices joined in an opinion authored by Justice Sotomayor, emphasizing that *Miranda* rested the "heavy burden" on the government to prove a defendant's knowing and intelligent waiver of his right to remain silent. The dissent contended that it is the prosecution that must prove an express or implied waiver, and on these facts they had failed to do so. Thus, this decision "turns *Miranda* upside down" for it "construes ambiguity in favor of the police," now placing the burden on the suspect to unambiguously invoke his right to remain silent and presuming waiver in the absence of such invocation.

Critics of the majority decision express concern that this ruling will allow a serious undermining of the *Miranda* principles. Will law enforcement agencies decide, as a matter of policy, that it is sufficient to simply give the warnings and then proceed to interrogation, without allowing a suspect a true opportunity to choose between invocation and waiver? Or will most continue with usual police practices of obtaining an explicit waiver before proceeding to interrogate? Only time will tell what impact this decision will have in the field, in the courtroom, and on suspects' rights.

Since the 1966 issuance of *Miranda v. Arizona*, the Court has decided scores of *Miranda* cases that clarify, limit, or buttress the holding. Over four decades later, these cases still fill a vital part of the Court's docket. By all indications, *Miranda* jurisprudence will continue to evolve over the coming years.

Pro: Arguments in Support of the *Miranda* Ruling

While supporters of the *Miranda* ruling would rely on much of the same reasoning set forth in the *Miranda* opinion, the context for the reception of *Miranda* into American society bears remark. Supporters of the 1960s Warren court embrace *Miranda* as one of the critical criminal procedure decisions made by that Court, the sum total of which revolutionized the criminal justice system. Those decisions included *Mapp v. Ohio* (1961), in which the Court ruled that evidence obtained illegally under the Fourth Amendment could no longer be admitted in state prosecutions, as well as the *Gideon v. Wainwright* (1963) case, specifying that indigent defendants facing state felony charges have the right to have counsel appointed to represent them under the Sixth Amendment.

For those in the civil rights movement, these holdings by the Court mirrored a new consciousness, a growing awareness that the law and the criminal justice system did not always treat everyone fairly, and that indigent people and people of color might be especially ill-treated. Observers of the criminal justice system have noted that many of the cases involving a denial of criminal procedure rights came from the southern states and that the individuals involved were often indigent African Americans. An early draft of the *Miranda* opinion included a reference to this. For these observers of the system, *Miranda* and the other decisions applying the Bill of Rights to the states marked important progress in the protection of individual rights against the state and federal government.

Con: Criticism of the *Miranda* Ruling

The critics of *Miranda* were many, and their reaction to *Miranda* was swift and severe. The criticism began internally. Miranda had divided the Court as closely as it is possible, with only five of the nine justices joining to form the majority: Chief Justice Warren (author) with Justices Black, Brennan, Douglas, and Fortas. Of the four justices who disagreed with the ruling

(Clark, Harlan, Stewart, and White), three filed separate dissenting opinions. Justice Clark's opinion was a partial concurrence—he agreed with the result in one of the four cases—but primarily a dissent, for he disagreed with the institution of the *Miranda* rules. Clark contended that police brutality is rare and that the efforts of law enforcement are "not fairly characterized" by the majority opinion. He submitted that the "totality of the circumstances" standard for determining whether a statement is involuntary should remain the standard. Objecting to the Court deciding to fashion a constitutional rule that he argued would interfere with such an effective and important tool of law enforcement, he warned that "[s]uch a strict constitutional specific inserted at the nerve center of crime detection may well kill the patient."

Justice White, joined by Harlan and Stewart, authored another dissent, declaring that the *Miranda* ruling was without foundation and precedent, for it "has no significant support in the history of the privilege or in the language of the Fifth Amendment." Further, while the "human dignity of the accused" is important, as recognized by the majority, so too is "society's interest in the general security." White detects a "deep-seated distrust of all confessions" in the majority opinion, an attitude he rejects. He states, there is "nothing wrong or immoral, and certainly nothing unconstitutional" in most interrogation processes. In an accusation repeated in the body politic, White contends that *Miranda* will "measurably weaken the ability of the criminal law to perform these tasks. It is a deliberate calculus to prevent interrogations, to reduce the incidence of confessions and pleas of guilty, and to increase the number of trials." In addition, in "some unknown number of cases," a killer or a rapist will be set free to repeat those crimes. The third dissent, authored by Justice Harlan and joined by Stewart and White, echoes some of the same concerns in the other two dissents, including seeing "no adequate basis" to extend the privilege against self-incrimination to custodial interrogations. Harlan decries the conclusion that Mr. Miranda's confessions are now inadmissible as evidence against him, a sacrifice to the Court's "own finespun conception of fairness, which I seriously doubt is shared by many thinking citizens in this country." This dissent closes with the assertion that if policy needed to be written about the law of confessions, that should be addressed by the legislature, rather than by the Court.

See Also: 6. Exclusionary Rules.

Further Readings

Brennan, William J., Jr. "State Constitutions and the Protection of Individual Rights." *Harvard Law Review*, v.90/3 (1977).

Buchwalter, James L. "Construction and Application of Constitutional Rule of *Miranda.*" *American Law Reports, Federal*, v.17/2d 465 (2007).

Cassell, Paul G. "The Paths Not Taken: The Supreme Court's Failures in *Dickerson.*" *Michigan Law Review*, v.99/5 (2001).

Gold, Susan D. *Miranda v. Arizona (1966): Suspects' Rights (Supreme Court Decisions Series).* Breckenridge, CO: Twenty-First Century Books, 2005.

Helmholz, H., Charles M. Gray, John H. Langbein, Eben Moglen, and Henry E. Smith. *The Privilege Against Self-Incrimination: Its Origins and Development.* Chicago: University of Chicago Press, 1997.

Kamisar, Yale. "On the Fortieth Anniversary of the *Miranda* Case: Why We Needed It, How We Got It—and What Happened to It." *Ohio State Journal of Criminal Law*, v.5 (2007).

Kelly-Gangi, Carol. Miranda v. Arizona *and the Rights of the Accused: Debating Supreme Court Decisions.* Berkeley Heights, NJ: Enslow Publishers, 2006.

Levine, Samuel J. "*Miranda, Dickerson*, and Jewish Legal Theory: The Constitutional Rule in a Comparative Analytical Framework." *Maryland Law Review*, v.69 (2009).

Miller, Jeremy M. "Law and Disorder: The High Court's Hasty Decision in Miranda Leaves a Tangled Mess." *Chapman Law Review*, v.10 (2007).

Rogers, Richard, Kimberly S. Harrison, Daniel W. Shuman, Kenneth W. Sewell, and Lisa L. Hazelwood. "An Analysis of Miranda Warnings and Waivers: Comprehension and Coverage." *Law and Human Behavior*, v.31 (2007).

Stuart, Gary L. *Miranda: The Story of America's Right to Remain Silent.* Tucson: University of Arizona, 2008.

Stuntz, Willliam. J. "*Miranda*'s Mistake." *Michigan Law Review*, v.99/5 (2001).

Thomas, George C., III, and Richard A. Leo. "The Effects of *Miranda v. Arizona*: 'Embedded' in our National Culture?" *Crime and Justice*, v.29 (2002).

14

Plea Bargaining

Bradley Campbell
California State University, Los Angeles

In the United States, defendants plead guilty in 90 percent or more of criminal cases. In most such cases, defendants are treated leniently in exchange for pleading guilty—a practice known as plea bargaining, which may involve altering charges or reducing sentences. This process may be explicit or implicit. Charge bargaining is a form of plea bargaining, in which the prosecutor agrees either to reduce the charges—for example, by changing the charge from murder to manslaughter—or drop one or more of the charges against the defendant. Sentence bargaining occurs where the prosecutor offers to recommend that the judge impose a more lenient sentence. Explicit plea bargaining occurs when charges are altered or sentences reduced based on an explicit agreement between the prosecution and defense. Implicit plea bargaining, however, involves no such agreement—and thus no actual bargaining. Instead, defendants plead guilty with the understanding that they will be treated more leniently. Plea bargaining, then, is not a unitary phenomenon. It includes a variety of different practices, but what they all have in common is that defendants who plead guilty ultimately receive lighter punishments than those who go to trial. Though widespread in the United States, plea bargaining has been controversial. Defenders argue that the practice allows the criminal justice system to process cases efficiently and allows the prosecution and defense to work out mutually beneficial agreements. But since the prevalence of plea bargaining means that trials

187

are rarely used to resolve cases, critics argue that the practice undermines the presumption of innocence and other ideals on which the adversarial trial system is based.

The Development and Spread of Plea Bargaining

Plea bargaining of any kind was unknown in the United States or elsewhere prior to the 19th century. By the late 19th century, however, plea bargaining was common (but not dominant) throughout the United States. At this time, there was a mixed system with frequent (but short) trials, explicit charge bargaining, and implicit plea bargaining. By the early 20th century, most cases were handled with guilty pleas (apparently as a result of implicit bargaining), and by the late 20th century, trials had become extremely infrequent, and explicit plea bargaining had become the most common way of handling cases.

Historians have offered several explanations for these changes. Some see the rise of plea bargaining as the result of greater professionalization in the criminal justice system. With professional prosecutors and defense attorneys taking a leading role in the process, pre-trial proceedings became more important than trials for establishing evidence of guilt. The trial as an amateur fact-finding process thus became less necessary, and in most cases, it benefited neither party to take the case to trial. Others have argued that growing caseloads prompted the need for a more efficient way of handling cases, or alternatively, that the expansion of due-process rights and the expansion of adversarial norms made trials much too costly, time consuming, and uncertain to be used as a routine procedure.

Plea Bargaining in America and Internationally

Today, plea bargaining is used in the United States to handle the overwhelming majority of criminal cases. But recently, the practice (or some variant of it) has spread to other countries—even in some cases to those that have inquisitorial rather than adversarial legal systems. In the late 1990s, for example, Argentina introduced a procedure called *procedimiento abreviado,* which is very similar to American plea bargaining. This allows the prosecution and defense to negotiate a sentence, although the sentence cannot exceed six years imprisonment. It is more limited than American plea bargaining, since it would not be used to handle the most serious crimes. Germany also has a practice that resembles plea bargaining. In these bargains, or *Absprachen*, a defendant agrees to confess at trial in exchange for a limited sentence. This differs from American plea bargaining in that there are no pleas of guilty—only confessions at trial—and the agreement is negotiated by the trial judge and defense rather than by the prosecution and defense. Italy's system of plea bargaining, called *pattegiamento*, allows the defense and prosecution to agree on a sentence, which must be ratified by a judge, and which can involve a reduction of no more than one-third of the regular sentence. Like American plea bargaining, this involves an arrangement made by the prosecution and defense, but it has more limitations than American plea bargaining. Unlike the American, Argentine, or German versions, it involves neither a guilty plea nor an admission of guilt on the part of the defendant. The French practice of *composition* is also similar to plea bargaining, but it diverges much more from the American practice. *Composition* also allows the prosecution and defense to negotiate an end to the case. If they come to an agreement, the defendant admits guilt and pays a fine, does community service, helps the victim, or whatever else the parties agree to. Unlike true plea bargaining, *composition* does not have the effect of a guilty verdict, but instead involves a dismissal of the case if the defendant fulfills the agreement. Also, unlike American plea bargaining, it may only be used in cases involving specified, nonserious offenses.

Pro: Arguments in Support of Plea Bargaining

Supporters of plea bargaining sometimes defend it simply on practical grounds. In this view, the adversarial trial is the ideal method of fact-finding and sentencing, but is too costly and time consuming for widespread use. This defense of plea bargaining is the most conventional and least enthusiastic about the practice itself. Since supporters see plea bargaining as necessary rather than ideal, pragmatic defenders may even agree with the opponents that plea bargaining is inherently flawed in various ways. Primarily, they view the increase in trials that would result from abolishing plea bargaining as creating far greater problems. If every case were tried, crowded trial dockets and financial burdens would make the system unworkable, and thus the adversarial trial—always the ideal—cannot be the normal practice. This is the view given by the U.S. Supreme Court in *Santobello v. New York*, one of several cases in the 1960s and 1970s that gave plea bargaining constitutional approval. Noting the enormous costs of full-scale trials, the Court described plea bargaining as essential to the administration of justice.

This defense of bargain justice—that it is necessary for economic reasons—is compatible with many of the criticisms. It is still incompatible, however, with claims that plea bargaining is not just inherently flawed (or not ideal), but inherently unjust. Supporters are often concerned with specifying the conditions under which plea bargaining can operate in a way that protects the rights of the accused—which has safeguards similar to those present in trials. The voluntariness of the plea agreement, for instance, is crucial. Just as a confession may not be forced, and any forced confession would be inadmissible as evidence in a trial, guilty pleas are only legitimate, in this view, so long as they are not coerced. For instance, while upholding the legitimacy of plea bargaining, the Supreme Court has stipulated that negotiated guilty pleas must be entirely voluntary. Prosecutors are not permitted to trick defendants by making false promises or to renege on their side of the bargain. Rule 11 of the Federal Rules of Criminal Procedure also focuses on the voluntariness of the negotiated plea by requiring the court to address defendants in open court to determine that no promises have been made outside the plea agreement and no force has been used.

The Issue of Coercion

Those who defend plea bargaining do not see the practice as necessarily coercive. Thus, they argue that the sentencing differential upon which such bargaining is based—the assumption that those convicted in trials receive more severe sentences than those who plead guilty—does not in itself affect the voluntariness of the plea. In *Brady v. United States*, for instance, the Supreme Court held that a guilty plea, to avoid a death sentence if convicted in trial, was not the result of coercion. Since they do not view all plea bargains as coercive, and since they believe that only voluntary pleas are acceptable, supporters of plea bargaining have attempted to distinguish the ordinary negotiation practices that may convince defendants to plead guilty, from unacceptable practices that would coerce them into doing so. One common distinction is between threats of severity versus offers of leniency. Either of these would result in a sentencing differential and in more guilty pleas. Defendants would plead guilty either to avoid punishment (a more severe sentence) for taking a case to trial or to obtain a reward (a less severe sentence) for avoiding trial by pleading guilty. From the defendant's standpoint, these may appear the same, and they can be difficult to distinguish empirically. Still, the idea is that while threats of punishment are coercive and therefore improper, offers of leniency are not. In this view, what makes plea bargaining voluntary is that no one is actually penalized for going to trial, only rewarded for pleading guilty. While supportive of plea bargaining generally, those who take this view may oppose certain practices they view as coercive, such as overcharging defendants or withholding or distorting information about the case in order to encourage a guilty plea. Overcharging would mean that those who are convicted in trial would be treated more severely than they would in a system without plea bargaining, and withholding information would mean they might make the plea agreement based on an overestimate of their likelihood of conviction at trial.

In the Shadow of Trials

Defenders of plea bargaining believe it is crucial to not inflict punishment for taking a case to trial. They assume that defendants who are convicted after trial will receive more severe sentences, but so long as this does not result from an added-on penalty, there is no injustice—convicted criminals are merely sentenced according to ordinary legal standards. Therefore, it is important that anyone who wishes may always have his or her case decided by trial. The right to trial, though seldom exercised, thus protects the integrity of the plea-bargaining process. It ensures that pleas are voluntary and that plea agreements will approximate the results of trials.

In this view, plea bargaining is legitimate because it occurs in the shadow of trials. It does not matter that most cases are disposed of with guilty pleas and that trials occur only infrequently. What is important is the ever-present possibility of trial, which actually makes bargaining possible. Either the state or the accused can refuse to bargain altogether, and either may reject any offer that is undesirable. Whether they do so depends on the result they expect at trial; the agreements they reach reflect the outcome of any hypothetical trial. When the state's case is weak, the prosecutor must offer the defendant a lighter sentence to obtain a guilty plea. The safeguards present in the adversarial system are thus present in the bargaining process. For example, if the rules of evidence governing trials would prohibit much of the prosecutor's evidence, this would make a guilty verdict at trial less certain—something the prosecutor would take into account in making an offer. Therefore, plea bargaining protects the rights of the accused, since the agreed-upon sentence is based on the likelihood that the accused would receive a given sentence after a trial.

Proponents of this view argue that since plea bargaining occurs in the shadow of trials, any injustices that result from it are inherent not to the plea bargaining process, but to the adversarial system itself. Innocent persons may plead guilty, but they do so believing (correctly) that there is some chance they will be convicted at trial. Likewise, guilty persons may receive much lighter punishments than they deserve, but they might instead be acquitted if their cases were tried. Trials are uncertain, and they do not necessarily free the innocent or convict the guilty. So long as people are not punished for refusing to plead—if trials affect the results of plea bargaining, rather than plea bargaining affecting the results of trials—plea bargaining is no more illegitimate than the adversarial trial process that guides it.

Plea Bargains as Contracts

Another argument, the idea that plea agreements should be assessed on the same basis as any contract, draws from these ideas, but goes further to offer a more full-throated defense of plea bargaining. This view of plea bargains as contracts sees plea bargaining not just as necessary and defensible, but desirable. Criticisms of plea bargaining often focus on matters such as constitutional rights, due process, and other issues, and assume that plea agreements, since they occur outside the trial process, are illegitimate. Defenses of plea bargaining often share the same assumptions, and attempt to defend the practice on these terms. But the contract view posits that voluntary agreements should be presumed legitimate except in certain circumstances. For example, contracts of enslavement are prohibited, as are contracts infected by duress; however, such circumstances do not apply to plea bargaining, and the assumption is that as in other voluntary contracts, the agreements are mutually beneficial—that both parties are better off under the terms of the bargain. This is, in fact, the conventional view regarding civil cases. Although civil plaintiffs and defendants have the right to take their cases to court, they may trade this right for concessions and agree upon a settlement.

From this perspective, there is nothing inherently illegitimate about plea bargains. Just as in a civil case, each party has rights that may be bargained away. The defendant may plead guilty or else force the state to prove its case in trial, while the prosecutor may or may not seek the maximum sentence. The rights of each party result in risks to the other. If there is a trial, the defendant risks being found guilty and receiving the maximum sentence, while the prosecutor risks a costly trial and acquittal. The plea agreement reassigns these risks in a way that is more acceptable to both parties than taking their chances at trial.

Beyond the benefits to the two parties, the contract view is that plea bargaining also benefits society broadly. This is not simply because there are not enough resources to take every case to trial (the common, more tepid defense), but because plea bargaining is an effective method of allocating resources. It allows the state to more effectively use its resources, however great or small they are. If the goal of criminal law is deterrence through punishment, then plea bargaining allows the criminal justice system to obtain the maximum deterrence possible from whatever resources it has been given.

Substantive Justice

Each of these perspectives holds that plea bargaining is compatible with the adversarial system of justice. The idea may be that adversarial trials are desirable but too costly for widespread use, that the possibility of trials protects the integrity of plea bargaining, or that legal adversaries use their rights as bargaining chips in negotiation. Other proponents of plea bargaining, however, see plea bargaining as valuable precisely because of its divergence from the norms of adversarial justice. The argument is that that plea bargaining may facilitate substantive rather than procedural justice, and allows the participants to avoid the formalism of the adversarial system. It is a way of handling most cases that is more satisfactory to both parties and better achieves the aims of the law.

In this substantive justice view, plea bargaining allows for a flexibility that better serves the interest of justice, similar to discretion at other stages of the criminal justice process. Just as police have flexibility in whether to make arrests, for example, prosecutors and defendants have flexibility in charging and pleading. This discretion allows prosecutors not just to avoid prosecuting the innocent, but also to make distinctions among the guilty. The overwhelming majority of people they are dealing with are not only factually guilty, but also have no grounds to contest the case. In many cases of negotiated pleas, then, there may be little actual bargaining involved. Rather, in this view, the prosecution and defense work together to establish the worth of a case—the penalty a particular offense deserves—without being constrained by the written law, which is too broad to make proper distinctions among those guilty of the same offense. Plea agreements are normally mutually satisfactory to both parties, not simply because they are mutually beneficial contracts, but because when negotiation is based on shared values, the parties can move beyond tactical considerations to decide upon an outcome that is mutually perceived as just. They can take into account what really happened, not just what is legally relevant. Conducted this way, plea bargaining better fulfills societal goals—to detect and discourage crime—while also serving the interests of defendants by helping restore their relationship to society. In this view, plea bargaining is not inferior to adversarial trials, nor is it conducted in their shadow, but instead may have a legitimacy and effectiveness that the adversarial process.

Con: Arguments in Opposition to Plea Bargaining

Unlike supporters of plea bargaining, opponents see guilty pleas resulting from negotiation as inherently coercive. They reject the distinction between penalties for going to trial and rewards for pleading guilty as purely theoretical. In either case, it is the sentencing differential that encourages guilty pleas. Whether this is conceived of as a threat or an offer is irrelevant to the decision-making process. Those convicted in trials still receive sentences that are more severe—sometimes many times as severe—than those who plead guilty. No matter what the penalties are, the essence of plea bargaining is that a defendant must choose between settling for a lighter penalty or risking one that is a more severe. One critic of plea bargaining compares this to the situation of someone who is robbed at gunpoint and agrees to hand over a wallet to avoid the risk that the gunman will shoot. In this situation, the gunman, like the prosecutor, forces someone to choose between an unpleasant, yet certain outcome, and a much more unpleasant, but less certain outcome. The defendant's choice in plea bargaining, like that of the robbery victim, is not truly voluntary.

Diverging From the Shadow of Trials

Critics of plea bargaining have also challenged the idea that guilty pleas occur in the shadow of trials—that sentences resulting from negotiation are based solely on the likely post-trial sentence, the likelihood of conviction, and a fixed discount for pleading guilty. In this view, plea bargaining in fact diverges from the shadow of trials because plea negotiations are affected by numerous factors that would not be present (or would not be as important) in determining the outcome of trials. For example, plea bargains may be affected by information deficits. That is, defendants may not be able to assess the likely outcome of conviction at trial if they are not privy to any evidence held by the prosecutor. They are, in effect, bargaining while blindfolded.

In such cases, defendants may go to trial believing the case against them is much weaker than it is; or, more likely, they may be encouraged to plead guilty based on the false belief that that their case is unwinnable. In either case, it is an erroneous belief about the likelihood of conviction that determines the decision.

In addition, while the public and the accused are the actual parties to the case, prosecutors and defense attorneys take a leading role in negotiating plea agreements—and their interests may differ from those of their clients. This problem, known as the *agency cost* by economists, can occur any time someone is represented by someone else, and indeed, agency costs may also affect the outcome of trials. But agency costs may be particularly important in plea negotiations. Prosecutors, for example, have an interest in winning a case once they take it to trial. However, while bargaining, they may have a personal interest in reducing their workload by arranging pleas in most cases along with an interest in trying their strongest cases to build their reputations. Likewise, defense attorneys may have financial interests in settling cases rather than taking them to trial, and thus may pressure clients into accepting plea agreements even in cases where the likelihood of conviction is slim. Plea agreements may then reflect the personal and professional interests of prosecutors and defense attorneys rather than the likely outcomes of adversarial trials.

Plea bargaining also diverges from the shadow of trials, according to the critics, because by its very nature it links punishment to a tactical decision on the part of the defendant—whether to accept the risk of going to trial along with the hope of an acquittal. To the extent that defendants are similar in their risk assessments, plea bargains will reflect possible trial outcomes. But defendants, in fact, differ psychologically. Some are more optimistic than others, and some more risk-averse. Decisions about whether to plead guilty, and what sentence to accept, are thus affected by these legally irrelevant factors, which would have less if any affect on the outcome of a trial.

The Contract View Fails the Public

Because they see plea bargaining as inherently coercive, as well as unreflective of trial outcomes, opponents of plea bargaining also reject the idea that plea bargains are contracts that benefit both parties. The contract view rests on the idea that plea bargains are voluntary, but opponents see plea bargaining as illegitimate because it penalizes people for exercising their rights. Since plea bargains occur outside of the shadow of trials, they do not enjoy the safeguards of the adversarial system. Rules of evidence, for example, may not shape the plea agreement if the defendant lacks knowledge of the prosecutor's evidence. Plea bargaining allows the state to obtain convictions without proving its case, as required by adversarial norms.

But the problem goes much deeper than this, according to the critics. Agency costs not only ensure that the pleas differ from trial outcomes, they also undermine the conception of plea bargains as legitimate contracts. This is because contracts are acceptable only insofar as the parties negotiating the contract are the only ones affected by the decision—when they internalize costs and benefits. But as prosecutors are only agents of the public, their decisions affect the allocation of public goods such as convictions and punishments. Thus, even when plea bargaining benefits both the prosecutor and the defendant, it may fail to serve the interests of the public. First, it undermines the public interest in deterring crime by giving inadequate sentences to the majority of guilty defendants. This is especially true if, as defenders claim, plea bargaining only involves lowering the sentences of those who plead guilty rather than raising the sentences of those who are convicted at trial. In this case, if the sentences of those convicted in trials are appropriately effective in deterring crime and are no larger than deserved, then the overwhelming majority of criminals—those who plead guilty rather than go to trial—receive sentences that are much too low to achieve the aims of the law.

Hawks and Doves

The idea that plea bargaining undermines the public's interest in deterrence by giving light sentences is sometimes called the *hawkish* objection to plea bargaining. But critics also argue that plea bargaining undermines the public's interest to protect the innocent, which is referred to as the *dovish* position. These positions are not incompatible, since according to the critics, the criminal law's purpose is not to obtain a certain number of convictions, but to sort the innocent from the guilty and to punish the guilty appropriately. Plea bargains, then, while resulting broadly in sentences that are too lenient, also fail to avoid convicting the innocent. Unlike the adversarial trial, they are not designed to do so, since by avoiding the trial the prosecution avoids having to prove the case. Where cases are weaker, prosecutors offer larger concessions to the defendant. Since cases against innocents are especially likely to be weak, and since defendants are more likely to accept drastically reduced sentences, the plea-bargaining system in fact operates as if it is designed to convict the innocent. From this viewpoint, plea bargaining is undesirable even though those involved are usually satisfied with the outcome. Both innocent and guilty defendants alike may be happy to avoid the risk of trial, but a system that allows them to do so fails to achieve societal goals of deciding cases according to uniform and fair procedures.

Result of an Overadversarial System

Most critics of plea bargaining, like most defenders, see the adversarial system as ideal. But while the defenders argue that the plea bargaining system operates according to adversarial norms, critics argue that its procedures and outcomes differ dramatically from those of trials. Another criticism of plea bargaining, however, sees plea bargaining as the unfortunate result of an overadversarial system of justice. Like other critics, John Langbein, a professor of law and legal history at Yale Law School, sees plea bargaining as inherently involuntary—similar in kind (though not degree) to the use of torture in medieval Europe to extract confessions from the accused. In either case, guilty pleas result from a promise of less punishment. But torture and plea bargaining are similar in another way as well: They both arose as methods of obtaining convictions in legal systems where safeguards to protect the accused made the trial system unworkable. In medieval Europe, the law required either two eyewitnesses or a voluntary confession to obtain a conviction. However, this standard of proof was too high to obtain convictions even in most cases where there was clear evidence of the defendant's guilt. Eventually, torture was used to overcome these safeguards, to encourage people to "voluntarily" confess.

Likewise, the legal system in the United States during the 19th and 20th centuries became increasingly adversarial. As more and more safeguards were developed to protect the innocent, the trial system became unworkable for most cases. Like the system of torture in continental Europe, plea bargaining is a nontrial procedure that enables prosecutors to obtain convictions without adhering to the formal law. Both systems—torture and plea bargaining—fail to protect the innocent from coercion and weaken the moral force of the law. Therefore, a trial system with overly high safeguards for protecting the innocent results in a system where most cases are decided without trials, where safeguards are set too low. For Langbein, the solution is not to decide all cases with full-scale adversarial trials, but to replace plea bargaining with a streamlined, nonadversarial procedure.

See Also: 11. Jury System; 12. Mandatory Sentencing.

Further Readings

Alschuler, Albert W. "The Changing Plea Bargaining Debate." *California Law Review*, v.69/3 (1981).

Alschuler, Albert W. "The Defense Attorney's Role in Plea Bargaining." *The Yale Law Journal*, v.84/6 (1975).

Alschuler, Albert W. "The Prosecutor's Role in Plea Bargaining." *The University of Chicago Law Review*, v.36/1 (1968).

Alschuler, Albert W. "The Trial Judge's Role in Plea Bargaining, Part 1." *Columbia Law Review*, v.76/7 (1976).

Baldwin, John, and Michael McConville. "Plea Bargaining and Plea Negotiation in England." *Law and Society Review,* v.13/2 (1979).

Ball, Jeremy D. "Is It a Prosecutor's World? Determinants of Count Bargaining Decisions." *Journal of Contemporary Criminal Justice*, v.22/3 (2006).

Bibas, Stephanos. "Plea Bargaining Outside the Shadow of Trial." *Harvard Law Review*, v.117/8 (2004).

Black, Donald. *The Social Structure of Right and Wrong*. San Diego, CA: Academic Press, 1998.

Brereton, David, and Jonathan D. Casper. "Does It Pay to Plead Guilty? Differential Sentencing and the Functioning of Criminal Courts." *Law and Society Review*, v.16/1 (1981–82).

Brunk, Conrad G. "The Problem of Voluntariness and Coercion in the Negotiated Plea." *Law and Society Review*, v.13/2 (1979).

Casper, Jonathan. "Having Their Day in Court: Defendants' Evaluations of the Fairness of Their Treatment." *Law and Society Review*, v.12/2 (1978).

Church, Thomas W. "In Defense of 'Bargain Justice.'" *Law and Society Review*, v.13/2 (1979).

Easterbrook, Frank H. "Criminal Procedure as a Market System." *The Journal of Legal Studies*, v.12/2 (1983).

Feeley, Malcolm M. "Perspectives on Plea Bargaining." *Law and Society Review*, v.13/2 (1979).

Feeley, Malcolm M. "Pleading Guilty in Lower Courts." *Law and Society Review*, v.13/2 (1979).

Feeley, Malcolm M. *The Process Is the Punishment: Handling Cases in a Lower Criminal Court*. New York: Russell Sage Foundation, 1992.

Friedman, Lawrence M. "Plea Bargaining in Historical Perspective." *Law and Society Review*, v.13/2 (1979).

Haller, Mark H. "Plea Bargaining: The Nineteenth Century Context." *Law and Society Review*, v.13/2 (1979).

Heumann, Milton. *Plea Bargaining: The Experiences of Prosecutors, Judges, and Defense Attorneys.* Chicago: University of Chicago Press, 1977.

Kipnis, Kenneth. "Criminal Justice and the Negotiated Plea." *Ethics*, v.86/2 (1976).

LaFree, Gary D. "Adversarial and Nonadversarial Justice: A Comparison of Guilty Pleas and Trials." *Criminology*, v.23/2 (1985).

Langbein, John H. "Torture and Plea Bargaining." *The University of Chicago Law Review*, v.46/1 (1978).

Langbein, John H. "Understanding the Short History of Plea Bargaining." *Law and Society Review*, v.13/2 (1979).

Langer, Maximo. "From Legal Transplants to Legal Translations: The Globalization of Plea Bargaining and the Americanization Thesis in Criminal Procedure." *Harvard International Law Journal*, 45 (2004).

Padgett, John F. "The Emergent Organization of Plea Bargaining." *American Journal of Sociology*, v.90/4 (1985).

Padgett, John F. "Plea Bargaining and Prohibition in the Federal Courts, 1908–1934." *Law and Society Review*, v.24/2 (1990).

Schulhofer, Stephen J. "Plea Bargaining as Disaster." *The Yale Law Journal*, v.101/8 (1992).

Scott, Robert E., and William J. Stuntz. "Plea Bargaining as Contract." *The Yale Law Journal*, v.101/8 (1992).

Utz, Pamela J. *Settling the Facts: Discretion and Negotiation in Criminal Court.* Lexington, MA: Lexington Books, 1978.

Vogel, Mary E. "The Social Origins of Plea Bargaining: Conflict and the Law in the Process of State Formation, 1830–1860." *Law and Society Review*, v.33/1 (1999).

15

Polygraphs

Christine S. Scott-Hayward
New York University

A polygraph, or lie detector, is an instrument that attempts to determine whether a person is telling the truth by measuring and recording physiological changes in the body while the subject answers a series of questions. The word *polygraph* literally means "many writings" and comes from the fact that the instrument simultaneously records a number of different body responses, and the responses are graphically recorded. Polygraph tests are based on the theory that lying causes stress, which in turn causes physiological changes in the body. Sensors are attached to the body to mechanically record these changes (in breathing, blood pressure, pulse, and perspiration), which are then measured to indicate whether the subject of the exam is answering the questions truthfully. Polygraph use is controversial due to the lack of scientific consensus on its effectiveness, and most courts do not admit the results of polygraph tests into evidence in criminal trials.

History of the Polygraph

The modern polygraph was developed in the 20th century in the United States and is used in a variety of contexts, both civil (such as employment screening) and criminal (such as as an interrogation tool as well as part of the treatment and supervision of people convicted of sex offenses).

However, attempts to develop a lie detector instrument that would record physiological changes resulting from the telling of a lie actually began as early as the 19th century. Cesare Lombroso, an Italian criminologist, was one of the first to develop such an instrument, which he used to measure changes in pulse and blood pressure during questioning. In 1915, William Marston, then an undergraduate at Harvard University, conducted experiments on his fellow students in which he found that he could determine who was telling the truth based on whether or not their blood pressure rose. Marston continued working on lie detection post-graduation, and published a number of articles and books on the topic.

Polygraph Groundbreakers: Larson and Reid

Although some of Marston's claims were repudiated by later students of the polygraph, his work was important, in part because of its impact on John Larson, a Berkeley, California, police officer with a Ph.D. in physiology who is credited with inventing the first modern polygraph machine. In 1921, after reading one of Marston's articles, Larson developed an instrument capable of continuously recording multiple physiological responses (blood pressure and respiration) to a series of questions. The new device played a major role in solving a series of thefts on the campus of the University of California in 1921, and thereafter was adopted as an interrogation tool by the Berkeley Police Department under Chief August Vollmer.

Larson's machine was later refined by one of his former assistants, Leonarde Keeler, who added a measurement of electrical skin conductivity and developed a portable instrument. In 1930 Keeler moved from Berkeley to Chicago, where he met John E. Reid, who had developed a polygraph machine similar to the Larson/Keeler machine. Reid had a law degree and was a polygraph examiner at the Chicago Police Scientific Crime Detection Laboratory until 1947, when he left to start his own company, John E. Reid and Associates. Although Keeler played an important role in developing polygraphy, Reid became the leader in the field and was a strong advocate of the polygraph until his death in 1983. He testified as an expert in many cases across the country. In addition, he authored numerous articles and books on the polygraph and criminal interrogation with two main collaborators: Fred E. Inbau, a professor of law at Northwestern University; and Fred Horvath, a polygraph examiner with John E. Reid and Associates. Reid also made significant modifications to the testing procedure.

Procedures of the Polygraph

Most modern polygraph examinations consist of a pre-test interview, during which the examiner familiarizes the subject with the testing procedure and may collect preliminary information about the subject, which is later relied upon by the examiner, particularly during a control question test. After the examination is conducted, the examiner will analyze and, depending on the technique used, score the test results and render an opinion as to the truthfulness of the subject. There are a variety of polygraph examination techniques used today.

The first polygraph testing technique was the Relevant-Irrelevant Test (RIT), developed by Larson, which was the dominant method until the 1950s. It is still used today, but by a minority of examiners. This method consists of two types of questions. The relevant questions relate to the issue under investigation, while the irrelevant questions are on neutral topics such as name, age, and location of the test. The polygraph measures the physiological responses to both questions, and if the responses to both questions are similar, the subject is considered to be truthful. If the responses to the relevant questions are stronger than to the irrelevant questions, then the subject is considered to be deceptive. This method, which has been subject to few validity studies, has been criticized because of the high number of false positives—the machine showing truthful subjects to be lying.

In response to some of the concerns with the RIT, in 1947, John Reid published an article outlining the comparative response method of questioning in a polygraph exam. This method, now known is the control question test (CQT) is still used today, and is the most commonly used method in police interrogation. Like the RIT, the CQT includes relevant and irrelevant questions, but also includes what are called *lie control* questions. These questions relate to behavior that most people are expected to have engaged in, but will lie about, such as: "have you ever stolen money?" or "have you ever lied to get out of trouble?" The test is passed if the physiological responses during the lie control questions are larger than those during the relevant questions. If the reverse is scored, the subject is considered to be deceptive. Unlike the RIT, the CQT is numerically scored. The CQT has been the subject of a large number of validity studies, but accuracy rates have varied considerably.

An alternative method of testing, known as the Guilty Knowledge Test (GKT) or Concealed Information Test (CIT), was developed by David Lykken in the late 1950s. This method tests the subject on his or her knowledge of the crime that would not be known to an innocent person. The subject is given multiple-choice answers and is rated based on how he or she reacts to the correct answer. This method is considered more valid by some supporters; however, it has yet to be used systematically in the criminal justice field.

Finally, although not a polygraph per se, voice-stress analysis (VSA) is another type of lie detection technique. VSA devices were developed in the latter half of the 20th century by former U.S. Army personnel. They attempt to detect the existence of truth, deception, and/or stress from voice and speech. This device is simpler to conduct than a polygraph test, since all that is required is a voice or a recording of a voice, and it can be conducted without the knowledge of the subject. It is used predominantly in law enforcement, for example by both the Central Intelligence Agency and the Federal Bureau of Investigation.

The Use of Polygraphs in the Criminal Justice System

In the criminal justice system, polygraphs are primarily used in two settings. The first is by the police, as part of the interrogation process. Most police interrogation manuals, including the widely used *Criminal Interrogation and Confessions* (which sets out the Inbau and Reid nine-step method of interrogation), recommend using an interview to determine guilt or innocence, followed up by an interrogation based on the presumed guilt of the suspect. During the interview step, investigators may ask a suspect if they are willing to take a polygraph test to ascertain a suspect's guilt or innocence based on how the suspect responds. Investigators are taught that a guilty suspect will generally refuse to take a polygraph test, while an innocent suspect will be eager to take a test that he or she believes will demonstrate his or her innocence. In addition, polygraph tests can be conducted by the police as part of this first step, and if the results are unfavorable, they can then be used to confront the suspect with his or her apparent lies.

Polygraph tests can also be used during the second phase, the actual interrogation. For example, Inbau and Reid teach nine steps of interrogation, which include confronting the suspect with his or her certain guilt, offering explanations or excuses that might justify the crime, and showing sympathy. Step three is handling denials. The manual suggests that one way to deal with a suspect who is denying responsibility for the crime is to offer the suspect the opportunity to take a polygraph test. If a suspect refuses to take a test, the interrogator can point out the incriminating nature of the refusal, which, if the suspect is guilty, may lead to a confession.

Polygraphs may also have a rehabilitative purpose, and are used in the federal systems and in some states as a component of treatment for people in prison and under community supervision (including probation, parole, and post-release supervision). The use of polygraphs is most common among people convicted of sex offenses, and is often a mandatory condition of probation or release from prison (whether through parole or other supervised release). Some states also use polygraphs in some capacity in prison treatment programs, although this is not as widespread; fewer than half the states report this type of use. Polygraphs are more common in the community, where at least two-thirds of states rely on them. States report multiple purposes for polygraph use, including assessing the suspect's ability to admit the full extent of his or her crime, assessing his or her criminal history, obtaining information about victims, and most commonly, assessing the extent to which a person is complying with treatment and supervision requirements.

The Admissibility of Polygraphs in Criminal Cases

While there is no per se ban on the admissibility of polygraph evidence in court, both federal and state courts have traditionally been reluctant to admit test results as evidence. The first court to consider the admissibility of the results of a polygraph exam was the District of Columbia Circuit Court of Appeals in its 1923 opinion in *Frye v. United States*. In this case, the defendant had initially confessed to murder, but later recanted his confession and offered results from a polygraph test conducted by William Marston to support his innocence. The court declined to admit the results because the test was not recognized in the scientific community. In its decision, the court developed a more general rule on the admissibility of scientific evidence, holding that such evidence was only admissible if the principle had gained general acceptance in the relevant field.

Relying on *Frye*'s general acceptance rule, both state and federal courts almost uniformly excluded most polygraph evidence, with two limited exceptions. First, courts in some states and federal circuits allowed the admission of polygraph evidence if both parties agreed, known as admission by stipulation. Second, some state and federal courts allowed the admission of polygraph evidence for the purpose of impeaching or corroborating witness testimony where the character of truthfulness of the witness has been questioned.

Daubert *and* Scheffer: *A Split in the Federal Circuits*

The *Frye* general acceptance rule governed the admissibility of polygraph exams and other scientific evidence until 1993, when the Supreme Court invalidated it in *Daubert v. Merrell Dow Pharmaceuticals, Inc.* In that case, the Court held that the Federal Rules of Evidence (enacted after *Frye*), particularly Rule 702, now governed the admissibility of scientific evidence. Under Rule 702, scientific evidence is admissible in court by a qualified expert witness if the evidence "will assist the trier of fact to understand the evidence or to determine a fact in issue." The Court held that in applying this rule, courts should weigh a number of factors, including but not limited to (1) whether the theory of technique could be, and had been tested; (2) whether the theory or technique had been subjected to peer review and publication; (3) the known or potential rate of error; and (4) general acceptance in the relevant scientific community. From being the sole determining factor under *Frye*, general acceptance became just one factor among many to be considered under *Daubert*.

Unlike *Frye*, *Daubert* did not specifically concern polygraph evidence, which the Supreme Court has only rarely considered. When it has, however, it has expressed skepticism about its reliability. In 1998, in *United States v. Scheffer,* the Court directly addressed the admission of polygraph evidence in a case concerning Military Rule of Evidence 707, which contains a per se ban on the use of polygraph evidence in military trials. The Court held that this ban did not violate a defendant's constitutional due-process rights. In reaching this decision, the Court noted the disputed reliability of polygraph results, pointing out that "there is simply no way to know in a particular case whether a polygraph examiner's conclusion is accurate, because certain doubts and uncertainties plague even the best polygraph exams." A number of judges also rejected the admission of polygraph evidence because it infringed on the jury's role in determining credibility.

As a result of *Daubert* and *Scheffer*, there is now a split in the federal circuits. Some circuits still retain outright general bans on the admission of polygraph evidence, holding that polygraph evidence is unreliable and not generally accepted in the scientific community. Others continue to admit stipulated polygraph evidence for the impeachment or corroboration of a witness's testimony. A third group of courts hold that *Daubert* requires a case-by-case analysis of the particular polygraph evidence, and may allow the admission of polygraph evidence without stipulation. However, despite this new standard of expanding the admissibility of scientific evidence, including polygraph evidence, in practice not much changed. Even in circuits where there is no outright ban, courts generally still decline to admit the polygraph. The reasons given by courts vary, and range from the concern that polygraphs tend to prejudice juries, to questioning the reliability of polygraphs and holding that the results of an exam may be irrelevant, ambiguous, or misleading.

At the state level, courts are also split. A majority of states still have general bans on polygraph admission, while approximately 20 states use the admission-by-stipulation standard, requiring that both parties stipulate in writing to the admissibility of the results prior to conducting the test. The purpose of admission is rarely to establish the guilt or innocence of the person accused of a crime, and instead is usually for impeachment or corroboration. At both the state and federal level, polygraph evidence may be admissible at the discretion of the court or presiding official in informal hearings such as probation revocation, where the rules of evidence do not apply.

The Exception: New Mexico

New Mexico is the only state that allows polygraph evidence to be admitted without both parties' stipulation. In 2004, in *Lee v. Martinez*, the state supreme court undertook a comprehensive *Daubert* analysis and held that the results of a polygraph exam could be admitted into evidence. In that case, the defendant sought the introduction of the results over the opposition of the prosecutor. The test in question was conducted using the control-question technique, and so the court focused solely on that technique in its analysis.

The court relied heavily on a 2003 National Academy of Sciences report on the polygraph, discussed in more detail below, and concluded that the CQT is testable, has been subject to peer review and publication, and has interquartile (midspread) accuracy rates ranging from 83–90 percent, with a median accuracy rate of 85 percent. The court also noted that under New Mexico law, there are additional standards for the admission of polygraphs, which ensure that only a qualified, licensed polygraph operator can perform a polygraph exam and testify in court about the results. In addition, both the pretest interview and the test itself must be audio- or video-recorded in full. Finally, the court examined the issue of general acceptability and determined that although the CQT has not been generally accepted within the scientific community, neither has it been uniformly rejected, and as such the general acceptability factor carried little weight in its analysis. The court concluded that the CQT is reliable and admissible as evidence so long as the conditions set out in New Mexico law are met. Thus, each court must conduct a case-specific analysis in determining whether to admit the results of a polygraph examination.

Pro: Supporting the Validity of the Polygraph

Although there is a heated debate in the scientific community on the validity of polygraph examinations, a large number of field and laboratory studies have been conducted on its validity. In 2003, the National Academy of Sciences conducted such a review, uncovering research reports of almost 200 studies—102 of which were of sufficient quality to be included in its review. Overall, the median accuracy rate in those studies was 86 percent, with an interquartile range of 81–91 percent.

The American Polygraph Association (APA), the leading polygraph professional association, provides information on 80 studies, which it has compiled since 1980, and reports accuracy rates ranging from 80–98 percent. The APA further points out that many studies report inconclusive tests as errors, which can lead to accuracy rates appearing lower than they actually are.

Relying on these 80 studies, the APA believes that lies can be accurately detected by a valid examination, which requires a combination of a properly trained examiner; a polygraph instrument that at least records cardiovascular, respiratory, and electrodermal activity; and the proper administration of an accepted testing procedure and scoring system. Under these circumstances, the APA holds that the polygraph can be a useful tool in a variety of areas in the criminal justice system. Many police departments agree, and see polygraphs as a useful interrogation aid that can help induce confessions. Even critics of the validity of polygraphs themselves recognize the usefulness of polygraphs for this purpose.

Rehabilitation and Recidivism

In terms of rehabilitation, there is some evidence that the use of polygraph monitoring might reduce recidivism. There are at least two studies that find some impact of polygraph testing on recidivism. A 2001 Oregon study compared people on community supervision in one county who took part in a program that combined polygraph monitoring with treatment and specialized supervision, with those in another county who did not receive the same combination of services. The study found that people in the first group were 40 percent less likely to be convicted of a new felony. However, because the effects of the specific elements of treatment were not isolated, it is unclear exactly what role polygraph monitoring played.

Another study, from 2007, looked at the impact of polygraph use on recidivism rates of a group of adult males convicted of sex offenses. The group was receiving treatment and under community supervision, and half the participants were subject to polygraph monitoring. The study found an effect on nonsexual violent recidivism—fewer people in the group who were subject to polygraph monitoring were charged with nonsexual violent offenses. However, there were no significant differences between the groups with respect to the number charged with sexual offenses.

Con: Questioning the Validity of the Polygraph

Since its inception, the validity of the polygraph has been questioned, particularly in the scientific community. Recent surveys of members of two scientific organizations, the Society for Pyschophysiological Research and the American Psychological Association's Division of General Psychology, show that only about a third of those surveyed believed that the CQT was scientifically sound.

The Error Rate

Many critics are concerned with the potential for errors, which are usually referred to as false positives or false negatives. False positives occur when a person is telling the truth, but is nonetheless reported as being deceptive. Some argue that false positives occur because of the similarity of physical changes caused by emotional factors, such as feelings of guilt, to those caused by lies. False negatives occur when a deceptive subject is reported as truthful. This sometimes happens because the subject has been able to "beat" the polygraph by artificially augmenting responses to control questions.

Given that it is the test most commonly used by investigators, the CQT has been the subject of most of the research in this area. In particular, critics question the two assumptions that underlie the CQT: first, that innocent people are more responsive to control questions than relevant questions; and second, that guilty persons respond more intensely to relevant questions than control questions. William Iacano, an expert in psychophysiology, argues that there is no evidence that the first assumption is true, and in fact, that being confronted with a false accusation can lead to a similar physiological response as telling a lie. With respect to the second assumption, Iacano points to the ability of guilty individuals, with less than 30 minutes instruction, to recognize control questions and employ countermeasures such as curling the toes or lightly biting the tongue while answering control questions. One study showed that after instruction, 50 percent or more guilty individuals were able to defeat the test.

Poor Research Standards

These concerns cause many to doubt the validity of the CQT, but critics also note that it is virtually impossible to accurately estimate the test's validity because of the poor quality of the research. A 2003 National Research Council report found that the majority of polygraph research was unreliable, unscientific, and biased. It noted that most of the relevant studies were below the quality typically needed for funding by the National Science Foundation or the National Institutes of Health. The report concluded that many of the research studies that the American Polygraph Association relied upon were significantly flawed.

One problem with polygraph research is that many research studies involve laboratory experiments conducted with undergraduate students who simulate a crime. These studies are criticized for many reasons, including the trivial consequences of failing a test, and the fact that the tests are so far removed from real life that they fail to offer any insight into how polygraphs work in the field. There are also problems with many of the field studies that have been conducted, mainly because it is very difficult to establish ground truth—who is guilty and who is innocent. Generally, ground truth is established by looking at cases where confessions have identified the guilty parties. The polygraph charts of these individuals are then rescored blindly. However, this fails to identify cases in which the original examiner made an error, because generally, if the guilty party beats the initial test, he or she us unlikely to be interrogated in an effort to extract a confession. Thus, the only cases selected for study are those in which the original examiner was correct and a verifying confession was obtained.

For these reasons, the high accuracy rates cited by many proponents of the polygraph have been questioned. The only field study conducted that established ground truth through confessions not dependent on the polygraph test outcome found an accuracy rate of just 57 percent, compared to rates of up to 98 percent cited by the APA and others.

VSA has been subject to even more criticism than the polygraph. A recent meta-analysis of 24 empirical studies over 30 years found no evidence of the validity or reliability of voice-stress, analysis-based technologies for the detection of deception in individuals.

No Uniform Training Standards or Procedures

Another criticism that has been leveled at polygraphs is that there are no uniform training standards or special procedures. Although the APA and other professional organizations such as the American Association of Police Polygraphists do publish standards and conduct special courses, organizations do not have the ability to enforce compliance with these standards. Furthermore, in many states, individuals do not have to belong to a professional organization in order to administer exams. More than 20 states do not require a polygraph examiner to be licensed or certified.

Finally, while many critics of polygraphs recognize the important role that polygraphs play as an interrogation tool, polygraphs and other lie detectors have been important factors in some false confessions. One well-known example is the case of 18-year-old Peter Reilly, who was told that the results of his polygraph examination showed him to have murdered his mother. Based on this, Reilly eventually confessed, was convicted of manslaughter, and spent two years in jail before his confession was shown to be false when it was proven that he was elsewhere at the time of the murder. By then, the trail had grown cold, and the murder remains unsolved.

Another false confession linked to a polygraph exam is that of Michael Crowe. Crowe, age 14, became a suspect in the murder of his 12-year-old sister, Stephanie, who was stabbed to death in her California bedroom in 1998. Despite reports of another suspect, Crowe was taken into custody and questioned with neither his parents nor an attorney present. During the interrogation, Crowe was given a VSA test and told that the test was in infallible lie detector. Detectives told him—falsely—that he had failed the test. Although he had no memory of having committed the crime, Crowe came to believe that he must be guilty, and eventually confessed. Crowe was later exonerated prior to his trial after Stephanie's blood was found on the clothing of the original suspect.

See Also: 7. Expert Witnesses and Hired Guns; 8. Eyewitness Testimony and Accuracy; 18. Sex Offender Registry.

Further Readings

Alder, Ken. *The Lie Detectors: The History of an American Obsession.* New York: Free Press, 2007.

American Polygraph Association. "The Official APA Website." www .polygraph.org (Accessed March 2010).

Bhatt, Sujeeta, and Susan E. Brandon. "Review of Voice Stress Based Technologies for the Detection of Deception." http://www.polygraph .org/files/Bhatt__Brandon_2008_voice.pdf (Accessed March 2010).

Blum, George L. "Annotation: Admissibility in State Criminal Case of Results of Polygraph (Lie Detector) Test: Post-Daubert Cases." *American Law Reports,* v.6/10 (2010).

Bush, John C. "Warping the Rules: How Some Courts Misapply Generic Evidentiary Rules to Exclude Polygraph Evidence." *Vanderbilt Law Review,* v.59/2 (2006).

Committee to Review the Scientific Evidence on the Polygraph, The National Academy of Sciences. *The Polygraph and Lie Detection.* Washington, DC: National Academies Press. 2003.

Daly, Reagan. "Treatment and Reentry Practices for Sex Offenders: An Overview of States." New York: Vera Institute of Justice, 2008.

Daubert v. Merrell Dow Pharmaceuticals, Inc., 509 U.S. 579 (1993).

Frye v. United States, 293 F. 1013 (D.C. Cir. 1923).

Gallini, Brian R. "Police 'Science' in the Interrogation Room: Seventy Years of Pseudo-Psychological Interrogation Methods to Obtain Inadmissible Confessions." http://works.bepress.com/cgi/viewcontent .cgi?article=1006&context=brian_gallini (Accessed February 2010).

Gudjonsson, Gisli H. *The Psychology of Interrogations and Confessions: A Handbook.* Chichester, England: Wiley, 2003.

Iacono, William G. "Forensic 'Lie Detection': Procedures Without Scientific Basis." *Journal of Forensic Psychology Practice,* v.1/1 (2001).

Inbau, Fred E., John E. Reid, Joseph P. Buckley, and Brian C. Jayne. *Criminal Interrogation and Confessions.* Sudbury, MA: Jones and Bartlett Publishers, 2004.

Lee v. Martinez, 96 P.3d 291 (N.M. 2004).

Lykken, David T. *A Tremor in the Blood: Uses and Abuses of the Lie Detector.* New York: Plenum Press, 1998.

Thurman, John E. "Annotation: Admissibility in Federal Criminal Cases of Results of Polygraph (Lie Detector) Test: Post-Daubert Cases." *American Law Reports, Federal,* v.140 (2008).

United States v. Scheffer, 523 US 303 (1998).

Vigliucci, Vincent V. "Note: Calculating Credibility: *State v. Sharma* and the Future of Polygraph Admissibility in Ohio and Beyond." *Akron Law Review,* v.42 (2009).

16

Restorative Justice

William R. Wood
California State University, Fullerton/University of Auckland

R estorative justice is both a philosophy and loosely aligned set of interventions that focus less on crime as the breaking of laws than as the harming or breaking of human relationships. Emerging in the 1970s and 1980s as an alternative to more traditional youth and adult justice practices, restorative justice interventions such as victim–offender mediation, sentencing circles, and family group conferencing are largely organized around the principles of victim participation and redress, offender accountability and reintegration, and community participation in local justice practices. Such practices are thought to meet the needs of these three groups more directly and comprehensively than more traditional rehabilitative or punitive approaches, and these three groups are seen as the primary social actors through which both crime redress and crime reduction can be best achieved.

Primarily, restorative justice seeks to include victims in their own cases, ideally in settings that afford them the possibility of meeting with those who have harmed them, and more generally toward the goal of repairing these harms. Restorative justice also seeks to provide opportunities for offenders to be accountable for these harms; to make amends to those they have harmed, when possible; and to reintegrate into their communities after they have made amends. Finally, restorative justice seeks to include local communities into justice processes to the extent that they may help support victims, provide opportunities for offender reintegration, and when possible, participate in the shaping of justice policies and community approaches to crime.

In the last three decades, restorative justice has moved from an alternative or peripheral position in justice practices to one that has gained both credibility and widespread use in the United States, Canada, Europe, Australia, New Zealand, and elsewhere. The concept of restorative justice rests on some basic theoretical positions and assumptions, and is used in a variety of restorative interventions and programs. Further, proponents and critics alike have analyzed the strengths (pros) and weaknesses (cons) of this approach to justice.

Basic Premises of Restorative Justice

The most basic premise of restorative justice is that the concept of crime can be better understood as harm. In all ways that people harm one another, criminal or otherwise, restorative justice views successful redress as comprised of three basic elements: namely, the accepting of responsibility for harms caused; the making of amends; and, to the degree possible, the successful return or restoration of involved parties to their social roles and lives.

Much of the theoretical work in restorative justice has focused on the reasons why contemporary justice systems fail in these three goals. Restorative justice emerged in large part out of the work of practitioners who focused primarily on developing interventions that addressed these problems. By the 1980s, restorative justice literature was regularly identifying several problems in justice practices, specifically (1) the exclusion of victims from participating in and having knowledge of their cases, (2) the failure of criminal justice systems to provide or allow for meaningful redress for victims, (3) the revictimization of victims by policing and prosecutorial agencies, (4) the problems in adversarial forms of justice that discourage offenders from taking responsibility for their offenses, (5) the lack of means by which offenders could take responsibility and make amends to those they have harmed, (6) the lack of successful offender reintegration, and (7) the forging of justice policies that excluded and often harmed local communities to the benefit of the state.

Early advocates of restorative justice linked these problems to deficiencies in justice practices, as well as to theories of crime control and justice used to justify these policies. In particular, works by Norwegian criminologist Nils Christie, the Australian criminologist John Braithwaite, and the

American sociologist Howard Zehr were seminal in shaping the theoretical impetus and legitimization of restorative justice in the 1970s and 1980s. While these works were not the only authoritative ones on the topic, each provides insight into the basic premises of restorative justice as a set of practices that seek to include and make amends to victims, encourage offenders to accept responsibility and make amends, and to include local communities in the shaping and participation of justice interventions.

Conflict as Property

Christie's work centered on the idea of conflict as property. Conflict, he argued, had been historically transformed by the modern criminal justice systems from something that people "owned" as victims or harmed parties, to something to be solved or addressed by the state itself—not only for reasons of expediency, but for other goals such as crime reduction and public order, political capital, and revenue. The professionalization of justice practices, in his estimation, represented a lost opportunity for potential individual participation both for victims of crime, and more generally, in the loss of opportunity for community members to affirm collective norms and values.

For Christie, this loss was especially relevant for victims of crime. While the state may have a duty to victims in terms of reducing victimization, he argued, it generally cannot be vested in the outcome of particular cases in the same way a victim may be. The state is generally interested in depriving the offender of money or liberty as a matter of deterrence, revenue, or justice. It is decidedly less concerned with or even able to allow the victim an opportunity to participate in the "ownership" of her own conflict. Christie's article provided significant historical and theoretical justification for the use of practices such as victim–offender mediation, which enabled victims to gain knowledge of their cases, participate in the shaping of agreements as to amends, and directly receive the benefits of such agreements.

The Work of Braithwaite and Zehr

While Christie's work emphasized victims and local communities as "owners" of conflict, the work of John Braithwaite emphasized the idea that Western justice systems do little to afford offenders any concrete means by which to make amends to those they have harmed, and to reintegrate into the communities where trust has been broken. Central to Braithwaite's work was the concept of shame, which he argued is present in both informal types of social control as well as within formal criminal justice practices. Western societies, Braithwaite argued, had effectively uncoupled shame and punishment to the degree that today, punishment practices are essentially private ones that seek to restore order and social homeostasis through rehabilitation, or through the administration and application of pain away from public view. In either case, however, be it rehabilitation or punishment, there is too little emphasis on setting forth specific and concrete requirements by which an offender may cross the line back into conventional behavior and group acceptance.

In contrast, Braithwaite argued for the use of "reintegrative shaming," or approaches that incorporated the participation of family members, local community members, and victims to make the sense of shame more immediate, as well as to make the possibility of reintegration more concrete. In Braithwaite's estimation, immediacy stemmed from the idea that the esteem of family members, community members (particularly those who know the offender), and even victims matter more to most offenders than the opinions or judgments of justice professionals. The process of reintegration is made more real through the setting forth of specific actions to repair harms caused to victims and to the community that signify both to the offender and to the community that the obligation incurred through the offense has been fulfilled.

Howard Zehr's book *Changing Lenses,* published in 1980, remains the most widely cited work in restorative justice. Zehr argued that restorative justice could be conceptualized as a distinct justice paradigm centered on the principle of harm, and not crime, as the primary theoretical and organizational impetus for most justice interventions. Critical of what he (and many others) called modern forms of "retributive" justice, Zehr argued that such an approach emphasized the rule of law, crime control, and punishment at the expense of victims, offenders, and communities.

Zehr recognized that while some crimes were so heinous as to require "special handling," and some offenders so dangerous that they must be removed from society, he argued that such cases had in fact set the norm for how Western societies approached crime control on the whole. In the vast number of cases, he argued, there was ample opportunity for a new, normative set of guiding justice principles centered on the questions of how particular programs might repair harms done to victims, support the ability of offenders to make amends and reintegrate, and address community needs and obligations surrounding crime.

History of Restorative Justice

The term *restorative justice* is usually attributed to a work by Albert Eglash in 1977, where he contrasted what he called "retributive" and "restorative" forms of justice. In this work, Eglash voiced concern over the use of punishment in modern justice systems that neither addressed the damage caused to crime victims, nor allowed for offenders to participate in making amends for these damages outside the possibility of financial restitution. Using the concept of "creative restitution," Eglash argued that victims could be better served, and offenders could be better afforded opportunities to take responsibility for their actions, in settings that focused less on punishment and more on the restoration of such harms through a variety of restorative possibilities beyond financial recompense.

Victim–Offender Reconciliation Programs

While Eglash is credited with the term, by the mid-1970s, there were already several programs in the United States and Canada that were bringing youth offenders and victims together in informal reconciliation settings. In the late 1960s and early 1970s, concern over the labeling of youth offenders as "delinquent" and the effects of institutionalizing youth led to the development of programs such as diversion, as well as alternative programs to be used in lieu of formal court processes. One such alternative was the use of victim–offender reconciliation, developed in part in Ontario, Canada, in 1974, where two youths who had vandalized several family properties were taken to these homes to meet with victims and decide upon appropriate restitution. Similar victim–offender reconciliation programs (VORPs) were established in Indiana and Minnesota in the 1970s.

Early VORP interventions were largely informal, working either as an alternative to courts or as an alternative within courts. As the use of VOPRs grew in the 1970s and 1980s, they were often conducted by people from conflict-resolution or civil-mediation backgrounds who had been trained in the use of mediation as an alternative to the costs and lengthy duration of formal litigations and courts. Such approaches centered primarily on needs instead of laws, and advocated face-to-face meetings between parties in lieu of paid litigators as a means to better meet these needs. By the 1980s, dozens of reconciliation or victim–offender mediation (VOM) programs existed in North America; by the early 1990s, these programs numbered in the hundreds; and by the turn of the century, a national survey in the United States found over 1,000 such programs in existence.

Victims' Rights Movements and Indigenous Justice

VOMs represent only one strand in the development of restorative justice, however. Two others were the emergence of victims' rights movements, and the growth of indigenous justice practices in New Zealand and Canada. In the 1970s and 1980s, victims' rights groups won important concessions in dozens of U.S. states, including the right to restitution, the right to speak at sentencing and to present victim impact statements, the right to knowledge about their cases and the release of offenders, and certain privacy rights. Such legislation was important to restorative justice as it provided legitimacy for the use of agreements between victims and offenders as to restitution and other amends. It also opened the door for the further use of victim–offender meetings in some states and municipalities where such meetings had been barred due to lack of victim standing or due process concerns.

The reemergence of indigenous justice practices in the 1980s, particularly in Canada and New Zealand, stemmed from the growing antipathy of native communities toward colonial and racist criminal justice policies, and the belief that such policies, however reformed, could not meet the needs of people whose history of justice was decidedly more communitarian than that of Western legal systems. The adopting of Family Group Conferencing (FGC) in New Zealand in the late 1980s, for example, was predicated in part on the problem of the overrepresentation of Maori youth in the juvenile justice system. While FGCs were not explicitly Maori, they were nevertheless seen as a step toward addressing Maori criticisms of individuated justice in New Zealand's justice system—a system contrary to social and cultural histories where families stood alongside offenders and were participants in decisions as to proper redress or recompense, and were expected to help see these through.

Throughout the 1990s, diverse approaches to restorative justice grew markedly in the United States, Canada, Europe, Australia, and New Zealand. During this same decade, restorative justice arguably moved from a peripheral approach to a more dominant one as it was recognized, researched, and in some cases, supported increasingly within, rather than outside, of formal justice organizations. By the end of the 1990s, some 19 U.S. states had adopted legislation authorizing its use, and over half of U.S. states had incorporated restorative justice into program plans for youth or adult justice practices.

Restorative Justice Interventions

While there is considerable debate within the literature regarding how big the restorative justice tent should be in terms of programs and interventions, there are nevertheless some fairly agreed-upon premises shared between advocates and practitioners. Victims must be given an opportunity to voice the effects of crime in their lives, directly to offenders if they wish, but also to the court and justice systems that may be involved. When an organization, program, or intervention lacks this component—even where it may have other possible benefits for victims, offenders, and community members—it is generally seen as not adhering to basic restorative justice principles. Victims and offenders are not equal parties in this sense, and the deliberate intent to include victims within the criminal justice process, and to make victims' needs a primary focus of restorative interventions, is the most fundamental difference between this approach and civil uses of mediation or conflict resolution.

Offenders must not only admit guilt, but are also required to be accountable for harms they have caused. Ideally, accountability means a face-to-face meeting with the victim or victims, but it also may include restitution or other types of service with or without a face-to-face meeting. Such actions help to restore harms caused to victims, as well as potentially reintegrate the offender back into the community. This stems from the premise within restorative justice that the needs of victims, not the needs of justice systems, should be primarily addressed through such interventions, and that the process of restoring harms should allow for concrete means by which the offender can return, figuratively or literally, back into his or her community.

Community members are often asked to participate in restorative practices in order to give support to the victim, to help offenders understand the importance of making amends, and to actively engage in the construction of local justice expectations and policies. Community members may also be asked to participate in cases with no identifiable victims, or where the crime affects the community in an immediate sense. Arguably, where the roles of victims and offenders are clearer, the roles of community members are more ambiguous. Some types of interventions explicitly include community members or representatives; others do not. Some municipalities use community accountability or community restorative boards, comprised of community volunteers. While restorative justice literature is virtually unanimous on the importance of including community members, the means by which specific programs or interventions do so vary widely.

Victim–Offender Mediation

One commonly used practice in restorative justice is victim–offender mediation (VOM). This intervention brings together offenders, victims, and mediators with the primary goal of allowing the victim a means to explain the harms the offender has caused, to inquire into the motives of the offender, and to address further concerns the victim may have regarding personal safety. A secondary and not uncommon goal of VOM is the forging of an agreement between the victim and the offender regarding restitution and other appropriate means of redress.

VOMs are usually conducted by staff trained in mediation techniques. Some VOMs are conducted cold (i.e., without prior meeting and preparation of victims and offenders prior to mediation), although a majority of mediations involve having mediators meet at least once with both victims and offenders prior to the VOM. While the formats of such meetings vary, they often involve a basic structure, set forth in advance by the mediator, clarifying the purpose and procedure of the meeting as well as the roles of participants.

Family Group Conferencing

Family group conferencing (FGC) is another commonly used intervention, particularly in Australia and New Zealand. Unlike VOMs, FGCs regularly include family members of both offenders and victims, as well as other community representatives and even law enforcement. The inclusion of a larger number of people, where conferences can regularly reach 12 people or more, reflects indigenous practices to include family members to signify collective responsibility for the making of amends.

Aside from their larger size, another primary distinction between VOMs and FGCs is the use of facilitators or coordinators in lieu of mediators, reflecting the idea that such conferences are less between two parties than among several. The premise for this approach, most often used in juvenile cases, rests on the idea that the family of the juvenile plays an important role in ensuring that he or she understands the effects of their actions, and successfully fulfills their obligation to the court and the victim. The inclusion of family members of both the offender and victim, as well as community members and other individuals, is thought to strengthen social bonds and is seen as able to exert a less formal but more immediate and consistent form of social control than that exercised by juvenile courts and policing agencies.

Sentencing Circles

This type of intervention is most closely aligned with indigenous practices of justice, particularly in Canada and the northern United States, that stress a multi-tiered method of culpability and reintegration for the offender, and support for the victim. Unlike VOMs, sentencing circles often involve several meetings leading up to the large circle meeting that includes victims, offenders, family members, community members and leaders, prosecutors, and other vested parties. Prior to this meeting, the offender may be asked to meet with members of the circle to admit blame and explain possible means by which to restore harms. Victims usually meet with members of the circle to receive support and guidance. Finally, prior to the meeting of all parties, members of the circle meet to decide upon a sentencing plan and meeting agenda.

Community Restorative Boards

Another common restorative justice approach is the use of community restorative or accountability boards, which are comprised of community members who are often trained in restorative justice goals. Offenders appear in front of these boards as a condition of their sentence. Community boards are often used when there is no identifiable victim of a crime (i.e., drug possession) or when victims cannot participate in VOMs. Normally, community boards place less emphasis on sentencing per se, and more emphasis on deciding upon a course of action by which the offender can make amends through the setting of an agreement between the board and the offender. Although the structure and use of these boards varies, they are becoming increasingly utilized within juvenile and adult courts, where the agreement itself becomes part of the condition of diversion or probation.

Restorative Community Service

Aside from the restorative interventions discussed, more traditional interventions such as community service and restitution have also been re-oriented toward restorative justice goals within the United States, Canada, and Europe. This has not been without debate within restorative justice literature, however, and not all restorative justice advocates see such interventions as falling within the scope of restorative justice.

Those who do advocate the use of community service have argued that such an approach must be oriented around the making of amends to the community, particularly in cases where offenses may have damaged community or public property or values, and must in some way utilize these programs to bring offenders into interaction with community members. Work crews and other more traditional forms of service are thus seen as falling outside the purview of a restorative approach to service.

Pro: Arguments in Support of Restorative Justice

In the last 20 years, the corpus of empirical work on restorative approaches has grown markedly. As a result, there is a much clearer picture as to the merits of its claims and to the effects of such interventions on victims, offenders, and communities.

On the whole, this research suggests that perhaps the greatest strength of this approach lies in the localizing of justice practices in response to problems or deficits in more traditional justice practices. In the 1970s and 1980s, restorative justice approaches started in the United States and elsewhere largely as local and grassroots initiatives, which were driven less by policy or polity than by individuals and small groups seeking to meet the needs of victims, encourage offenders to make amends, and include local communities in restorative practices. The diverging shape and substance of restorative interventions were, and remain, a response to problems in peoples' immediate lives, and differences between types of restorative interventions reflect distinct social and cultural traditions and milieus.

Research on restorative justice suggests important improvement over more traditional justice practices in the areas of victim involvement and satisfaction, offender recidivism and program completion, and community involvement in justice practices. Controlled studies of victim involvement in restorative justice interventions have consistently found increased victim satisfaction in terms of participating in the outcomes of their cases, being afforded the opportunity to address offenders, and having knowledge of their rights and the justice process. Research has also found that while restorative interventions may increase the likelihood that offenders will fulfill restitution or other obligations, victims tend to find more value in the increased opportunity to participate and have a say in the outcome of their cases.

While concerns over the requisite participation of victims have been a focal point of critics, little research suggests that victims are in fact coerced into restorative interventions. Rather, the larger problem has been that of "all or none," insofar as victims have often seen participation in such interventions as their only chance to participate in their own cases. In this regard, many restorative programs have moved toward a gradated approach to victim involvement, where victims may choose to meet directly with offenders, or be involved in less direct ways such as suggesting appropriate community service or other obligations.

Offender Agreements and Recidivism

Research on offender participation in restorative justice has tended to focus on two areas, namely recidivism and offender completion of agreements. By and large, research has found moderate or negligible negative correlations in each, but it has also found few cases where restorative interventions actually increase recidivism or decrease completion. Restorative interventions, at the very least, do not encourage further offending and in fact frequently discourage it, and do so within interventions that better meet the needs of victims, communities, and offenders. Given the political and criminological emphasis on recidivism as perhaps the primary indicator of success in criminal justice programs, such findings tend to support the claim that restorative interventions may better meet the needs of these groups without jeopardizing public safety.

Offender perceptions of their own involvement in restorative practices have been less studied than offender outcomes in recidivism and completion. Existing studies suggest that while offenders by and large find their involvement meaningful, and appear to be willing to participate in programs that ask them to admit culpability and make amends, they also may feel doubly punished in restorative programs that ask them to participate in addition to other regular sanctions.

Research on community involvement in restorative practices has consistently found that both attitudes toward offenders and preferred approaches to crime control do not mirror the conventional wisdom. In programs that require offenders to work or interact with community members, community volunteerism and support has tended to overwhelm the capacity of such programs. Several studies suggest that, contrary to the practice of removing offenders (particularly nonviolent offenders) from community interactions, community members want to be involved in restorative practices and want to work with offenders. Community restorative or accountability boards have been successfully used in dozens of municipalities in the United States and elsewhere as a means of addressing less serious offenses, and arguably constitute the most concrete example of what Nils Christie has called the opportunity for "norm clarification" on the part of local communities.

Con: Arguments Against Restorative Justice

While restorative justice has gone a long way in the last three decades toward establishing empirical support and legitimacy, it is not without its critics, who have repeatedly voiced concern over its inability to structurally transform existing justice practices, and its blurring of formal and informal mechanisms of social control. Restorative justice also faces what some have called substantial fault lines within and between advocates and practitioners, particularly as it has become increasingly institutionalized within juvenile and adult justice systems.

Whose Justice?

Arguably, the most pointed problem facing restorative justice is the question of "whose justice." Critics of restorative justice have written extensively on the question of its potential to structurally counter justice practices in the United States and elsewhere that disproportionately incarcerate and punish minorities. Empirical work on the benefits to victim satisfaction, decreased recidivism, positive offender reintegration, and community involvement has been tempered by those who have pointed to the tendency of restorative justice to be used in white, middle-class communities where violent and serious crime rates are low, community cohesion is high, and substantial resources exist to support such programs. Few examples of successful restorative justice programs exist, for example, in urban ghettos that evidence both high rates of violent crime and incarceration, substantial distrust of policing and justice agencies, and few community resources. Given its history and foundations in traditions of social justice, this remains perhaps the largest problem facing restorative justice in the early 21st century.

Due Process, Fair Sentencing, and Mainstreaming

Other problems in the use of restorative justice have centered on questions of due process. Of primary concern has been the use of restorative justice as a means of coercing offenders to implicate themselves without full knowledge of their rights and the potential criminal and civil consequences of doing so. There is also concern that the increasing use of restorative justice within formal justice agencies may induce a net-widening effect. Offenders may be given the opportunity to participate in restorative justice as an alternative to being charged when, in reality, such charges would not withstand legal scrutiny.

Restorative justice also faces questions regarding fair sentencing. Critics have argued that this approach may lead to wildly different sentences for similar offenses, particularly where such programs may be used as an alternative to existing courts. Differing sentences bring to light problems of social equity, not only in terms of the expectations of all offenders, but also in terms of social inequalities that tend to punish minority and poor offenders disproportionately. In some cases as well, restorative justice agreements between victims and offenders have resulted in forms of double punishment, where offenders have been bound to victim–offender agreements on top of court-ordered sanctions they would have nevertheless received had they not chosen to participate.

The growth of restorative justice in the last two decades has also given rise to tensions and fault lines within and between advocates and practitioners. Of particular concern is the fear that as restorative justice continues to grow, it will itself become usurped or co-opted by criminal justice agencies and organizations. Mark Umbreit, the founding director of the Center for Restorative Justice and Peacemaking, has identified several potential problems related to the mainstreaming of restorative justice interventions, including: (1) the shift away from victim-driven interventions toward programs that serve the needs of justice systems, (2) cost-cutting measures that reduce or eliminate pre-mediation meetings with offenders and victims, (3) the growing focus on restitution as the sole or primary outcome of victim-offender meetings, and (4) the risk of what he calls the "McDonaldization of victim-offender mediation."

What is at stake in the internal arguments about the problems and promises of integrating restorative justice into juvenile and adult justice agencies is what one scholar has called "a dismal pattern of good intentions gone awry" in the histories of other reform or alternative-justice movements. Restorative justice in this sense is struggling with the problem of becoming a brand among many, frequently applied to justice programs and interventions that make few changes other than their label. There are no police who patrol the use of the restorative justice label, and increasingly, it has been applied to any and all sorts of interventions that remotely include victim restitution, offender job-training or rehabilitation, and community service, in ways that do not meet even the most amenable guidelines of restorative justice.

It is also facing questions of whether or not the benefits to those who participate—victims, offenders, and community members—can realistically

begin to address structural patterns of inequality that have created a bifurcated system of justice. In places where it has been used, research suggests
that it has provided marked improvement over more traditional justice interventions. Yet in other areas, its promises remain decidedly more oblique.
The relative dearth of such programs in inner cities or impoverished areas is
one example, but another is the place of serious violent crime and the trauma
that accompanies such victimization. It may very well be that restorative
justice is able to transform, as Howard Zehr suggests, normative principles
for a vast number of crimes, and this unto itself would be remarkable. But
criminological research long ago identified the link between social marginality and heightened patterns of violent offending and victimization—patterns
that drive both the prison industrial complex and cycles of victimization.
Until it begins to make inroads into these patterns, restorative justice is likely
to be regarded as a reform movement, perhaps much needed, but also (as
many reform movements) limited to transformation within certain social and
cultural regions, and not the transformation of them.

See Also: 12. Mandatory Sentencing; 14. Plea Bargaining; 20. Victim
Rights and Restitution.

Further Readings

Bazemore, Gordon, and Mark Umbreit. *Conferences, Circles, Boards,
    and Mediations: Restorative Justice and Citizen Involvement in the
    Response to Youth Crime.* Washington, DC: Office of Juvenile Justice
    and Delinquency Prevention, and St. Paul, MN: Center for Restorative
    Justice and Mediation, University of Minnesota, 1999.
Braithwaite, John. *Crime, Shame and Reintegration.* Cambridge:
    Cambridge University Press, 1989.
Christie, Nils. "Conflict as Property." *British Journal of Criminology*, v.17
    (1977).
Office of Juvenile Justice and Delinquency Prevention, and Gordon
    Bazemore. *Balanced and Restorative Justice for Juveniles: A Framework
    for Juvenile Justice in the 21st Century.* Washington, DC: Office of
    Juvenile Justice and Delinquency Prevention, 1997.
Raye, Barbara. "How Do Culture, Class and Gender Affect the Practice of
    Restorative Justice? (Part 2)." In *Critical Issues in Restorative Justice,*

edited by H. Zehr and B. Toews. Monsey, NY: Criminal Justice Press, 2004.

Umbreit, Mark. *Victim Meets Offender: The Impact of Restorative Justice and Mediation (Evaluation of Four Programs in the United States).* Monsey, NY: Criminal Justice Press, 1994.

Van Ness, Daniel, and Karen H. Strong. *Restoring Justice.* Cincinnati, OH: Anderson Publishing, 2002.

Zehr, Howard. *Changing Lenses: A New Focus for Crime and Justice.* Scottdale, PA: Herald Press, 1990.

17

Sentencing Disparities

Christine Martin
University of Illinois at Chicago

D isparity and discrimination in sentencing is often used interchangeably. A definition of disparity is that it is a difference in treatment or outcome that does not necessarily involve discrimination. However, there is no question that racial disparity exists in sentencing. For example, a 2004 report on felony sentences in state courts by the U.S. Bureau of Justice Statistics (BJS) indicated that offenders convicted of a felony were most likely to receive incarceration sentences.

Men accounted for 82 percent of those convicted of a felony and whites, who made up 82 percent of the adult U.S. population, comprised only 59 percent of felony convictions. In contrast, African Americans, who were only 12 percent of the U.S. population, comprised 38 percent of felony convictions. A 1998 U.S. Department of Justice study of federal convictions reported that the mean prison sentence for African American offenders (91.1 months) was substantially higher than the mean sentences for whites (48.9 months) or Hispanics (48.9 months), and this trend is similar in state courts.

These statistics illustrate the disparity in sentencing that is reflected in the racial disproportion of convictions and sentence lengths for African Americans compared with non-African Americans. After decades of research conducted on the subject of racial and ethnic disparity in sentencing, there are still conflicting findings concerning this disparity. Some researchers have found that African Americans are treated more leniently than whites. Some have found that African Americans are treated more harshly, while others have found that there is no substantial race effect on sentencing outcomes. An added complexity to the issue of sentencing disparity is the role that ethnicity plays independent of race.

Inconsistencies in the Research

There have been diverse reactions from researchers to the inconsistency of findings concerning racial disparity in sentencing (RDS). Some researchers pinpoint the variables used to test the existence of RDS as the source of the inconsistent findings, while others identify flaws in the methodology as the reason for inconsistent findings. Still others suggest that the theoretical premise of the investigation of RDS is inadequate. Inconsistencies in RDS findings have spanned decades, but the bottom line is that racial disparity in sentencing still exists, and conflicting explanations as to why disparity exists still remain.

Methodological Flaws in Sentencing Research

Because of the number of research studies published on race and punishment, certain flaws in past methodology have been discovered and should be dealt with when investigating RDS. Three examples of these kinds of methodological limitations in past research on this topic include the problem of selecting a sample that is too small, selecting a sample in a biased way, and omitting important variables from the research design.

The problem of selecting a sample that is too small to support the investigation of RDS typically occurs with samples that are drawn from populations that are largely homogeneous, with limited variation in the types of cases available in the population. For example, samples of homicide cases from single jurisdictions, such as a single city or county, often have a too-small number of cases with the necessary racial or ethnic characteristics to support the investigation of RDS.

For example, a sample selected in research conducted in Philadelphia in 1976 on the death penalty was too small to investigate the relationship between the victim and offenders' race on death sentencing decisions because there were not enough cases with African American victims and white offenders.

The problem of selecting a sample that is collected in a biased way is typically an issue when the sample is selected from a pool of cases that are in the later stages of criminal justice processing such as at conviction or sentencing, as opposed to at arrest or arraignment. Selecting cases from convicted or sentenced offender populations may conceal racial or ethnic disparity that might have occurred earlier at the arrest stage or pretrial stages of the case. As a result, RDS findings may not demonstrate the way that race or ethnicity impacts earlier decisions in case processing, such as how race or ethnicity impacts how severely a defendant is charged, which in turn may play a part at sentencing.

The problem of omitting relevant variables from the research design is dependent on the availability of data, which often cannot be helped. However, there are a few key variables that are important for investigating RDS that were largely missing from the earliest research on the topic. These variables include the victim's race, mitigating or aggravating factors, legal circumstances, and offender and victim ethnicity.

One final concern regarding methodological issues in RDS research is the use of jail and prison sentences as a single measurement of incarceration. Researchers have suggested that combining jail and prison sentences into a total incarceration category is problematic because the two types of sentences are qualitatively different, and combining them can lead to different conclusions as to what influences sentencing decisions.

Variables Used in Sentencing Research

In most of the very early research on racial disparity in the criminal justice system, the offender's race was the only variable used to investigate disparity or discrimination. Recent studies have shown that racial inequality in sentencing is largely influenced by the victim's race as well, and that a combination of the two is imperative to the understanding of disparity in criminal justice outcomes, including sentencing.

Other important factors that have been missing from early RDS research are the mitigating, aggravating, and legal circumstances surrounding the incident. In Illinois, mitigating and aggravating factors are taken into account at the sentencing stage in homicide cases, after the verdict or finding of guilt has been established, once the defendant has been convicted of first-degree murder, and when the death penalty is considered. The sentencing phase is completely separate from the conviction phase, which establishes guilt or no guilt. Aggravating factors, which include such things as the murdered individual being a police officer or a prison guard, and mitigating factors, which include such things as the defendant not having any prior criminal history, are taken into account in the courtroom and should be considered when investigating RDS.

The defendant's prior conviction record is a particularly important legal variable that should be accounted for in sentencing research, because it may indicate that racial disparity in sentencing is based on the criminality of the offender instead of racial or ethnic discrimination. For example, if one group of offenders is more likely to have serious prior convictions than others, they may receive harsher sentences than the others as a result; therefore, sentencing decisions would then be as much, if not more, a matter of prior record then of disparate sentencing decisions.

Theoretical Premises of Sentencing Disparity

Two fundamental theoretical premises that seem evident in the research on RDS are the black criminality argument and the discrimination argument. The discrimination argument suggests that racial discrimination is at the root of sentencing disparity, and that race has a direct and/or indirect relationship with sentencing outcomes.

The black criminality argument suggests that blacks are more criminal than anyone else, and that legitimate legal factors such as prior convictions are at the root of the disparity. Some researchers suggest that social class plays a major role in the racial disparity of sentencing. They believe that class, not just race, makes much of the difference. For example, one researcher suggested that racial disparity stems from more severe punishment of certain types of crimes that are committed by people with lower social status, such as street crimes, which are committed disproportionately by African Americans. Crimes such as white-collar crimes, which are committed more by whites, who have higher social status, are punished less severely. Thus, racial disparity from this perspective is a socioeconomic or class issue. In sum, some researchers consider class, not race, to be at the heart of sentence disparity; others believe that African Americans are simply more criminal than non-African Americans; and still others believe that racial discrimination is the root cause of sentence disparity.

More contemporary theories used to help explain RDS place attention on court workers' decision making during case processing. One theory in particular, referred to as focal concern theory, suggests that court workers, including judges, base decisions on three concerns: blameworthiness, protection of the community, and practical constraints and consequences. Blameworthiness is associated with the defendant's culpability and the guarantee that punishment fits the crime. The concern for community protection, which is visible in the emphasis on incapacitation and deterrence, considers the offender's future behavior in terms of dangerousness and recidivism to be of primary importance. Practical constraints and consequences are concerns about cost to the criminal justice system, disruption of the offender's societal ties to his or her family, and the impact of offender recidivism on the workgroups' public status. Because these focal concerns are influenced by the defendant's position in the social structure, disparate treatment based on racial or ethnic status may occur.

In addition to these focal concerns, the working conditions experienced by courtroom actors, including time constraints, workload, and resource issues, and an overload of pre-sentence information with sparse definitive information about the background and character of the defendant, generates an atmosphere of ambiguity and uncertainty for making satisfactory decisions. These constraints and uncertainty cause court workers to adopt a perceptual shorthand for decision making. This shorthand makes the most of attributes about the case and the defendant's characteristics, such as race and ethnicity. Once established, this phenomenon becomes a patterned way of thinking that is resistant to change. Through this process, disparity in outcomes for some racial and ethnic groups materialize. Judges often characterize nonwhite defendants as more dangerous and culpable than white defendants, and some scholars have illustrated that judges rely on stereotypes of nonwhite defendants to assess blameworthiness in lieu of a gap in available information about them.

As a result, judges and other courtroom decision makers will likely impose harsher sentences on African American and Latino defendants than on whites, because they are perceived as being more dangerous, more likely to recidivate, and less likely to be deterred. Focal concern theory was developed to explain the decision-making behavior of judges in the sentencing stages of case processing.

Ethnicity and Disparity in Sentencing

In 2009, the U.S. Census Bureau counted 48.4 million Hispanics, or 15 percent of the U.S. population; since 2002, Hispanics have been the largest minority group in the United States. RDS researchers have identified a gap in research that integrates ethnicity with race in criminological investigations. There has historically been a lack of reliable measures of ethnicity in governmental data on crime and punishment. The race categorization for Hispanic victims and offenders in the Federal Bureau of Investigation (FBI) database and other official sources of criminal data are designated as black, white, or other.

There is an important and independent role that ethnicity plays in sentencing outcomes that has been demonstrated through research. Some scholars have shown that to properly identify black–white differences in sentencing outcomes, it is required that ethnic groups be included in the analysis. In one study where Latinos were compared with whites and blacks, the outcomes were not the same as when their numbers were included in these groups. When Latino subjects were combined with whites into one large, white race group, which is often the case in race and ethnicity data, the differences in outcomes between blacks and whites were cancelled out or reversed.

Contemporary research has shown that case-processing outcomes for Latinos have a different pattern than that for African Americans or whites. Outcomes for Latinos vary based on contextual factors such as their geographic location or the type of offense they are charged with. Researchers have perceived the nuances inherent in studying ethnic and immigrant groups that pose a different set of problems than when studying race groups in the United States. For example, while populations of race groups are widespread across the United States and more easily aggregated for national-level investigations, populations of immigrant and ethnic groups are often limited to certain regions of the country, and their experiences with the criminal justice system vary from one location to the next. Despite the importance of studying ethnic differences in sentencing outcomes, and despite recent progress made toward that end, studies examining racial and ethnic differences in outcomes continue to be rare.

Disparities in Sentencing and Sentencing Guidelines

One systemic issue that is tied to RDS comes from sentencing reform that emerged during the Reagan administration of the 1980s in response to increased punitive enforcement mediated by a war on crime and drugs. Vast increases in arrests and imprisonment of nonwhite, street-level drug dealers and a continuous movement toward harsher penalties and incarceration characterized this war on crime and drugs. The tenets of the campaign were enforced through policy that included mandatory sentencing; three-strikes laws; and an overall sentencing-reform movement, one component of which included sentencing guidelines.

A principal goal in the creation of sentencing guidelines was to increase uniformity in sentencing by restricting the discretion of judges and requiring that sentences be based primarily on characteristics of the offense and the offender's prior record. Reformers also sought to eliminate unwarranted disparities and institutionalize principles of just deserts and deterrence as the basis for criminal sentencing. A study was conducted using homicide sentences to determine how effective sentencing guidelines were in deterring RDS.

In 1993 The BJS conducted a study that provided evidence that African American homicide offenders received longer sentences than their non-African American counterparts, even after the implementation of sentencing guidelines that were designed to help alleviate racial disparity.

In 1980, guidelines governing how defendants should be sentenced had been implemented by only one state: Minnesota. By 1996, nine states had changed their sentencing structure from the traditional, indeterminate sentencing structure to the presumptive or determinate sentencing structure currently being adopted in federal and state courts throughout the country.

Determinate sentencing is a response to criticisms aimed at traditional sentencing practices or indeterminate sentencing, which gave considerable discretion to judges. It is designed to provide uniform sentencing that is in proportion with the offense and to eliminate racial, ethnic, and gender bias in sentencing. This was accomplished by creating a legislative sentencing commission, which predetermined the terms of imprisonment, probation, and mandatory supervised release previsions for every crime classification.

The BJS study measured racial disparity in homicide sentencing before and after the implementation of determinate sentencing guidelines in three states, including Illinois. Even though the average length of a prison sentence for each racial group decreased by at least 30 percent under sentencing guidelines, racial disparity in the length of prison sentences remained. The average prison sentence for African Americans pre- and post-sentencing guidelines was still longer than that for whites or Latinos.

Research conducted in 1990 examined racial bias in capital sentencing and provided evidence that racial inequality exists in the punishment of homicide. Research findings from two periods were reviewed: those using data before the U.S. death penalty ban in 1972, and those using data from cases after the death penalty was reestablished in 1976. There were two consistent conclusions drawn from these research studies regardless of the period, which is that racial discrimination continues to exist in capital sentencing outcomes, and that this discrimination is greatly impacted by the race of the victim.

After attempting to control for bias in homicide sentencing through sentencing guidelines, bias still remained against African Americans. In addition, empirical research on capital cases, which are homicide cases that end in death penalty sentences, also reveal that African American offenders are discriminated against when it comes to sentencing.

RDS and the War on Drugs

The most obvious culprit of the existence of RDS is not based on research findings, theory, or approaches to studying RDS, but is established in the practical administration of public policy. The War on Drugs, which has been fought primarily in minority communities, is rooted in politics and increased punitive enforcement of crack cocaine drug offenders.

In keeping with the anticrime slogans of its presidential campaign, the Reagan administration established a war on drugs and crime in the 1980s that was characterized by vast increases in arrests and imprisonment of street-level drug dealers and a continuous movement toward harsher penalties and incarceration. The tenets of the campaign were enforced through policy that included mandatory sentencing, three-strikes laws, an overall sentencing-reform movement, and a significant move toward prison construction. African Americans were disproportionately represented in drug-related punishments.

Crack Versus Powder

Findings from the National Household Survey on Drug Abuse showed that African Americans, whites, and Hispanics use drugs in roughly the same proportions as they are represented in the general population. For example, the survey revealed that in 1998, among the nation's 10 million users of illicit drugs, approximately 72 percent were white, 15 percent were African American, and 10 percent were Hispanic. These percentages were similar to the groups' percentages of the U.S. population. In 2000, 69 percent of the population was white, 12 percent were African American, and 12 percent were Hispanic. The disproportion in punishment of African American drug offenders had to do with the type of cocaine that they were using and selling, which was crack cocaine as opposed to powder cocaine.

One prevailing response of the criminal justice system to crack cocaine violations has been the establishment of harsher punishment for crack than for other forms of the same drug. African American offenders disproportionately violated drug laws prohibiting the use and selling of crack as opposed to powder cocaine. Eighty-two percent of crack cocaine defendants in 2007 were African American, compared with nine percent who were white. In contrast, 80 percent of powder cocaine defendants were white, and 14 percent were African American.

Some researchers warn that African Americans living in urban environments have borne the brunt of the War on Drugs because they have been targeted, arrested, and imprisoned in disproportionate numbers. Not only have African Americans and other nonwhites been arrested for drug offenses at a disproportionately high rate, but drug offenders in these racial and ethnic groups have also been sentenced more harshly than white drug offenders. There is ample evidence to support the argument that the War on Drugs has been fought primarily in minority communities. Since 1976, the number of persons arrested for drug offenses has more than doubled; the number of whites arrested for drug offenses increased by 85 percent, while the number of blacks arrested for these offenses increased fourfold. The proportion of all black drug arrestees also increased, from 22 percent in 1976 to 39 percent in 1994. These racial differentials in arrest rates are reflected in prison populations. Between 1986 and 1991, the proportions of blacks and whites in state and federal prisons reversed, from 53 percent white and 46 percent black to 53 percent black and 46 percent white. This reversal in a short period of time has been attributed to the War on Drugs.

Disparity in sentencing of crack cocaine offenders compared with powder cocaine offenders is a reflection of the disparity in punishment for these two kinds of offenses. Federal penalties for suppliers and users of crack cocaine were more severe than comparable powder cocaine offenses. Under federal law, the punishment for one gram of crack cocaine equated to the same punishment for 100 grams of powder cocaine. This unequal punishment of crack versus powder cocaine resulted in African American drug violators receiving average sentence lengths that were 40 percent longer than the average prison sentence for whites.

The U.S. Supreme Court has recently boosted judges' discretion to impose more lenient criminal sentences, including shorter terms for crack cocaine offenses. This ruling is part of a recent trend toward giving judges greater leeway in setting prison time, which loosens the restrictions placed on their discretion by the sentencing guidelines established in the 1980s. Crack cocaine offenders are being retroactively released from prison and continue to be studied and managed by the criminal justice system through funded reentry research and going-home projects. These studies and projects are aimed at helping ex-offenders successfully integrate back into the community.

In this new turn of events, the court emphasized the lack of grounds for the disparate treatment of crack and powder cocaine offenders, but did not change basic criminal laws that treat crack and powder cocaine crimes differently. The 100-to-1 difference was narrowed in November 2007 to a crack:powder cocaine ratio that varied, depending on the offense, from 25:1 to 80:1. The narrower ratios, applied retroactively, will result in the early release of 19,500 inmates over the next 30 years.

Pro: Positive Outcomes of Racial Disparity Research

One major benefit associated with the topic of RDS is the diligence of social scientists in their attempts to establish the cause and cure for this disparity. Much has been discovered concerning this topic, especially in the ways that researchers should conduct these investigations. The methodological flaws accounted for in modern research on the topic are imperative to understanding RDS, and if included in research and theories that have been developed, may help explain and enhance the understanding of the existence of RDS. In addition, sentencing guidelines were established to help eliminate RDS, and now research is being conducted to determine if that purpose has been realized.

A benefit to offenders who are affected by RDS is the recent move by the criminal justice system to rectify RDS, particularly for drug offenders. Crack cocaine offenders are punished more harshly than both powder cocaine and methamphetamine offenders. However, this trend is now being partly corrected.

The federal government has freed the first of thousands of federal inmates convicted on crack cocaine charges based on these amended U.S. Sentencing Commission guidelines that retroactively reduced their sentences. Of the 19,500 offenders eligible nationwide for reductions in sentences, 1,944 are in federal prisons in Virginia; and in Illinois, there are 997 prisoners eligible for release.

Con: Negative Outcomes of Racial Disparity Research

RDS continues to be a problem in the United States; in particular, racial disparity in sentencing continues to exist for African Americans, even after post-sentencing guidelines. In addition, adverse effects of the punitive approach to dealing with drug offenders, particularly crack cocaine offenders, are currently unfolding. Reentry and recidivism are activities that go hand-in-hand when describing these ex-offenders. Mandatory sentences for crack offenders have been served, and record numbers of prisoners are reentering their communities. These ex-offenders, their families, and their communities did not benefit from prevention or rehabilitation programs.

Enough time has passed to witness the full results of the criminal justice system's response to crack violations and get-tough policies developed in the 1980s. The punitive decisions for harsher penalties and increased incarceration are now being undone, but only after the prisoners have served their time. Many have written and warned about the adverse effects that these get-tough policies would have and have had on the prisoners' children, families, communities, and their futures. Prisoners are now being released back into the population, which has become a new issue for the criminal justice system.

See Also: 4. Drug Laws; 12. Mandatory Sentencing; 9. Three-Strikes Laws.

Further Reading

Chambliss, William J. *Power, Politics, and Crime.* Boulder, CO: Westview, 2001.

Chilton, Roland, and Wendy C. Regoeczi. "Impact of Employment, Family Structure, and Income on NIBRS Offense, Victim, Offender, and Arrest Rates." *Justice Research and Policy,* v.9/2 (Fall 2007).

Demuth, Stephen, and Darrell Steffensmeier. "Ethnicity Effects on Sentence Outcomes in Large Urban Courts: Comparisons among White, Black, and Hispanic Defendants." *Social Science Quarterly,* v.85/4 (2004).

Durose, Matthew R., and Patrick A. Langan. "Felony Sentences in State Courts, 2004." *Bureau of Justice Statistics Bulletin* (July 2007).

Engen, Rodney L., and Sara Steen. "The Power to Punish: Discretion and Sentencing Reform in the War on Drugs." *American Journal of Sociology,* v.105/5 (March 2005).

Martin, Christine. "Crack, Powder Cocaine, and Meth: The Criminal Justice System's Response to Drug Violations." *Law Enforcement Executive Forum,* v.8/5 (2008).

Martinez, Ramiro, Jr. "Moving Beyond Black and White Violence: African American, Hatian, and Latino Homicides in Miami." In *Violent Crime: Assessing Race and Ethnic Differences*, edited by Darnell F. Hawkins. New York: Cambridge University Press. 2003.

McDonald, Douglas C., and Kenneth E. Carlson. *Sentencing in the Federal Courts: Does Race Matter? The Transition to Sentencing Guidelines.* Washington, DC: U.S. Department of Justice, Office of Justice Programs, Bureau of Justice Statistics, 2003.

Reiman, Jeffrey H. *The Rich Get Richer and the Poor Get Prison: Ideology, Class, and Criminal Justice.* Boston: Pearson/Allyn and Bacon, 2007.

Spohn, Cassia C. "Thirty Years of Sentencing Reform: The Quest for a Racially Neutral Sentencing Process." *Criminal Justice 2000: Policies, Processes, and Decisions of the Criminal Justice System.* U.S. Department of Justice Office of Justice Programs. 2000.

Steffensmeier, Darrell, and Stephen Demuth. "Ethnicity and Judges' Sentencing Decisions: Hispanic-Black-White Comparisons." *Criminology,* v.39/1 (2001).

18

Sex Offender Registry

Mary K. Evans
University of Nebraska at Omaha

Public interest in controlling violent offenders has been a focus of society and lawmakers throughout American history. Specifically, over the past 25 years, the citizens of the United States have voiced an adamant desire to monitor and control convicted sex offenders living in the community. This desire for control has been largely driven by extensive media coverage of previously convicted sex offenders committing horrific crimes against children. The kidnappings, rapes, and murders of children like Jacob Wetterling, Polly Klaas, and Megan Kanka represent a few of the highly publicized incidents that fueled public outrage, advocacy, and much of the legislation that manages the sex offender population today.

Specifically, the most profound piece of legislation that exists today requires convicted sex offenders to register their personal information with law enforcement so it can be placed on a sex-offender registry. Sex-offender registration, and the practice of community notification, is intended to facilitate police investigations and increase the publics' ability to protect itself by warning potential victims if a convicted sex offender lives in the neighborhood. It has been roughly 25 years since contemporary sex-offender legislation came into existence; therefore, it is an appropriate time to examine the history, evolution, and current state of such legislation; present relevant constitutional challenges; and finally, review the pros and cons of such legislation to date.

The History of Sex Offender Legislation

Sex-offender registration laws are thought to be new and innovative policy reforms that address the behavior of sex offenders, but in actuality, registration laws are simply old polices that have been rewritten to meet the challenges of today. For instance, in 1937, Florida became the first state to enact a criminal registration statute that required offenders of all types, including sex offenders, to register their addresses with law enforcement agencies upon criminal convictions in an effort to prevent reoffending. Ten years later, California enacted the nation's first statewide sex-offender registration law, requiring sex offenders to register their whereabouts with police. Shortly after, Arizona passed its own sex-offender registration law; while Alabama, Ohio, and Nevada all enacted sex-offender registration laws between 1957 and 1967. Very little is known about the application of these early registration laws or the degree to which they affected criminal behavior. Despite this lack of information, states returned to the concept of sex-offender registration after a number of violent offenses occurred that involved child victims.

In 1989, Earl Shriner drew national media attention for sexually assaulting a seven-year-old Seattle boy, mutilating his genitals, and leaving him for dead. Shriner had formerly been institutionalized for murder in the 1960s and convicted of child molestation in 1977, 1987, and 1988. The repetitive nature of Shriner's crimes influenced the passage of Washington's Community Protection Act (1990), a comprehensive piece of legislation that required convicted sex offenders to register their personal information with law enforcement upon reentering the community in an effort to promote public safety against sexual predators. Washington's legislation is referred to as the first contemporary attempt to register sex offenders' whereabouts so they can be monitored years after they have completed their sentence.

A crime was also committed against 11-year-old Jacob Wetterling in 1989. Jacob was abducted near his home in Minnesota by an armed, masked stranger as he was playing outside with his brother and friend. To date, Wetterling has not been found. This case resembled that of another boy in a neighboring town who was abducted and sexually attacked earlier that year. Although it is not known who abducted Wetterling, many thought it could have been one of the many parolees living in a local halfway residential facility that housed convicted sex offenders. Although Jacob's abduction drew much attention to the repetitiveness of sex-offender behavior, it was the homicides of Polly Klaas and Megan Kanka that brought this issue to the forefront of the national policy agenda.

In 1993, the media widely disseminated the story of Polly Klaas, a 12-year-old girl who was abducted from her bedroom in California, sexually assaulted, and killed. She was found to have been murdered by a convicted sex offender who was living in the community. One year later, the media reported that seven-year-old Megan Kanka was missing from her New Jersey home. Megan was later found sexually assaulted and murdered. Jesse Timmendequas, a twice-convicted sex offender, was also convicted in her murder. Public outrage resulted when investigators learned that Timmendequas lived across the street from Megan with two other convicted sex offenders. Advocates on behalf of Megan questioned how convicted sex offenders could live anonymously in a neighborhood filled with families and children. As a result, the family agonized over the question of whether Megan would be alive today if they knew Timmendequas lived across the street from their home.

As both girls were both found to have been murdered by convicted sex offenders who had been released from prison and were living in the community, their parents actively lobbied state and federal legislators for remedies to address the repetitive nature of sex-offender behavior. The results of their efforts have produced much of the federal and state sex-offender policies that exist today.

Contemporary Sex Offender Registry Legislation

Wetterling Act and Megan's Law

In 1994, the federal Jacob Wetterling Crimes Against Children and Sexually Violent Offender Registration Act mandated that 10 percent of a state's funding under the Edward Byrne Memorial State and Local Law Enforcement Assistance grant program be used for establishing a statewide system for registering and tracking convicted sex offenders. The act also "strongly encouraged" states to collect DNA samples from registered sex offenders, which would be typed and stored in databases, and used to clear crimes. States quickly began complying with the Wetterling Act by requiring blood samples and registry information from only those sex offenders convicted of violent sex acts against children. As a result of the Kanka homicide, New Jersey adopted similar legislation, entitled Megan's Law, which was passed in 1994 with the belief that parents should have the right to know if a dangerous sexual predator moves into their neighborhood. The initial Wetterling Act was amended to include a federal version of Megan's Law in 1996, and required states to make relevant information on released sex offenders available to the general public.

Inconsistent Procedures, Specific Types of Information

Every state has created and/or expanded their registry to include persons convicted of violent or nonviolent sex crimes, regardless of their victims' ages. This federal legislation, however, did not provide detailed instructions to states concerning how to fulfill registration and community notification requirements. As a result, states differed in their implementation of Megan's Law, producing inconsistent practices and enforcement between states. Generally speaking, state registration notification can be divided into three categories: broad community notification, notification to those at risk, and passive notification. States have chosen to release sex-offender registry information in a number of ways. For example, some state statutes mandate proactive notification, others merely authorize it, while others permit notification only in response to community requests. Community notification of sex-offender registry information can include, but is not limited to, print media reports in newspapers, neighborhood flyers, email notification, phone calls, door-to-door campaigns, community meetings, and/or state-sponsored Websites.

Despite the lack of federal guidance on how notification procedures should occur, the legislation was exact in addressing the types of information gathered by law enforcement agencies. Specifically, sex offenders are required to provide a photograph and register their addresses, offenses, and other relevant information, such as their telephone numbers, social security numbers, employment information, and fingerprints to local authorities when they move into a new jurisdiction. States do not release all registration information to the public. Photos and addresses are always provided to the public, but social security numbers of registered sex offenders are not.

Sex Offender Levels

Finally, although all sex offenders are required to register with law enforcement, not all sex offenders are subject to the practice of community notification. Some states, like Iowa, notify community members of all registered sex offenders despite their crime or likelihood to reoffend. Other states, like Nebraska, use a tier-based system that classifies sex offenders based on the risk they pose to the community, and only notifies community members of those most likely to reoffend: Level III sex offenders.

The tier-based system utilizes specific levels to differentiate sex offenders' risk to the community. Level I offenders are assessed at minimal risk to the community. Information obtained on Level I offenders is only available to law enforcement to aid in monitoring and investigations of registered sex offenders. Level II sex offenders are those who have been assessed to pose a moderate risk to the community. Notification goes beyond law enforcement to include specific entities where children are likely to congregate. Specific entities can include, but are not limited to, schools, daycares, churches, or other neighborhood organizations. Finally, Level III offenders are considered to pose the greatest threat to society. Registration information regarding Level III sex offenders is provided to the general public in order for them to take precautions to minimize victimization.

Updated Legislation

An additional amendment to the Wetterling Act included the Pam Lychner Sexual Offender Tracking and Identification Act (1996). This amendment was considered to be the first step toward creating a national registration system to facilitate the tracking of registrants from state to state by the FBI and state law enforcement agencies. Other sex offender registration policies that have been enacted over the past 10 years include the Campus Sex Crimes Act (2000), which requires registered sex offenders to provide law enforcement with information on schools they have attended, are attending, or are employed. More recently, the Prosecutorial Remedies and Other Tools to end the Exploitation of Children Today Act of 2003, also known as the PROTECT Act, was created in an effort to prevent the abduction of children and to eliminate sexual exploitation of children by sexual predators. The PROTECT Act allowed for new investigative tools to both law enforcement and prosecutors in the management and monitoring of sexual predators; mandated the practice of Internet-based community notification in all states; and created the national AMBER Alert Program, which helps locate abducted individuals.

Recently, however, the Wetterling Act and its amendments were replaced with a more comprehensive and uniform piece of federal legislation. In 2006, President George W. Bush signed the Adam Walsh Child Protection and Safety Act (AWA), which amended the Wetterling Act of 1994 and Megan's Law of 1996. The new law expands previous federal sex-offender policies by imposing mandatory minimum penalties for those who sexually exploit children. The Sex Offender Registration and Notification Act (SORNA), a provision of the AWA, specifically deals with the registration of sex offenders. The purpose of the SORNA is to establish and maintain a nationwide network of sex-offender registries and notification procedures in an attempt to inform the public and thereby prevent victimizations. SORNA is thought to build on existing state law in a number of ways. First, it expands states' jurisdictions to federally recognize and register sex offenders on Native American reservations. It also increases penalties and expands the types of crimes for which registration is required. Additionally, the AWA normalizes the requirements for registration nationwide, in terms of duration and accuracy of information. The law requires that sex offenders provide more extensive personal registration information to be publicly released, and requires sex offenders to frequently verify registration information. If registered sex offenders do not comply with the new registration requirements, they will be charged with a felony.

The Tier System

SORNA is different from previous legislation in that it standardizes registration and community notification practices for all states. The tier system used under SORNA does not classify offenders based on individualized assessments of risk for reoffending, but rather by the type of crime for which offenders are convicted. Under this conviction-based approach, all persons required to register are subject to community notification regardless of assessed risk to the community. The new standardized levels classify the tier under which a sex offender must register, from least to most serious:

Tier 1: Sex offenders other than Tier II or Tier III (required to register for a period of 15 years).

Tier 2: Sex offenders other than Tier III with an offense punishable by imprisonment for more than one year and comparable to or more severe than the following federal offenses involving a minor: sex trafficking, coercion and enticement, transportation with intent to engage in criminal sexual activity, and abusive sexual conduct. Also included are any offenses involving the use of a minor in a sexual performance, solicitation of a minor to practice prostitution, or production or distribution of child pornography (required to register for a period of 25 years).

Tier 3: Sex offenses punishable by imprisonment for more than one year and comparable to or more severe than the following federal offenses: sexual abuse or aggravated sexual abuse, abusive sexual contact against a minor less than 13 years old, offenses involving kidnapping of a minor (parent or guardian excepted), or any offense that occurs after one has been designated a Tier II sex offender (required to register for life).

Although all tiers proscribe a mandatory duration for registration, these durations can be mitigated. If Tier 1 sex offenders maintain what the act refers to as a "clean record" for 10 years, there is a five-year reduction of registration time. Tier 2 sex offenders do not get a reduction and must register for a fixed period of 25 years, whereas Tier 3 sex offenders must register for life, with no exceptions. Furthermore, the tiers determine the time intervals in which registration information must be verified with law enforcement. Tier 1 sex offenders must verify information with law enforcement once a year, those in Tier 2 every six months, whereas those in Tier 3 must verify information every three months.

Under SORNA, every state must include the following information for every offender in their registry: a physical description of the sex offender; the convicted offense; the criminal history of the offender, including dates of arrests and convictions and correctional or release status; a current photograph; fingerprints and palm prints; a DNA sample; a photocopy of a valid driver's license or identification card; and any other information required by the attorney general. Further, the Walsh Act mandates juvenile registration (i.e., juveniles above the age of 14). Some states, such as Illinois, have long required the registration of juveniles, so the AWA simply creates uniformity nationwide. In sum, the SORNA provision in the AWA standardizes the ways in which states have previously responded to the Wetterling Act and Megan's Law of the 1990s. This standardization can be seen in the ways in which sex offenders are defined, when sex offenders must register upon convictions, the types of information states must gather about released sex offenders, and the types of punishments for offenders upon failure to comply. Finally, the AWA requires each jurisdiction in the United States to provide registry information to the public via the Dru Sjodin National Sex Offender Public Website.

Through the above provisions, SORNA theoretically will decrease victimization rates and increase public safety through much-improved monitoring and tracking techniques for registered sex offenders. SORNA attempts to close gaps and potential loopholes in past sex offender legislation by holding sex offenders accountable for updating registration information. This means increased penalties for violating registration requirements and requiring the registration of both adult offenders and juveniles over 14 years of age. Only juveniles who are adjudicated delinquent for offenses equivalent to rape or attempted rape are required to register. Juveniles who are adjudicated delinquent for lesser sexual assaults or nonviolent sexual contact are not required to register. By July 27, 2010, all states were expected to implement SORNA requirements or risk losing state funding.

The Legality of Sex Offender Legislation

Constitutional challenges to sex-offender registration statues included allegations that they violate the Ex Post Facto Clause and the due process guarantees provided by the U.S. Constitution. Ex post facto, meaning "from a thing done afterward," is prohibited by Article I of the Constitution. Generally, this clause prohibits making conduct criminal retrospectively. A law is considered ex post facto if there are changes in punishment and/or it inflicts a greater punishment than the law stated when the initial crime was committed. Sex offenders who were found guilty of an offense before the specific registration statute was passed argued that mandated registration and community notification should not apply to them because it violates the Ex Post Facto Clause.

Similarly, the Fourteenth Amendment to the U.S. Constitution guarantees that states shall not deprive citizens of life, liberty, or property without due process of the law. Due process includes both substantive due process and procedural due process. Sex-offender registration and community notification laws have been challenged on both of these grounds. Generally, substantive due process guarantees that individual rights and liberties cannot be taken away without proper justification. Sex-offender registration laws have been challenged on the grounds they are unjustified intrusions of the offender's rights to privacy, liberty, and anonymity. Sex offenders argue that public notification of their personal information as required by registration and community notification statutes are unjustified intrusions. Likewise, procedural due process monitors the legal process that is due to individuals before their rights can be infringed. A balancing act must be accomplished between an individual's interest and the state's interest of protecting the public. Sex offenders have used this line of reasoning to argue that sex-offender registration and community notification results in a substantial loss of liberty due to the stigmatizing label of being a registered sex offender. Additionally, sex offenders argue that the state's interest is not sufficient to justify this deprivation with providing proper procedural protections (i.e., a hearing, notice, and assistance of counsel) before implementing statute requirements upon an individual.

Two Cases of Constitutional Challenge

Although these constitutional issues were raised as early as 1994, it was not until 2003 that the Supreme Court heard two significant cases challenging the above-mentioned constitutional issues surrounding sex-offender registries and community notification.

In *Connecticut Dept. of Public Safety v. Doe* (2003), John Doe filed suit against the state of Connecticut claiming that the state's sex-offender registry law violated his procedural due process guaranteed under the Fourteenth Amendment. In particular, John Doe argued that he was entitled to a hearing on his current dangerousness before being subject to the law's registration requirements. He also claimed that the law violated the Ex Post Facto Clause of the U.S. Constitution. Lower courts granted John Doe's motion on the due process claim, but rejected the ex post facto claim. The state of Connecticut then appealed the procedural due process affirmation to the Supreme Court. The state of Connecticut argued that John Doe failed to show that he had been deprived of a liberty that necessitated due process protection. John Doe claimed that the act of registration and community notification damaged his reputation unfairly. The Court did not favor John Doe's claim, and instead rejected his claim that it violated his right to procedural due process.

Another significant constitutional challenge to sex-offender registration laws was in *Smith v. Doe* (2003). On May 12, 1994, Alaska enacted the Alaska Sex Offender Registration Act, which contains two retroactive components: a registration requirement and community notification system requiring all convicted sex offenders in the state to comply. The law also requires the offender to give personal information (e.g., name, aliases, addresses, photographs, physical description, place of employment, and date of birth) to the state in order to carry our proper community notification. If the offender does not comply with such requirements, the state is legally able to seek criminal prosecution. It was argued that Alaska did not have a mandatory sex-offender registration and community notification requirement at the time of the offender's release from prison—before the law was enacted. Lower courts agreed, indicating that the act violated the Ex Post Facto Clause because its effects were punitive despite the legislature's stated intent to the contrary. However, the Supreme Court held that because the Alaska State Sex Offender Registration Act is civil and nonpunitive, its retroactive application does not violate the Ex Post Facto Clause because the clause is only applied to criminal proceedings. Both court cases were victories for advocates of sex-offender registration and community notification laws in the United States.

Pro: Arguments in Support of Sex-Offender Registration

Advocates for sex-offender legislation and registration often refer to the tragic victimizations of the past to reaffirm the necessity of registration laws to protect the most vulnerable populations, especially children. Specifically, proponents of sex-offender registration policies maintain that the public has the right to know about serious potential risk to its safety and the safety of its children. These policies face widespread support among citizens throughout the United States. They argue that parents should know if convicted sex offenders are living in their neighborhood so they can then take preventative measures against victimization and warn their children about particular people in their neighborhood. Additionally, proponents argue that law enforcement should be given every tool necessary to investigate crimes. Sex-offender registries offer police a ready list of suspects should a sex crime occur in the neighborhood in which a registered offender lives.

Additionally, proponents argue for registration policies, as current laws that punish sexual offenders are not punitive enough and allow for sex offenders to reenter society to reoffend. Theoretically, registering sex offenders and monitoring their whereabouts inhibits their opportunities of offending, particularly those who are deemed most at risk to reoffend. Proponents feel that such laws put sex offenders on notice while also providing a sense of security for citizens. By registering sex offenders, it limits the opportunity to operate in secrecy or be in occupations in which they interact with children (such as Boy Scout leader, daycare provider, or teacher). In other words, the laws provide an external control measure and may be an obstacle the sex offender must overcome in order to reoffend.

Advocates also contend that sex offender registration can serve as an internal control measure for the sex offender. Simply having to register may show the sex offender that he must be responsible for his own actions. In turn, this may lead the sex offender to obtain treatment within the community and allows the offender to be open and honest about his crimes. At the same time, there are advocates who claim sex offenders are likely to reoffend and that treatment is not the solution, as treatment does not always work. They contend that some sex offenders have a compulsion to offend and are simply incapable of self-control. There is an assumption among proponents of sex-offender legislation that sex offenders are likely to recidivate. These advocates propose lengthier sentences and increased monitoring of sex offenders other than simple registration. To that end, advocates of sex-offender registration policies feel that if the law can prevent just one act of sexual violence from occurring, it is worth the effort.

Con: Arguments Against Sex Offender Registration

Critics of sex offender registration policies do not make light of sexual victimization. Instead, critics argue that sex-offender registration policies seem intuitively correct, but are in fact based on mistaken assumptions. On the surface, sex-offender registration policies are intended to provide closer supervision of sex offenders and deter future instances of sexual victimization; however, critics argue that registration policies provide a false sense of security, produce numerous unintended ramifications, and do not reduce instances of victimization. In fact, some argue that sex-offender policies may, in fact, increase instances of victimization.

Sex-offender registration policies were enacted to prevent the horrific crimes that inspired such legislation. Critics point out that while these were highly publicized crimes, they were committed by offenders not known to their victims. A report conducted by the U.S. Bureau of Justice Statistics indicates that only 14 percent of all sexual assault cases reported to law enforcement agencies involve offenders who were strangers to the victim. In other words, registration laws may do very little to protect children from the serious risk of sexual violence that occurs in the home or by acquaintances. Similarly, if a citizen examines the local registry to find that no sex offenders live in their neighborhood, they may assume they are safe. Likewise, the registry information for those offenders who have absconded will not be accurate. Critics point out that sex-offender registries only notify the public of convicted offenders, or those who have come into contact with law enforcement. The reality is that sex offenders may live in the neighborhood but are not known to local law enforcement because they have never been caught. Critics also argue that that registration laws will do little to deter future sex offenses; crime will be displaced to areas where the identity of the sex offender is unknown. A willing sex offender will simply drive farther from home to commit a crime. As a result, critics urge that the empirical realities of sexual victimization need to be shared with the public, so that registry information does not provide them with a false sense of security.

Additionally, critics often mention the numerous unintended consequences of sex offender legislation. For example, critics cite that sex offender registration and the extension of community notification creates a "scarlet letter" for sex offenders living in the community. There is a stigma attached to being publicly identified as a sex offender. Critics are concerned about this public label and associated stressors sex offenders face upon reentering the community. For example, being a registered sex offender may limit opportunities to acquire housing or a job. There are many accounts of registered sex offenders in America who are unable to secure housing and they end up homeless; thus, they are registered, but with no locatable address. Likewise, obtaining an adequate job is difficult for many registered sex offenders, as they often are rejected because of their criminal status. Additionally, sex offenders often find themselves socially isolated, which may prove detrimental. Social ties to the community are essential, critics argue, for any offender who reenters the community after incarceration.

Vigilante attacks are also a concern for critics of sex-offender registration policies. There have been numerous crimes committed against registered sex offenders that range from minor harassment to murder. Additionally, family members of registered sex offenders have also faced vigilante attacks simply because they are related to a sex offender. These stressors inhibit a successful transition back into the community and can increase a sex offender's likelihood to reoffend—the opposite intent of the legislation. Many critics understand that sex-offender legislation will not vanish; however, they urge reforming existing policies to reduce the possibility of unintended consequences.

A number of empirical examinations have indicated that registration and community notification laws are limited in their ability to reduce incidents of sexual victimizations. One recent empirical examination conducted by researchers for the state of New Jersey, the birthplace of Megan's Law, has concluded that the sex-offender registration policies in their state have failed to reduce recidivism rates of registered sex offenders. The results of these studies indicate that, although well intended, such laws have done little, if anything, to increase public safety.

❖

See Also: Mandatory Sentencing; Three-Strikes Laws.

Further Readings

Adam Walsh Child Protections and Safety Act of 2006, *Public Law* No. 109-248. 64.

Campus Sex Crimes Prevention Act. *Public Law* No. 106-386, Division B, Title VI, section 1601 d_, 114 Stat. (2000).

Connecticut Dept. of Public Safety v. Doe, 538 U.S. 1 (2003).

Department of Justice. *Federal Register: The National Guidelines for the Sex Offender Registration and Notification.* Washington, DC: Department of Justice, July 2008.

Finn, Peter. *Sex Offender Community Notification.* Washington, DC: National Institute of Justice, 1997.

Greenfeld, Lawrence. "Sex Offenses and Offenders: An Analysis of Data On Rape and Sexual Assault." Bureau of Justice Statistics. (February 1997). http://www.ojp.usdoj.gov/bjs/pub/pdf/soo.pdf (Accessed December 15, 2009).

Human Rights Watch. *No Easy Answers: Sex Offender Laws in the U.S.* New York: Human Rights Watch, 2007.

Jacob Wetterling Crimes Against Children and Sexually Violent Offender Registration Act. *Public Law* No. 103-322 (1994).

Jenkins, Phillip. *Moral Panic: Changing Concepts of the Child Molester in Modern America.* New Haven, CT: Yale University Press, 1998.

Megan's Law, Pub. L. No. 104-145. 110 Stat. 1345 (1996).

Pam Lychner Sexual Offender Tracking and Identification Act of 1995. Public Law No. 104-236, 110 Stat. 3093-94 (1996).

Prosecutorial Remedies and Other Tools to End the Exploitation of Children Today Act. Public Law No. 108-21 117 STAT. 650 (2003).

Smith v. Doe, 538 U.S. 84 (2003).

Terry, Karen. *Sexual Offenses and Offenders: Theory, Practice, and Policy.* Belmont, CA: Wadsworth, 2006.

Terry, Karen, and J. Furlong. *Sex Offender Registration and Community Notification: A "Megan's Law" Sourcebook.* Kingston, NJ: Civic Research Institute, 2008.

Wright, Richard. *Sex Offender Laws: Failed Policies, New Directions.* New York: Springer, 2009.

19

Three-Strikes Laws

Jennifer N. Grimes
Indiana State University

Few criminal justice policies evoke more debate and discussion than the enhanced sentencing provisions commonly referred to as "three strikes and you're out" laws. These laws have become a point of contention for criminal justice practitioners, researchers, activists, and attorneys concerning the justice and injustice of these sentence enhancements. The three-strikes sentencing policies, which became popular in the United States in the mid-1990s, enhance the punishment for repeat offenders by triggering a mandatory prison sentence for those individuals who have been previously convicted of a serious or violent felony; the sentence is significantly higher for repeat offenders versus first-time offenders committing the same act. From 1993 to 1995, 24 states and the federal government passed three-strikes provisions in response to the perceived increase in violent crime in the United States, although whether violent crime had actually been increasing during this time has been called into question. Habitual offender laws were not new to the American criminal justice system, and many states already had provisions in place increasing the punishment for repeat offenders. Despite this, politicians and lobbyists still opted to introduce new three-strikes laws in connection with the popular slogan to their state legislatures. The purpose of these laws was to increase the length of time that dangerous offenders such as rapists and murderers spent in prison for a third felony. The provisions of the three-strikes laws vary from state to state, with California's version of the law providing the harshest penalty for repeat offenders, regardless of whether or not the third felony was violent or serious.

The motivation for the adoption of three-strikes laws as a crime control measure centered on two philosophies of effective crime reduction: (1) incapacitation and (2) specific and general deterrence. Proponents of three-strikes laws argued that the extended sentences guaranteed to repeat offenders would increase public safety by removing chronic offenders from communities for much longer periods of time—sometimes for life. The three-strikes laws were also expected to fulfill the goal of specific deterrence by reminding offenders who already had previous offenses on their record that there would be serious repercussions for committing an additional felony.

It was also expected that the lengthy sentences handed down to chronic offenders would result in general deterrence by illustrating to those with or without existing criminal records the extent of what the criminal justice system response would entail upon commission of repeated criminal activity. The three-strikes crime control policies reflect the tough-on-crime rhetoric espoused by politicians and promoted by the mass media's emphasis on violent crime during the mid-1990s. While nearly half of the states passed three-strikes provisions during this time period, with the exception of California, the laws were mostly symbolic and not applied with any regularity. Since the adoption of these laws, many legal and ethical debates have been introduced regarding the ethics, fairness, and constitutionality of these laws.

The History and Development of Three-Strikes Laws

The first use of the three-strikes slogan as a crime control policy in a major American media outlet appeared in the *Seattle Times* on May 25, 1992. It would be almost one year before another article concerning three-strikes laws would be published in the *Seattle Times*. That article discussed the support that Initiative 593, the Three Strikes and You're Out proposal, was receiving from the National Rifle Association and other lobbying groups. After public debate regarding the problems associated with the adoption of this legislation, including the costs associated with increased and extended incarceration and the danger that the law may be applied toward nonviolent offenders, the first three-strikes law in the United States was passed by Washington voters in November 1993.

The Klaas Murder

Supporters of a three-strikes bill in California were unsuccessful in gaining support for a similar enhanced-sentencing initiative in 1993. Mike Reynolds, a wedding photographer from Fresno, spoke with Governor Pete Wilson in 1992 about sponsoring a three-strikes bill in California after the murder of his 18-year-old daughter Kimber by repeat offenders the previous year. At the time, there was little support or enthusiasm for the initiative, and Wilson said it was unlikely that the laws would change. Reynolds then approached his assemblyman, Bill Jones, but Jones was not optimistic that he could get the measure through the Democratic-controlled assembly. Jones enlisted the assistance of Democrat Jim Costa, but in April 1993, the measure didn't even make it out of committee. The possibility of the adoption of a three-strikes law in California seemed to have been defeated.

The political and social climate changed, however, after the 1993 kidnapping and murder of 12-year-old Polly Klaas. Reynolds and other three-strikes supporters were able to capitalize on the public outrage that resulted from the Klaas murder and channel it toward support for the three-strikes initiative in California. Klaas's killer—a habitual, violent offender out on parole at the time of the crime—served as the perfect symbol for the type of predator the public had to fear if the three-strikes initiative was not passed.

The Klaas kidnapping and murder was picked up by national media outlets, and the details of the crime played out repeatedly for audiences nationwide: a young girl, in the midst of a slumber party with friends, was kidnapped at knifepoint from her own bedroom. The kidnapping occurred on October 1, but Klaas's whereabouts remained unknown for over two months—during which time a steady stream of local and national news coverage reiterated the public's worst fear: Americans are not safe from crime, even in their own homes. Actress Winona Ryder brought additional attention to the case, offering a $200,000 reward for information leading to Klaas's whereabouts. Klaas's community mobilized in the search for the missing girl, and her case received continued nationwide media attention.

In December, a suspect was taken into custody—Richard Allen Davis, a 39-year-old repeat offender who had spent most of his life in prison. Much emphasis in the subsequent media coverage of the Klaas case focused on the fact that the suspect was a habitual offender. Davis provided a tip regarding the location of Klaas's body, and her remains were found on December 5, over 60 days after she disappeared. He was later convicted of her kidnapping and murder.

Californians quickly mobilized and adopted their own three-strikes provision in 1994. Proposition 184, an initiative entitled Three Strikes and You're Out, was enthusiastically embraced by California voters, even though the California legislature had already adopted the same law earlier that year. California, however, passed a more punitive version of the three-strikes law than Washington state, in that California's law only required that the first two convictions involve a strikeable offense (in California, this included most felony offenses and some drug offenses); any third felony conviction could result in a third strike and a sentence of 25 years to life. A later attempt to soften the impact of California's existing version of the three-strikes law by requiring the third felony to be a violent or dangerous crime was defeated by a narrow margin in 2004 following a heated media campaign. Further attempts by activist groups to bring another initiative to the California legislature to amend California's three-strikes laws did not garner enough signatures to introduce the bill to the California legislature.

The Legality of Three-Strikes Laws

Several challenges have been raised as to the constitutionality of three-strikes laws in general, but the most persistent criticisms have been directed at the law as it is written and enforced in California. The main argument concerning California's three-strikes law centers on the issue of whether an enhanced sentence of 25 years to life in prison for an act that would otherwise not garner such a punitive response from the criminal justice system is a violation of the U.S. Constitution's Eighth Amendment protection from "cruel and unusual punishment." Two cases were argued simultaneously before the U.S. Supreme Court on November 5, 2002, regarding the constitutionality of California's three-strikes provision: *Ewing v. California* and *Lockyer v. Andrade*. In both cases, the defendants had prior criminal histories that made them eligible for the three-strikes sentence enhancement, but their strikeable offenses were for nonviolent acts that many argued did not warrant a criminal sentence of 25 years to life. In the case of *Ewing v. California*, Gary Ewing was convicted of stealing three golf clubs worth just over $400 from a golf pro shop in El Segundo, California. Ewing was convicted of felony grand theft for the crime, although under California law, the prosecutor and trial judge had the discretion to charge Ewing with a lesser offense. The trial judge in the Ewing case denied Ewing's request to reduce the charge to a misdemeanor, and he was subsequently convicted and sentenced to 25 years in prison.

In the case of *Lockyer v. Andrade*, Bill Lockyer was convicted of stealing five videotapes from a K-Mart department store in Ontario, California. The prosecution decided to charge Andrade with two counts of petty theft with a prior conviction, making him eligible for the three-strikes sentence enhancement. Andrade's request to have the two petty theft charges classified as misdemeanors was denied by the trial court, and because under the California law any felony can qualify as a third strike, Andrade's conviction of two felony theft charges for the stolen videotapes made him eligible for sentencing under the three-strikes law. Andrade subsequently received two, consecutive 25-year prison sentences for the stolen videotapes, which were reportedly worth about $150. The defendants' legal argument in both the *Ewing* and *Lockyer* cases centered on the issue of proportionality in the punishment that was afforded in both convictions relative to the committing offense, thereby arguing that California's three-strikes law violated the Eighth Amendment.

On March 5, 2003, the Supreme Court delivered its decision in both the *Ewing* and *Lockyer* cases. In a 5–4 decision, the Court upheld both sentences and rejected the argument that California's three-strikes law was a violation of the Eighth Amendment protection against cruel and unusual punishment. In the *Ewing* case, Justice Sandra Day O'Connor delivered the majority opinion, stating, "Though three-strikes laws may be relatively new, our tradition of deferring to state legislatures in making and implementing such important policy decisions is longstanding." Justices Antonin Scalia and Clarence Thomas authored concurring opinions because they rejected the notion that the proportionality principle of the Eighth Amendment was intended to address the length of sentences; they argued that the issue of proportionality was only meant to address the types of punishments those convicted of crimes could receive, not the length of the sentence itself. The majority decision in the *Lockyer* case concluded that federal precedents failed to set a clear standard as to violations of the principle of proportionality. In addition, Lockyear's sentence still retained the possibility of parole, albeit remote.

Pro: Arguments in Support of Three-Strikes Laws

The primary impetus for the three-strikes laws is to keep dangerous and violent offenders in prison for much longer periods of time than previous sentencing schemes permitted—in some cases, for life. The basic premise is that by incarcerating offenders with extended prison sentences that offer little or no chance for parole, public safety is increased due to the incapacitation of individuals who are proven habitual offenders and/or a direct threat to public safety. The laws are a solution to the criticisms leveraged against the criminal justice system that prisons have become a "revolving door" for many offenders, and that even offenders who pose a substantial threat to the public are released after short prison terms due to plea bargains and liberal sentences. The empirical research on the crime reduction effects of the three-strikes laws has been mixed, with some research indicating that the laws have been effective in reducing crime, while other studies finding the data to be inconclusive or not fulfilling the crime reduction effect the laws were created to produce. Proponents of the law argue that regardless of the mixed empirical research, the sentence enhancements enable the criminal justice system to remove individuals who have proven to be unwilling or unable to refrain from law-violating behavior from the rest of a law-abiding society.

The Deterrent Effect

Another argument in support of three-strikes sentence enhancements involves the deterrent effect of these laws. Supporters argue that there should be no greater deterrent for an offender who is considering committing another crime than the knowledge that the criminal justice response to a new offense will be severe. Three-strikes laws trigger mandatory minimum sentences for habitual offenders; therefore, it is presumed that those with existing criminal records who have already demonstrated a disregard for the law—and who are likely to consider committing additional crimes—will be deterred from such actions. Proponents of these sentence enhancements also argue that offenders who are released from prison are well aware of the other prisoners who are serving long or life sentences because of three-strikes laws, and therefore many of these offenders will be deterred from recidivating. In other words, an offender's awareness of fellow prisoners who are serving long prison sentences under this enhanced sentencing scheme provides its own deterrent effect; offenders know they will also be aging behind bars if they commit a new offense that qualifies under a three-strikes sentencing provision.

Three-strikes laws also serve the purpose of incapacitating dangerous and repeat offenders who should have received longer sentences for previous offenses. While the media has critically portrayed rare or extreme cases of persons being sentenced under the three-strikes provision for seemingly minor crimes such as stealing videos, a piece of pizza, or a beer from a convenience store, the fact is that all offenders sentenced under these laws are chronic, habitual offenders who have committed serious crimes at one time in their criminal career. In addition, rapists, child predators, murderers, and other dangerous and/or violent offenders are finally removed from society due to three-strikes laws. A review of the offenses committed by persons sentenced under these enhanced sentencing schemes reveals that most of these offenders have been convicted of a serious or violent crime at some time in their criminal careers. The fact that the committing offense is not necessarily a violent one does not negate the fact that the law is working to incapacitate habitual offenders who have little or no regard for the law.

The three-strikes laws are also liberal in that in order to qualify for the enhanced sentencing, an offender must have three separate convictions, not just three different offenses. This means that offenders who previously had lesser charges dropped or were able to plea bargain their way to a lesser sentence are still slipping through the cracks of the criminal justice system and are not subject to sentencing under the three-strikes laws. In addition, most offenders have committed more offenses than those for which they were actually convicted; therefore, those who qualify for the enhanced sentences are still likely to have committed many more offenses than their official criminal record demonstrates. The notion that these laws unfairly target offenders for petty crimes misses the point that those sentenced under the three-strikes provision have multiple convictions and have likely committed many more offenses than the criminal justice system's official record reflects.

Finally, three-strikes laws remove much of the discretion from judges and prosecutors and require them to prosecute and incarcerate habitual offenders for longer periods of time. Judges who would have previously handed down light sentences will find their ability to do so further reduced, thus increasing public safety by ensuring that chronic offenders are removed from society. Judges take many extraneous factors into consideration when handing down sentences, such as the capacity of correctional institutions or the costs associated with lengthy incarceration. Three-strikes laws minimize these considerations by ensuring that judges are bound by the requirements that are triggered by these enhanced sentencing schemes. Proponents of these laws argue that the cost to incarcerate an offender or the burden this places on a state's criminal justice system should not be a consideration when public safety should be the top concern.

Con: Arguments Against Three-Strikes Laws

One of the concerns regarding the exceedingly long punishments afforded to criminals under these enhanced sentencing schemes is that three-strikes laws offer no incentive for offenders to rehabilitate while behind bars. Although the primary goal of the American penal system has shifted from rehabilitation to incapacitation, rehabilitation still plays a role in corrections. Offenders who are sentenced to exceedingly long minimum sentences with only a remote chance for parole have no motivation to take advantage of any of the rehabilitative services offered in correctional institutions. There is also no motivation for good behavior or otherwise controlling one's actions within the prison setting, thus increasing the dangerousness of the prison for both other prisoners and the correctional staff. The same danger can be said for law enforcement officers who are faced with an offender on the street who knows he or she is facing a mandatory three-strikes sentence. These excessively long sentences, often for nonviolent offenses, are likely to result in a sense of hopelessness among those convicted of or facing conviction under the three-strikes law, thus increasing the likelihood of dangerous or volatile confrontations with criminal justice professionals.

Burdensome Costs and Racial Disparities

Another criticism of three-strikes involves the staggering costs associated with incarcerating offenders for such extensive periods of time. The financial burden of three-strikes laws extends to the need to build new prisons and hire additional staff to supervise the increasing prison population. In addition to the cost per prisoner that a state faces for such an extensive, mandated prison sentence, healthcare for the aging prison population is another cost that must now be absorbed by the state. States are responsible for the health and welfare of the prisoners in their custody, and this responsibility extends to the aging and sick population as well. The astronomical costs associated with incarcerating three-strikes offenders is not limited to the incapacitation of young and healthy individuals who only require correctional supervision; the number of offenders aging behind bars and requiring extensive medical care is now compounding the costs associated with three-strikes laws, particularly in California. The fact that California spends more money on incarceration than on education has rightly garnered much criticism and concern.

Three-strikes laws are also unfair because they serve to exacerbate pre-existing racial disparities in the criminal justice system and, particularly, in the incarceration rate of minorities. The criminal justice system has long been recognized as having a disproportionate amount of contact with minorities, so the fact that three-strikes laws incorporate past convictions into the current sentencing scheme results in enhanced sentences for minorities who are convicted of strikeable offenses. For example, African Americans and Hispanics are disproportionately represented in the California penal system compared to their rate in the general population, and this disparity is also seen in other states. Whether the increased involvement in the criminal justice system is due to more crime being committed by minorities or bias in the criminal justice system may be open to debate, but three-strikes laws result in an increasing number of minorities being sentenced under these enhanced sentencing schemes. The result is increased devastation in already disorganized and disenfranchised minority communities.

Finally, critics address the disproportionality of this sentencing scheme. While the Supreme Court may have upheld the constitutionality of these habitual offender laws, this does not mean that the laws are fair or ethical. The incarceration of offenders for 25 years to life for nonviolent offenses, which on their own would have only merited a short time in jail or perhaps even probation for a first-time offender, is argued to be grossly unfair. Some offenders, especially those who committed multiple crimes in early adulthood when they were less mature, are subject to these enhanced sentences regardless of the severity of the third offense. Other offenders may be committing petty crimes due to extraneous social factors such as poverty or drug addiction.

Petty thefts such as the infamous case in which an offender's theft of one piece of pizza triggered a three-strikes sentence represent the disproportionality that supporters of these laws apparently did not anticipate. These laws were created to target violent offenders who pose a threat to public safety, not as a tool for long-term incarceration of every offender who commits repeated, but petty, crimes. The public was convinced of the need for these laws to protect them from violent offenders who were slipping through the criminal justice system under existing sentencing provisions. These laws would never have received such overwhelming public support if people had understood how many nonviolent offenders were going to be caught in the snare of these laws.

❖

See Also: 12. Mandatory Sentencing; 14. Plea Bargaining; 17. Sentencing Disparities; 18. Sex Offender Registry.

Further Readings

Applegate, Brandon K., Francis T. Cullen, Michael G. Turner, and Jody L. Sundt. "Assessing Public Support for Three-Strikes-and-You're-Out Laws: Global versus Specific Attitudes." *Crime and Delinquency,* v.42 (1996).

Austin, James, John Clark, Patricia Hardyman, and Henry D. Alan. "The Impact of 'Three Strikes and You're Out.'" *Punishment and Society: The International Journal of Penology,* v.1/2 (1999).

Austin, James, P. Clark, and D. A. Henry. "The Impact of Three Strikes and You're Out." *Punishment and Society,* v.1 (1999).

Beckett, K., and T. Sasson. *The Politics of Injustice: Crime and Punishment in America.* Thousand Oaks, CA: Pine Forge Press, 2000.

Benekos, P. J., and A. V. Merlo. "Three Strikes and You're Out! The Political Sentencing Game." *Federal Probation,* v.59 (1995).

Beres, Linda S., and Thomas D. Griffith. "Did 'Three Strikes' Cause the Recent Drop in California Crime? An Analysis of the California Attorney General's Report." *Loyola of Los Angeles Law Review,* v.32 (1998).

Beres, Linda S., and Thomas D. Griffith. "Do Three-Strikes Laws Make Sense? Habitual Offender Statutes and Criminal Incapacitation." *Georgetown Law Journal,* v.87 (1998).

Clark, J., J. Austin, and D. A. Henry. "'Three Strikes and You're Out': A Review of State Legislation." Washington, DC: National Institute of Justice, 1997.

Currie, Elliot. *Crime and Punishment in America.* New York: Henry Holt and Company, Inc, 1998.

Domanick, Joe. *Cruel Justice: Three Strikes and the Politics of Crime in America's Golden State.* Berkeley, CA: University of California Press, 2004.

Dyer, Joel. *The Perpetual Prisoner Machine.* Boulder: Westview Press, 2000.

Greenberg, David F. "Striking Out in Democracy." *Punishment and Society,* v.4 (2002).

Greenwood, Peter W., et al. *Three Strikes and You're Out: Estimated Benefits and Costs of California's New Mandatory-Sentencing Law.* Santa Monica: RAND, 1994.

Harris, J. C., and P. Jesilow. "It's Not the Old Ball Game: Three Strikes and the Courtroom Workgroup." *Justice Quarterly,* v.17 (2000).

Janiskee, Brian P., and Edward J. Erler. "Crime, Punishment and Romero: An Analysis of the Case Against California's Three Strikes Law." *Duquesne University Law Review,* v.39 (2000).

Johnson, Jeffry L., and Michelle A. Saint-Germain. "Officer Down: Implications of Three Strikes for Public Safety." *Criminal Justice Policy Review,* v.16 (2005).

Jones, William. "Why Three Strikes Is Working in California." *Stanford Law and Policy Review,* v.11 (1999).

King, Ryan, and Marc Mauer. *Aging Behind Bars: Three Strikes Seven Years Later.*Washington, DC: The Sentencing Project, 2001.

Kovandzic, Tomislav V., John J. Solan III, and Lynne M. Vieraitis. "'Striking Out' as Crime Reduction Policy: The Impact of 'Three Strikes' Laws on Crime Rates in U.S. Cities." *Justice Quarterly,* v.21 (2004).

LaFree, Gary. "Too Much Democracy or Too Much Crime? Lessons from California's Three-Strikes Law." *Law and Social Inquiry,* v.27 (2001, 2002).

Lungren, Dan. "Three Cheers for Three Strikes." *Hoover Institution Policy Review* (1996).

Males, Mike, and Dan Macallair. "Striking Out: The Failure of Calfiornia's 'Three Strikes and You're Out' Law." *Stanford Law and Policy Review,* v.65/11 (1999).

Marvell, T., and C. Moody. "The Lethal Effects of Three-Strikes Laws." *Journal of Legal Studies,* v.30 (2001).

Mauer, Marc. *Race to Incarcerate.* New York: The New Press, 1999.

Merritt, Nancy, Terry Fain, and Susan Turner. "Oregon's Get Tough Sentencing Reform: A Lesson in Justice System Adaptation." *Criminology and Public Policy,* v.5 (2006).

Moody, Carlisle, Thomas B. Marvell, and Robert J. Kaminski. "Unintended Consequences: Three-Strikes Laws and the Murders of Police Officers." Unpublished manuscript, 2002.

Reynolds, Mike, Bill Jones, and Dan Evans. *Three Strikes and You're Out: A Promise to Kimber: The Chronicle of America's Toughest Anti-Crime Law.* Fresno, CA: Quill Driver Books/World Dancer Press, 1996.

Ricciardulli, Alex. "The Broken Safety Valve: Judicial Discretion's Failure to Ameliorate Punishment Under California's Three Strikes Law." *Duquesne Law Review,* v.41 (2002).

Schafer, J. "The Deterrent Effect of Three Strikes Law." *FBI Law Enforcement Bulletin,* v.68/4 (1999).

Schmertmann, Carl P., Amankwaa Adansi, and Robert D. Long. "Three Strikes and You're Out: Demographic Analysis of Mandatory Prison Sentencing." *Demography,* v.35/4 (1998).

Schultz, D. "No Joy in Mudville Tonight: The Impact of 'Three Strike' Laws on State and Federal Corrections Policy, Resources and Crime Control." *Cornell Journal of Law and Public Policy*, v.9 (2000).

Shepherd, Joanna M. "Fear of the First Strike: The Full Deterrent Effect of California's Two-and Three-Strikes Legislation." *Journal of Legal Studies*, v.31 (2002).

Shichor, David, and Dale K. Sechrest. *Three Strikes and You're Out: Vengeance as Public Policy*. Edited by David Shichor and Dale K. Sechrest. Thousand Oaks, CA: Sage, 1996.

Stolzenberg, Lisa, and Stewart J. D'Alessio. "Three Strikes and You're Out: The Impact of California's New Mandatory Sentencing Law on Serious Crime Rates." *Crime and Delinquency*, v.43 (1997).

Turner, Susan, Peter Greenwood, E. Chen, and T. Fain. "The Impact of Truth-in-Sentencing and Three Strikes Legislation: Prison Populations, States' Budgets and Crime Rates." *Stanford Law and Policy Review*, v.11 (1999).

Tyler, Tom R., and Robert J. Boeckmann. "Three Strikes and You Are Out, but Why? The Psychology of Public Support for Punishing Rule Breakers." *Law and Society Review*, v.31 (1997).

Vitiello, Michael. "Three Strikes: Can We Return to Rationality?" *Journal of Criminal Law and Criminology*, v.87 (1997).

White, Ahmed A. "The Juridical Structure of Habitual Offender Laws and the Jurisprudence of Authoritarian Social Control." *The University of Toledo Law Review*, v.37/3 (Spring 2006).

Worrall, John L. "The Effect of Three-Strikes Legislation on Serious Crime in California." *Journal of Criminal Justice*, v.32 (2004).

Zimring, Franklin E., Gordon Hawkins, and Sam Kamin. *Punishment and Democracy: Three Strikes and You're Out in California*. New York: Oxford University Press, 2001.

20

Victim Rights and Restitution

Wendelin M. Hume
University of North Dakota

In the United States the crime victims' movement started primarily at the grassroots level in the early 1960s, in conjunction with movements for both women and civil rights. In the beginning of the victim's movement, the main goals were to make society aware that crime victims exist, they may need help to overcome the trauma they experienced, and they need humane treatment in the hands of the criminal justice system. Changes began at the grassroots level with efforts such as separate court waiting rooms for victims, as well as various states instituting compensation and restitution initiatives for crime victims, beginning with California in 1965 and ending with Maine in 1992. Services offered to victims vary greatly from state to state, and there has been no standardized set of victims' rights, but rather a developing set of guidelines for the proper handling of victims. Over 32,000 statutes have been passed in the different states that define and protect the rights of crime victims. Some states, like California in 1982, have even passed state legislation that includes a victims' bill of rights. The federal government began paying attention to victims after the grassroots movement gathered strength, as demonstrated with the designation of a National Victims of Crime Week in 1981 and the establishment of the Presidential Task Force on Victims of Crime in 1982. Also in 1982, the federal government passed the Omnibus Victim and Witness Protection Act, and in 1984, it passed the Federal Victims of Crime Act.

As the crime victims' movement progressed, two new goals were established: to enhance victim participation within the criminal justice system, and to establish a set of victim's rights. While the federal government did pass a Victim's Rights and Restitution Act in 1990, there are still many questions about how many reforms should take place in the criminal justice system to enhance its service to victims without compromising the belief that the justice system should be neutral, and that it exists to serve society over the needs or desires of a single victim. One of the most controversial topics is the balancing of criminal victims' and criminal defendants' rights. One of the central debates is whether justice should be "blind," as symbolized by the figure of Lady Justice holding evenly balanced scales and a sword while blindfolded, which is how the system operates currently; or if the system should be impassioned with concern for those who have been injured at the hands of another, which would require the implementation of victims' rights and victim restitution programs.

Victim Rights Overview

While the term *rights* can have various definitions, when it comes to victims' rights, it is usually a power granted by law that entitles a victim to require another person, usually a criminal justice official such as a police officer or judge, to perform a specific act or to refrain from performing a specific act. For instance, police officers could be required to return personal property that was used as evidence in the case as quickly as possible (perform), or requiring the judge to not remove the victim from the courtroom during the trial (refrain).

Of course, crime victims cannot exercise rights they are unaware of or do not understand. The primary concept of victims' rights is the perception that America's current legal system is more concerned with the protection of the rights of criminal offenders and alleged offenders than with protecting the victims of criminal offenses. When a person is accused of a crime, there are numerous specific rights to consider in the U.S. Constitution, such as the right to remain silent or the right to have an attorney present during questioning; yet, for the victim, there are currently no rights specifically mentioned in the Constitution. Victim advocates would like to see rights for crime victims be at least as extensive as the rights of offenders, and that victims receive proper compensation or restitution from offenders or the government.

Victim rights have typically been statutory, though at times they have actually been written into the constitution of a particular state. Currently, at least 32 states have at least some mention of victim rights in their state constitution; however, these rights are not always enforced. Typical victim rights vary, but often include the right to receive information and protection; have access to transportation for their participation in the justice process; have their property returned in a timely manner; have courthouse waiting areas separate from the defendant and others; have input into decisions being made by law enforcement investigators, prosecutors, and judges; be notified when court hearings are being held as well as when offenders are being released; and have the right to attend the court hearings and trial.

Restitution Overview

In general, restitution is the act of restoring to the rightful owner something that has been taken away or lost. Typically, in the case of crime victims, what has been taken away (such as a sense of one's own sexuality after a rape) or lost (such as flesh and blood after a knife wound) cannot be restored, and so instead must be compensated. Restitution for crime victims is typically a type of financial compensation for crime-related expenses payable to a victim from an offender who was convicted of the crime. Restitution potentially satisfies the goals of justice by compensating victims while simultaneously requiring offenders to assume financial responsibility for the consequences of their criminal behavior. Out-of-pocket expenses that are usually considered valid for restitution include medical treatment for physical injuries, the loss of or damage to property, and sometimes the costs of mental health counseling. It generally does not cover costs for pain and suffering for issues like increased level of fear, pervasive lack of trust of others, or reoccurring nightmares. Restitution is typically restricted to those who have been victims of crimes of personal violence.

There are some issues with the collection of restitution. For instance, offenders may only have enough money to pay fines or restitution, but not both, in which case poorer, smaller counties may rather collect the fine revenue than be concerned about restitution to the victim. There may be some social-class inequities in who is sentenced to pay restitution, as those with better social standing may have jail time waived so that they may work and pay restitution, whereas poor or unemployed offenders for similar offenses are sentenced to serve time. Some criminal judges may resist ordering restitution if they feel that collecting damages is something that should be taken up in civil court, not in their criminal court. Many victims never receive restitution money because the offender is not caught, convicted, and sentenced to restitution, or the offender is unable or unwilling to earn enough money to hand over meaningful payments to the victim.

Typical Victim Rights

While victim rights vary from state to state, they are often subject to discretionary decisions made by criminal justice officials, and are often not enforced. Some typical rights include the following:

Receiving Information and Notification

Victims should be notified about the status of their case. The victim should be aware of whether the case is currently under investigation, if a court hearing has been scheduled, and when and where the court hearing is going to be held. Typically, there is more than one hearing, so the victim should be informed about the progress of the case during all stages of prosecution. The victim should be informed about the status and location of the alleged or convicted offender. The victim should also be told about services available in the community or state that can help them recover from the crime and how to apply for these services.

Reasonable Protection and Separate Waiting Areas

Victims of crime may have concerns about their personal safety as well as the safety of their family and loved ones. Victim concerns about safety may develop because of a psychological panic state that arises after the trauma of victimization, or be based on implied or real threats made by the alleged or convicted offender and their colleagues. Thus, a variety of approaches can be developed to promote safety for the victim not just while participating within the criminal justice system, but also while in the community and at their home.

Victims also have the right to be free of intimidation while cooperating with law enforcement in the prosecution of their case. Therefore, secure or safe waiting areas should be provided to victims while they are attending court proceedings.

Availability of Transportation

In order to attend court proceedings and participate with other aspects of an ongoing criminal investigation, victims may be in need of transportation to get from their residence to the courthouse or other justice offices. Transportation can be provided in a squad car, for example, or transportation expenses can be reimbursed.

Participation and Attendance in the Justice Process

The vast majority of criminal cases that are carried forward in court are resolved through settlements known as plea bargains. Bargaining is a process in which the district attorney and defense council meet in private to work out a compromise without having to hold a public trial. Typically, the victim is not involved in these negotiations. If the case does not reach a negotiation and instead proceeds to trial, often the victim is not allowed to attend the trial in case they will be called as a witness, and their testimony should not be influenced by what they had witnessed previously in the courtroom. The decision to allow a victim to participate or attend is often left to the discretion of the presiding judge.

Victims may have the right to be heard at various stages of the criminal justice process, ranging from plea bargain negotiations, to sentencing, and at any parole release hearing. One way for a victim to be heard is through their written statement such as a victim impact statement, wherein the victim describes how the crime affected him or her emotionally, physically, financially, and spiritually. Victims may also be allowed to provide a written statement to the judge at sentencing, wherein they offer their opinion about an appropriate sentence. Victims may also provide a statement to the paroling authority, sharing information that they feel may be relevant in reaching a decision about an inmate's possible release. Occasionally, these statements may be made orally as well as submitted in writing.

Restitution and Return of Property

Restitution is designed to help crime victims recover the out-of-pocket expenses that result from the crime, such as the costs of medical treatment. The court can order that the offender pay restitution to the victim based on the financial losses resulting from the crime. Victims have the right to have their property that was used as evidence in a criminal case

274 Courts, Law, and Justice

to be returned as promptly as possible. While the justice system may view the pieces of property as evidence, for the victim, the items may have significant emotional or heirloom value (such as an antique vase from the victim's grandmother) or even be vital for day-to-day activities (such as an automobile). It is important to the victims, therefore, that the items be returned as soon as possible.

Victim Services and Applying for Victim Compensation

Victims may not know what services are available to help them deal with the effects of the crime. While some services in a community may be available to all victims of crime, some services are available only if the victim reports the crime to the police within a specified time frame and cooperates with the investigation and prosecution of a criminal case. Occasionally, some specialized services are available to help victims of specific types of crime, such as a shelter for domestic violence victims. Given the variation in the services, which may or may not be available to any particular victim, it can be important to provide the victim with the appropriate information and relevant referrals.

Given that the offender may not be caught, and if apprehended, may not have the financial means to provide restitution to the victim, some states have developed victim compensation programs. These programs provide financial assistance to victims of violent crimes or to survivors of homicide victims. The programs may pay for expenses such as medical care, mental health counseling, lost wages and, in cases of homicide, funeral expenses. The state may help with expenses not already covered by insurance or other sources. Such programs have specific eligibility requirements that victims must meet to qualify for the benefits. Most programs require the victims to report the crime promptly to law enforcement and cooperate in the investigation and prosecution of the case. There is also a rather detailed application and filing requirement.

Expectation of Compliance and Legal Remedies

Victims should carefully document all interactions regarding their case in a personal case file. If there are questions about their rights or their case, they should have a meaningful dialogue with the justice officials responsible for the implementation of the particular issue. If this does not result in a satisfactory response, the victim may choose to speak with the officials' supervisor.

There may be additional remedies in accordance with state law, the particular agency's policies, or other sources such as state associations. Several states such as Colorado, Wisconsin, South Carolina, Connecticut, and Alaska have formal programs and procedures to investigate and act upon complaints by crime victims who believe their legal rights have been violated.

State Legislation for Victim Rights and Restitution

Much of the movement to establish victims' rights and restitution programs can be seen in a variety of state legislation efforts. A select sampling includes the following:

1965: California establishes the first victims' compensation program
1977: Oregon enacts the first legislation mandating arrest in domestic violence cases
1980: Wisconsin passes the first bill of rights for crime victims
1982: California adopts a constitutional victim bill of rights
1986: Rhode Island's new constitution gives victims the right to restitution, to submit victim impact statements, and to be treated with dignity and respect
1993: Maine is the last state to enact a crime victim compensation program
1999: Oregon is the 32nd state to pass a constitutional amendment that guarantees victims' rights

Federal Legislation for Victim Rights and Restitution

Some of the movement to establish victims rights and restitution programs has also taken place at the federal level. While some feel that the federal government should take the lead in showing concern for victims and establishing victim rights, others feel that these decisions should be left to the states. A selection of some of the federal legislation for victim's rights and restitution includes the following:

1974: Child Abuse Prevention and Treatment Act establishes a national Center on Child Abuse and Neglect within the federal government
1981: National Victims Rights Week is proclaimed by President Reagan

1982: Task Force on Victims of Crime is appointed by President Reagan

1982: Victim Witness and Protection Act provides criminal penalties for the intimidation of crime victims, provides a crime victims' Bill of Rights, and makes the granting of victim restitution a norm in federal sentencing

1984: Victims of Crime Act establishes a federally financed victim compensation fund

1990: Victim's Rights and Restitution Act incorporates a bill of rights for federal crime victims and explains about services that should be available to victims of crime

1990: Victims of Child Abuse Act features reforms to make the federal criminal justice system less traumatic for child victims and witnesses

1994: Violent Crime Control and Law Enforcement Act establishes a National Child Sex Offender Registry, calls for enhanced sentences for drunk drivers with child passengers, and provides funding for programs to combat violence against women

1996: Victims Bill of Rights Constitutional Amendment is introduced into Congress

1997: Victims Rights Clarification Act allows federal victims to both attend trial and appear as impact witnesses during the sentencing phase

2000: Victims of Trafficking and Violence Protection Act adjusts issues of worker exploitation resulting from trafficking in persons, increases prison terms for slavery violations, and requires courts to order restitution upon conviction

2000: Violence against Women Act is signed by President Clinton, and ensures that protection orders granted in one jurisdiction can be enforced in other jurisdictions, including tribal jurisdictions; strengthens services to victims of violence; and improves access to immigration protection for battered immigrant women

2004: Justice for All Act provides substantive federal rights for crime victims and mechanisms to enforce them

2005: Trafficking Victims Protection Reauthorization Act addresses both international and domestic trafficking in persons both adult and juvenile, with victim prevention efforts and enhanced prosecution of trafficking offenses

2006: Adam Walsh Child Safety and Protection Act establishes a comprehensive federal DNA database of material collected from convicted child molesters

Proposed Victim Rights Amendment

While individual pieces of state legislation and individual federal acts have had an impact on the treatment of crime victims by the criminal justice system and the services available to those victims, perhaps the most sweeping change of all would be an actual amendment to the U.S. Constitution. Though several resolutions have been made over the past decade to amend the Constitution to include wording that would protect the rights of crime victims, none of these resolutions have made it through their various potential hurdles, including the Committee on the Judiciary. The rights proposed within these resolutions typically are similar to the rights that several states have been working with, and may even have passed into their state's constitution. The wording of one such resolution, which was put forward in January 2003, reads as follows:

SECTION 1. The rights of victims of violent crime, being capable of protection without denying the constitutional rights of those accused of victimizing them, are hereby established and shall not be denied by any State or the United States and may be restricted only as provided in this article.

SECTION 2. A victim of violent crime shall have the right to reasonable and timely notice of any public proceeding involving the crime and of any release or escape of the accused; the rights not to be excluded from such public proceeding and reasonably to be heard at public release, plea, sentencing, reprieve, and pardon proceedings; and the right to adjudicative decisions that duly consider the victim's safety, interest in avoiding unreasonable delay, and just and timely claims to restitution from the offender. These rights shall not be restricted except when and to the degree dictated by a substantial interest in public safety or the administration of criminal justice, or by compelling necessity.

SECTION 3. Nothing in this article shall be construed to provide grounds for a new trial or to authorize any claim for damages. Only the victim or the victim's lawful representative may assert the rights established by this article, and no person accused of the crime may obtain any form of relief hereunder.

SECTION 4. Congress shall have power to enforce by appropriate legislation the provisions of this article. Nothing in this article shall affect the President's authority to grant reprieves or pardons.

SECTION 5. This article shall be inoperative unless it has been ratified as an amendment to the Constitution by the legislatures of three-fourths of the several States within 7 years from the date of its submission to the States by the Congress. This article shall take effect on the 180th day after the date of its ratification.

Pro: Arguments for Constitutional Victims' Rights

Prior to the establishment of the typical existing victims' rights, the victim's name and address were easily available as public records; offenders often harassed the victim; and victims were not apprised of the steps in the justice process, nor how long they would take nor how to prepare. Victims often came in contact with the offender in the hallways before the hearings, and victims often did not know the status of their cases following the hearings, or even if there were no hearings.

Many victim advocates argue strongly that crime victims deserve more rights within America's criminal justice system. They state that since the nation's ultimate goal is justice for all, more victim rights and enforceable victim rights are essential. These rights could include the ability for victims to participate in the plea bargaining process, perhaps even going so far as to be allowed a veto vote on any plea bargain proposed. Further, victim involvement in the sentencing process is seen to be improved with the expanded use of victim impact statements and victim statements of opinion. Proponents argue that victims should also have the right to attend the trial if they so choose, and abrogation of these rights should have remedies if members of the justice system violate their rights.

When the American colonies were first established, there was no public prosecutor, and instead, victims were parties to their own cases and acted on their own behalf during the course of the prosecution. At that time, victims possessed great discretion over whether or not to file a complaint, with whom to file a complaint, and even how the case should be moved through the system. Once prosecutors assumed the role as representatives of the state during the 1800s, crime victims were pushed to the side and only utilized if needed as a witness for the state.

However, crime is a violation of one person by another, not an offense against the state. Efforts over the past couple of decades at the federal and state levels have focused greatly needed attention on victim's rights and compliance issues. Every time a crime victim raises questions about their rights, it offers an educational opportunity for all those who are responsible for the implementation of victims rights to be sure that those rights are respected and the system is improved as it fulfills its responsibilities to victims. While in more recent history the victim has not been very involved in the criminal case, new state constitutional amendments and laws giving victims the right to be involved in criminal cases is beginning to change the view of the courts and the ability to legally enforce victims' rights.

In this view, an amendment to the U.S. Constitution would ensure that all victims have similar rights, no matter what state they reside in or became a victim in. It would also symbolically send an important message that the nation cares about those it failed to protect with its justice system. Crime victims' rights established by state legislation or even incorporated into a state constitution would still not be on equal footing with crime defendants' rights established by the Constitution, which would also guarantee that crime victims' rights would be enumerated and protected as the Bill of Rights protects the rights of those accused of crimes.

Con: Arguments Against Constitutional Victims' Rights

While the system does not deny the importance of a citizen who has been harmed by another, the system must stay steadfast in its mission to serve the whole of society and not cater to the desires of any one individual, whether the individual is an offender or a victim. The 200-year-old American legal system is based on the concept of public justice, wherein the hurt party is the state or government, which has a direct interest in protecting society and preserving order. In contrast, a private, individual hurt party would have only their own personal interests in mind. In addition, the discretion that exists in the hands of prosecutors in determining the conditions of a plea bargain, and judges in maintaining an orderly courtroom environment and determining a fair sentence, should not be curtailed by a citizen who may be in the midst of emotional turmoil and has little or no understanding of the overall workings of the justice system. Most of the laws as they are written now allow criminal justice officials considerable latitude with regard to the way they carry out their responsibility, and critics of a federal standard of victims' rights argue that it needs to stay this way.

There are numerous reasons for allowing the use of discretion by trained professionals in the field, and a concrete listing of victims' rights could curtail this discretion to the point that it would compromise the ability to carry out one's professional duties. Based on their emotional state and lack of understanding about the complexities of the justice system, victims often have unrealistic expectations and ask for services or decisions that are not practical or possible. Many other victims choose not to exercise their rights, even when they are made available, because they do not wish to get involved in the court system and may fear becoming more traumatized if the offender gets a slight punishment, despite the victim's best efforts to seek a stronger punishment. This unequal involvement of victims in justice decisions can lead to unequal sentencing of defendants, not only on the basis of the crime, but also on the writing or oratory skills of the victim or lack thereof.

While victims can use personal strategies to pursue actions they feel are their right to have made available, victims are generally not considered to be parties in the trial of the accused offender; through the prosecutor, the parties include the defendant versus the state. This lack of standing has historically prevented victims from taking legal action to enforce their own rights as victims, and highlights the fact that the prosecutor is fulfilling their role on behalf of all the citizens of the state. It is not the prosecutor's duty to use the states' resources and time to placate the desires of a single individual victim. It is also a strong concern that the passage of a federal statute or amendment would tilt the scales in favor of the victims, thus trampling on the rights of alleged offenders.

In ancient times, harms to a person or their property were regarded as a private matter. If victims and victim advocates believe more victims' rights or reform are needed to protect existing victims' rights, critics propose that perhaps it would be better to alter the civil legal system, which is already designed to give standing to the injured party without the oversight of the state.

In this view, the passage of a crime victims' rights amendment to the U.S. Constitution is anticipated to be detrimental to the criminal justice system, as it would make the criminal justice system in general and the courts in particular less efficient and effective. Additionally, there is concern that a victims' rights amendment may diminish the rights of the accused that is currently guaranteed in the Bill of Rights. Not only could the passage of a constitutional amendment have unintended and potentially undesirable consequences, but enforcement of the amendment would also be difficult, time-consuming, and expensive. An amendment to the Constitution is not taken lightly by critics, who do not see a compelling and clearly articulated need for it, given that there are numerous state and federal laws already in place that are seen as more than adequate to protect victims' rights.

Conclusion

The image of the scales of justice has been used by both sides of the victims' rights and restitution issue. Victim advocates feel that the scales have favored the offender, and only lately have they begun to level out by adding the rights of victims. Opponents to the victims' rights movement argue that too many victims' rights will trample on offenders' rights, and the enforcement of these rights will further impede America's already strained justice system. The challenge for the future is to find the appropriate balance between victims' rights and offenders' rights, while still maintaining the integrity and manageability of the nation's justice system.

See Also: 14. Plea Bargaining; 16. Restorative Justice.

Further Readings

Boland, Mary. *Crime Victims Guide to Justice.* Clearwater, FL: Sourcebooks, 1997.

Carmen, Andrew. *Crime Victims: An Introduction to Victimology.* Belmont, CA: Thomson Wadsworth, 2007.

Jerin, Robert, and Laura Moriarty. *The Victims of Crime.* Upper Saddle River, NJ: Pearson Education, 2010.

Kennedy, Leslie, and Vincent Sacco. *Crime Victims in Context.* Los Angeles, CA: Roxbury Publishing Company, 1998.

Moriarty, Laura J. *Controversies in Victimology.* Cincinnati, OH: Anderson Publishing, 2003.

Muraskin, Roslyn. *It's a Crime: Women and Justice.* Upper Saddle River, NJ: Pearson Education, 2007.

National Victims Constitutional Amendment Network. http://www.nvcap.org (Accessed February 2010).

Office of Justice Programs. "Crime Victims' Rights in America: An Historical Overview." (2008). http://www.ojp.usdoj.gov/ovc/ncvrw/1999/histr.htm (Accessed February 2010).

Roberts, Albert. *Helping Crime Victims: Research, Policy, and Practice.* Thousand Oaks, CA: Sage, 1990.

Wallace, Harvey. *Family Violence: Legal, Medical, and Social Perspectives.* Boston, MA: Pearson Education, 2008.

Index

Index note: Chapter titles and their page numbers are in **boldface**.

Abramson, Jeffrey, 153
Absprachen, 189
accident reconstruction, 95–96
acoustical evidence evaluation, 95
acquittals, 37–38, 41
Adam Walsh Child Protection and Safety Act (AWA), 247, 248, 249, 277
African Americans
    black criminality argument, 234
    DNA screenings and, 26
    heroin,cocaine and, 47
    racial profiling of, 26
    right to vote, 150
    sentencing disparities and, 231–232, 235–236, 237–239, 240
agency costs, 195
AIDS, 55
Alabama, 244
Alaska Sex Offender Registration Act, 251
alcohol-impaired driving, 63, 64, 68–72, 162
    See also **driving under the influence (DUI) penalties**
Amar, Akhil, 85
AMBER Alert Program, 247
American Association of Police Polygraphists, 211
American Civil Liberties Union (ACLU), 26
The American Jury (Kalven and Zeisel), 155

American jury system. *See* **jury system**
American Law Institute (ALI), 137
American Law Institute Test, 137
American Medical Association, 128
American Polygraph Association (APA), 208, 210
American Psychiatric Association, 139
American Psychological Association, 209
American Revolution, 118
Anslinger, Harry, 47
Anti-Drug Abuse Act, 49, 54
antifederalists, 118
Apodaca v. Oregon, 152
Argentina, 188
Arizona v. Evans, 82
arrestees
   DNA database and, 18, 20, 24–26, 27
   domestic violence and, 275
   drug, 6, 8, 47, 49
   DUIs, 62, 63, 65–66, 67, 72
   Miranda rights and, 179
   sex offender registry and, 249
   See also **mandatory sentencing; sentencing disparities**
Ashe v. Swenson, 35
assassinations, 125
asset forfeiture, 1–11
   acts and legislation, 3–5
   arguments against, 1, 8–11
   cocaine and, 3
   constitutional rights and, 9–11
   history of, 2–5
   key issues, 1–2
   pivotal cases, 9–11
   police budgets and, 5–6
   restoration to victims and, 8
   support for, 6–8
   taint doctrine and, 9
   types of, 2
   war on crime and, 1, 7, 17
   War on Drugs and, 8

Asset Forfeiture Fund, 7–8
audio recordings, 207
Australia, 222
automatic weapons, 117, 124
autrefois acquit, 32
autrefois convict, 32

background checks, 117, 122, 123, 125
Bajakajian, Hosep, 10
Ball v. United States, 37–38
ballistics, 93
bank fraud, 96
Bank Secrecy Act, 50
bans on guns, 124–125
    See also **gun control laws**
bargaining. *See* **plea bargaining**
Bartkus v. Illinois, 36
Baton Rouge (Louisiana), 26
Batson v. Kentucky, 152
battered spouse syndrome, 99
Bayesian model, 103
Becker, Howard, 47
Behavioral Risk Factor Surveillance Survey, 63
bench trials, 33
Bennis v. Michigan, 9–10
Benton V. Maryland, 33
Berghuis v. Thompkins, 183–184
Berkeley Police Department, 202
Bill of Rights, 32–33, 39–40, 149
    See also specific amendments
biological fluids, 94
Black, Hugo, 40
Black, Justice, 185
black criminality argument, 234
Blackstone, William, 32, 34
blameworthiness, 234–235
Blockburger v. United States, 34
blood alcohol content, 61, 62, 64–66, 67, 70
blood pressure, 201–202

blood samples
    DNA evidence and, 13, 14, 15, 19, 245
    as physical evidence, 26, 211, 271
blood types, 14, 94
blood-alcohol content, 61, 62, 64–65, 67
Boyd v. United States, 76
Brady, James, 125
Brady, Sarah, 125
Brady Handgun Violence Prevention Act, 125
Brady v. United States, 190
Braithwaite, John, 216–218
Breaking the Chains: People of Color and the War on Drugs, 51
breath specimens, 63, 64–65, 68
breath-testing devices, 64–65
Breed v. Jones, 39
Brendlin v. California, 82
Brennan, Justice, 185
Breyer, Stephen, 154
bright-line rule, 178
Burch v. Louisiana, 152
burden of proof, 10, 11
Burger, Warren E., 180
Burks v. United States, 41
Bush, George H.W., 52
Bush, George W., 123, 247

CAFRA. *See* Civil Asset Forfeiture Reform Act (CAFRA)
Calandra v. United States, 80
California
    African Americans and Hispanics in penal system, 26
    Compassionate Use Act, 53
    crime victim rights, 275
    DNA databases, 25, 245
    drug laws, 48, 52–53
    exclusionary rules, 77, 79, 82, 176
    eyewitness testimony policies, 112
    gun control laws, 127
    jury pools, 150
    juvenile courts and double jeopardy, 39

mandatory sentencing, 161, 164, 166, 168
medical marijuana and, 52–54
polygraphs and, 202, 211
sex offender registry, 244, 245
three-strikes law, 164, 166, 258, 259–261, 264–265
California v. Stewart, 176
See also **Miranda rights/ruling**
Canadian drug policies, 51, 54
Cardozo, Benjamin, 33
Carter Administration, 56
Castro, Joseph, 19
"cat out of the bag" ruling, 182
Center on Child Abuse and Neglect, 275
Centers for Disease Control, 63, 128
Central Intelligence Agency, 204
certainty-accuracy correlation, 105
Changing Lenses (Zehr), 218
Chapkis, Wendy, 53
chemical analysis, 93
chemical testing, 63, 64, 65–66
chemotherapy, 52–53
Chicago Police Scientific Crime Detection Laboratory, 202
Child Abuse Prevention and Treatment Act, 275
children
    endangerment of, 67
    eyewitness testimony and, 108
    gun control laws and, 124, 127
    kidnappings of, xiv, 243, 244–246, 247, 249, 254
    mandatory sentencing for crimes against, 162, 167
    molestation of, xiv, 243, 244–245, 249, 254, 255, 259–260
    murder of, xiv, 139–140, 144, 166, 243, 244–245, 249, 254, 259
    of prisoners, 241
    rape of, xiv, 243
    See also juveniles; **sex offender registry**
Chinese, 47
Cho Seung-Hui, 123
Christie, Nils, 216–217, 225
citizen screenings. *See* DNA screenings
City of West Covina v. Perkins, 10

civil asset forfeiture. *See* **asset forfeiture**
Civil Asset Forfeiture Reform Act (CAFRA), 4–5
civil deportation hearings, 81
Clark, Justice, 185
Clinton, William J., 127, 276
cocaine powder
    asset forfeiture and, 3
    drug laws and, 46–47, 49, 51, 54, 55–56
    mandatory sentencing and, 169
    physical evidence evaluation of, 93
    sentencing disparities and, 238–241
    See also crack cocaine
coercion, 14, 23, 78, 190, 197
    See also confessions
cognitive disability, 135–136, 137
    See also M'Naghten test
Coke, Lord, 32
cold cases, 17
college campuses, 125
colonial America
    jury system evolution, 149
    mandatory sentencing policies in, 160–161
Colorado, crime victim rights, 275
Colten v. Kentucky, 33
Columbine High School, 127
Combined DNA Index System (CODIS), 18, 19
Commentaries on the Laws of England: In Four Books With Appendix
    (Blackstone), 32, 34
Committee on the Judiciary, 277
community protection, 234–235
    See also public safety
community restorative boards, 221, 223
community service
    plea bargaining and, 189
    restorative justice and, 223–224, 225, 227
Compassionate Use Act (California), 53
competency, 92–93, 99
composition, 189
Comprehensive Crime Control Act (CCA), 4

Comprehensive Drug Abuse Prevention and Control Act, 3, 48
compurgators, 147–148
computer evidence evaluation, 95
conceal and carry laws, 122, 125–127
Concealed Information Test (CIT), 203
confessions
    coerced, 14, 23, 78, 190, 197
    false, 19, 23, 211
    illegally obtained, 79–80
    involuntary, 175–176
    Miranda warnings and, 174–177, 180, 182, 185
    plea bargaining and, 189, 197
    polygraphs and, 204, 205, 208, 210, 211
    recanting, 205
    voluntary, 176–177, 180, 197
confidence-accuracy correlation, 105
Connecticut, crime victim rights, 275
Connecticut Dept. of Public Safety v. Doe, 251
constitutional victims' rights, 277–281
contractual view of plea bargaining, 192–193
control question test (CQT), 203, 207, 209, 210
controlled substance list, 3
Controlled Substances Act, 48
coroners, 94
Cosby, William, 149
Costa, Jim, 259
crack cocaine
    drug laws and, 46–47, 49, 51, 54, 55–56
    mandatory sentencing and, 238–241
    sentencing disparities and, 238–241
    See also cocaine powder
crime labs, 93–94, 98
Crimes Without Victims: Deviant Behavior and Public Policy (Schur), 45
Criminal Interrogation and Confessions, 204
criminal statutes, 161
cross-race identifications, 105, 108
Crowe, Michael, 211
Crowe, Stephanie, 211
culture wars, 38

Dahmer, Jeffrey, 133–134

Daubert test, 91–92

Daubert v. Merrell Dow Pharmaceuticals, 91, 98, 205–207

Davis, Richard Allen, 166, 259

Davis v. United States, 181–182

de Tocqueville, Alexis. *See* Tocqueville, Alexis de

death penalty cases, 152, 232

death-qualified juries, 152

death row, 22, 98

Declaration of Rights (English), 118

decriminalization of illegal drugs, 46

delinquents, 219. *See* juveniles

Democracy in America (Tocqueville), 153

Department of Agriculture and Consumer Services (Florida), 126

detective/crime scene units, 93–94

determinate sentencing, 237

Dickerson v. United States, 174, 181

District of Columbia, 122, 136

District of Columbia v. Heller, 122, 129

Division of General Psychology (American Psychological Association), 209

DNA dragnets. *See* DNA screenings

DNA evidence, 13–28

    admissibility of, 19

    citizen screenings and, 2–7, 18–19, 20–21, 26–27

    databases and, 18, 20–21, 24–26, 27, 245, 277

    expert witnesses and, 94, 98

    eyewitness error and, 103–104, 108

    familial searches and, 20–21

    future of, 27–28

    history of, 14–15

    legal and ethical issues of, xiv, 20, 26–27

    post-conviction testing, 22–24

    science of testing, 16–17, 27–28

    sex offenders and, 245, 277

    specialized testing processes, 15–16

    storage of, 17–18

    support for database expansion, 24–25

    touch/transfer/low-level, 21–22

    types of, 15

DNA Index System, 18
DNA screenings, 2–7, 18–19, 20–21, 26–27
documentary evidence evaluation, 94–95
Dodson, Gary, 22
Doe, John, 251
domestic trafficking of persons, 276
Double Jeopardy Clause, 31–42
    attachment of, 33–34
    case dismissals and, 38
    exceptions to, 35–36
    Fifth Amendment and, 31
    government appeal and, 37–38
    history of, 32–33
    interpretation of, 31–32
    non-criminal proceedings and, 38–39
    opposition to, 40–42
    Petite Policy and, 36–37
    re-prosecution prohibitions and, 34–35
    support for, 39–40
double-blind lineups, 107
Douglas, Justice, 185
Doyle v. Ohio, 182
dragnets. *See* DNA screenings
driver's license suspension, 65
driving under the influence (DUI) penalties, 61–72
    administrative sanctions, 65–66
    blood alcohol content, 61, 62, 64–66, 67, 70
    databases and, 62–63
    deterrence and, 71–72
    effects or influences of, 63
    enforcement and sanctions, 70–72
    ignition locks, 68–69, 70, 71
    impaired driver control, 61–62, 63–64
    implied consent laws, 65–66
    mandatory sentencing policies, 162
    nonstandard penalties for, 67–69
    standard penalties, 67
    support for strong sanctions, 69–70
    testing for alcohol, 63, 64, 65–66

traffic fatalities and, 61–62, 69–70, 71
zero tolerance laws, 66–67
Driving while Intoxicated (DWI), 63
drug abuse, early intervention, 47
Drug Abuse Prevention and Control Act. *See* Comprehensive Drug Abuse Prevention and Control Act
drug arrests, 6, 8, 47, 49
drug czar, 49, 56
Drug Enforcement Agency, 7
drug laws, 45–56
    arrests, 6, 8, 47, 49
    cocaine and, 46–47, 49, 51, 54, 55–56
    criticism of, 50–52
    decriminalization of drugs and, 46
    history of, 46–49
    international policies, 54–55
    1960s and, 47–48
    policy changes in, 52–55, 56
    support for, 49–50
    War on Drugs and, 46, 48–49, 50–52, 55, 56
Drug Policy Alliance, 51
drug regulation, 3
drug trafficking, 50, 161
drug-related investigations, 5, 6, 9
drunk driving, 63, 64, 68–72, 162
    See also **driving under the influence (DUI) penalties**
Du Pont, John, 138
due process rights, 10, 33, 122, 175, 206, 226–227, 250
Duncan v. Louisiana, 151
Duren v. Missouri, 151
Durham test, 136–137, 144
Durham v. United States, 136–137

Edward Byrne Memorial State and Local Law Enforcement Assistance, 245
Eglash, Albert, 219
Eighth Amendment
    asset forfeiture and, 10
    three-strikes laws and, 261

Elkins v. United States, 77
embezzlement, 96
employment screenings, 201
England
    DNA database, 20
    DNA testing and exoneration, 22
    gun control in, 118, 120
    insanity defense in, 135
    jury system evolution, 147–149
    M'Naghten test, 135
    Navigation Act, 2–3
    Norman conquest of, 148
English House of Lords, 135
Equal Protection Clause, 152
equitable sharing, 4, 9
Eric Clark v. Arizona, 140
Escobedo v. Illinois, 175
ethanol, 63
ethnic disparity in sentencing. *See* **sentencing disparities**
European drug policies, 54–55
Ewing, Gary, 260
Ewing v. California, 260, 261
Ex Post Facto Clause, 250, 251–252
Exclusionary Rule, 41
exclusionary rules, 75–86
    current state of, 83
    Fifth Amendment context, 75, 76, 78
    Fourth Amendment context, 75, 76–78, 79, 82, 85
    fruit of the poisonous tree doctrine, 79–80
    limits on, 80–83
    opposition to, 85–86
    Sixth Amendment context, 75, 78–79, 81
    support for, 83–84
exoneration, 22–23
expert witnesses and hired guns, 89–100
    acoustical evidence evaluation, 95
    computer evidence evaluation, 94–95
    in criminal cases, 92–96
    documentary evidence evaluation, 94–95

financial evaluation and, 96
medical/biological evidence evaluation and, 94
opposition to using, 98–100
physical evidence evaluation and, 93–94
psychiatric/psychological evaluation and, 92–93
qualifications of, 89–91
reforms, 112
scientific reliability and, 91–92
support for using, 97–98, 100
traffic accident reconstruction and, 95–96
types of hired guns, 96–97
weapons and, 108–109
explicit charge bargaining, 188
Eyewitness Evidence: A Guide for Law Enforcement, 105
Eyewitness Evidence: A Trainer's Manual for Law Enforcement, 105
eyewitness testimony and accuracy, 101–112
administrator's behavior and, 106, 111
DNA testing and, 103–104
estimator variables in, 105–106, 108–109
history of, 102–104
increasing accuracy of, 104–106
lineups and, 101, 104, 107–108, 110–111
mistaken eyewitness testimony, 102, 103, 104, 106, 107–111
research on, 102–103
system variables in, 106–107, 109–110

fair cross-section requirement, 150, 151–152
fair sentencing, 227, 279
family group conferencing (FGC), 215, 222
fatal crashes, 61–62, 69–70, 71
Fatality Analysis Reporting System (FARS), 62
Federal Bureau of Investigation (FBI), 7, 62, 63, 123, 179, 204, 236
Federal Bureau of Narcotics, 47
Federal Circuit Courts. *See specific cases*
Federal Rule of Evidence 602, 89–90
Federal Rule of Evidence 701, 90
Federal Rule of Evidence 702, 90
Federal Rule of Evidence 703, 91
Federal Rules of Criminal Procedure, 190

federalist governmental structures, 36
felon DNA databases, 18, 20, 24–26, 27
females. *See* women
fiber analysis, 93
Fifteenth Amendment, 150
Fifth Amendment
    asset forfeiture and, 10
    DNA screenings and, 26
    Double Jeopardy Clause, 31, 32, 42
    exclusionary rules and, 75, 76, 78
    privilege against self-incrimination, 174–175
financial scams, 8
firearm possession, 161, 163
    See also **gun control laws**
Firearms Act, 120
first-tier trials, 33, 41
Florida v. Powell, 182
Fong Foo v. United States, 41
forensic science, 14–15
Fortas, Justice, 185
Fourteenth Amendment
    Due Process Clause, 10, 33, 122, 175, 206, 250
    Equal Protection Clause, 152
Fourth Amendment
    DNA screenings and, 26
    exclusionary rules and, 75, 76–78, 79, 82, 85
    search/seizure and, 64, 184
France, 189
fruit of the poisonous tree doctrine, 79–80
Frye test, 91–92
Frye v. United States, 91, 205, 206
functional lineup size, 110
furiosus (raging, raving beast), 135

Game Act, 118
genetic concordance, 13
genetic markers, 14
Germany, 119, 188–189
Gertz, Marc, 128

Gideon v. Wainwright, 79, 184
Gilbert v. California, 79
Glorious Revolution, 118
good faith exception, 41, 81–82
government surveillance, 20
grand juries (England), 148
Green v. United States, 40
Greenwald, Glenn, 54
guilty but mentally ill (GBMI) verdict, 137–138
Guilty Knowledge Test (GKT), 203
Gun Control Act, 125
gun control laws, 117–129
    conceal and carry laws, 122, 125–127
    Constitution and, 120–122
    criminals and, 117, 122, 123
    federal initiatives, 125
    firearm possession, 161, 162
    gun rights legislation, 125–127
    history of, 117–119
    international examples of, 119–120
    landmark cases, 122
    mentally ill and, 122, 123, 125
    opposition to, 117, 125–127, 128–129
    safe storage and distance, 124–125
    support for, 117, 127–128
    types of, 123–125
    waiting periods, 124
Gun License Act, 120
gun rights legislation, 125–127, 128
gun show loophole, 123
Gypsies, 119

hair
    DNA evidence and, 13, 16
    eyewitness identifications and, 110
Halper (defendant in *United States v. Halper*), 38–39
Hamilton, Andrew, 149–150
handguns. *See* **gun control laws**
handwriting analysis, 94–95

"hard" drugs, 51, 54
Harlan, Justice, 185
harm
    criminal acts and, xiii, 160, 167
    drug associated, 48, 51, 54–55
    See also **restorative justice**
Harris v. New York, 174, 181
Harrison Act, 47
hawkish objection, 196
Heath v. Alabama, 36
heroin, 3, 47, 51, 54
Hinckley, John, 125, 144
hired guns. *See* **expert witnesses and hired guns**
Hispanics, 231, 235–236, 238
Holland v. Illinois, 151
Holmes, Oliver Wendell, Jr., 37
Holocaust, 119
homosexuals, 119
Horvath, Fred, 202
Hudson et al., 38
Hudson v. Michigan, 83
human remains identification, 16

Iacano, William, 209–210
ignition locks, 68–69, 70, 71
Illinois, 162, 233, 237, 240, 249
Illinois v. Escobedo, 79
Illinois v. Krull, 82
immigrants, 276
Immigration Customs Enforcement, 7
impact witnesses, 276
implicit plea bargaining, 188
implied consent laws, 65–66
impoundment, 68, 70, 71
in personam asset forfeiture, 2
In re Gault, 39
in rem asset forfeiture, 2, 3, 4
Inbau, Fred E., 202, 204
incompetency, 92–93

indeterminate sentencing, 237
Indiana, 219
indigence, 179
inevitable discovery rule, 81, 82
Innocence Project, 22, 23
I.N.S. v. Lopez-Mendoza, 81
insanity, 92–93, 99
    See also competency
insanity defense, 133–144
    American Law Institute Test and, 137
    cognitive disability and, 135–136, 137
    Durham test and, 136–137
    guilty but mentally ill (GBMI) verdict, 137–138
    history of, 135–140
    irresistible impulse test and, 136
    landmark cases, 140
    M'Naghten test and, 135–137, 138–139, 140, 142, 144
    not guilty by reason of insanity (NGRI), 134–135, 138, 139, 142, 143, 144
    opposition to, 142–143
    postpartum psychosis and, 139–140
    post-traumatic stress disorder and, 139
    procedures involved in, 134–135
    reforms, 138–139
    support for, 140–141
international trafficking of persons, 276
interrogation practices
    custodial, 173, 177, 178, 180
    exclusionary rules, 85
    Miranda ruling and, 175–176, 177, 180
    psychological, 177
    right to counsel and, 175–176, 182
    self-incrimination and, 175–176
    See also **Miranda rights/ruling; polygraphs**
intoxication, 55, 63–64, 65, 90, 162
    See also **driving under the influence (DUI) penalties**
Intoxilyzer, 64
irresistible impulse test, 136
Italy, 189

Jacob Wetterling Crimes Against Children Sexually Violent Offender Registration Act. *See* Wetterling Act

jail time, 39

James II (king), 118

jeopardy. *See* **Double Jeopardy Clause**

Jews, 119

John E. Reid and Associates, 202

Jones, Bill, 259

Jones, Gary, 39

Judeo-Christianity, 40

junk science, 91, 99

juror eligibility, 146

juror screening, 146–147

jury pools, 150, 151, 152

jury summons, 146

jury system, 145–156
    fair cross-section requirement, 151–152
    history of, 147–149
    mechanics of, 146–147
    opposition to, 145, 154–156
    support for, 145, 153–154
    Supreme Court shaping of, 149–151

jury trials, 33

"just say know," 53

"just say no," 48, 53, 55

Justice for All Act, 276

Justices of Boston Municipal Court v. Lydon, 33, 41

juveniles, 39, 219, 222, 249, 250
    See also children

Kalven, Harry, Jr., 155

Kanka, Megan, xiv, 243, 244–245, 249, 254

Kaplan, John, 48, 51

Kassin, Saul M., 154–155

Keeler, Leonarde, 202

Kellermann, Arthur L., 127

Kennedy, John F., 125

Kennedy, Justice, 183

Kennedy, Robert, 125

Kent v. United States, 39
Kepner v. United States, 37, 41
kidnappings
    Ernesto Miranda and, 176
    of Jacob Wetterling, xiv, 243, 245–246, 247, 249
    of Megan Kanka, xiv, 243, 244–245, 249, 254
    of Polly Klaas, xiv, 243, 259–260
    Ralph Tortorici and, 143
    sex offender registry and, 249
King, Martin Luther, Jr., 125
Klaas, Polly, xiv, 166, 243, 244–245, 259–260
Kleck, Gary, 128
Knight (poker player in *Ashe v. Swenson*), 35

Landsteiner, Karl, 14
Langbein, John, 197
Larson, John, 202, 203
Latinos, 235
Lautenberg Amendment, 125
Lee v. Martinez, 207
legal blood alcohol limits, 61, 62, 64–66, 67, 70
legal drinking age, 66–67, 70
libel, 149–150
license plates, 68, 69, 70, 71
lie detectors. *See* **polygraphs**
life-in-prison sanctions, 161
Lindesmith, Alfred, 45, 47, 50, 55
Lindsay, R.C.L., 103
lineups, 101, 104, 107–108, 110–111
Lockhart v. McCree, 152
Lockyer, Bill, 261
Lockyer v. Andrade, 260, 261
Loftus, Elizabeth, 102–103
Lombroso, Cesare, 202
Lott, John, 128
Lykken, David, 203

machine guns, 117, 124
Mackey v. Montrym, 65

Madison, James, 32, 119
Madoff, Bernie, 8
Mafia, 6–7
mainstreaming, 227
male-male rape, 15
Malloy v. Hogan, 78, 175
mandatory sentencing, 159–170
  cocaine users and, 169, 241
  contemporary, 161–162
  costs of, 164, 169–170
  criminal victimization and, 165–166
  effectiveness of, 163–165
  future of, 170
  history of, 160–161
  opposition to, 167–170
  presence of discretion/bias and, 168–169
  public safety and, 165–166
  purpose of, 159–160
  rationale for, 162–163
  rigidity of, 169–170
  sentencing equity and, 166–167
  support for, 165–167
  three-strikes laws and, 159, 164, 166
Mao Tse-Tung, 119
Maori youth, 220
Mapp, Doralee, 78
Mapp v. Ohio, 77–78, 184
marijuana
  asset forfeiture and, 10
  decriminalization of, 46, 48
  distribution, 3
  European countries and, 54
  illegal possession of, 39, 47
  John Kaplan and, 51
  medical, 52
Marston, William, 202, 205
Maryland v. Shatzer, 182
mass murders, 127–128
Massachusetts Colony Constitution, 32

Massachusetts eye witness testimony policies, 112
Massiah v. United States, 78, 79
McDonald v. Chicago, 122, 129
McDonaldization of victim-offender mediation, 227
McDonald's (San Ysidro, California), 127
Medicaid fraud, 38–39
Medicaid programs, 7
medical marijuana movement, 52–53
medical/biological evidence evaluation, 94
Megan's Law, 245–246, 249, 254
    See also **sex offender registry**; Wetterling Act
Melendez-Diaz v. Massachusetts, 64–65
mental illness
    counseling costs, 271, 274
    genes for, 27
    gun control laws and, 117, 122, 123, 125–126, 127–128
    psychiatric/psychological evaluation of, 92–93
    See also **insanity defense**
Mexican Americans, 47
Michigan State Police v. Sitz, 64
Military Rule of Evidence 707, 206
Mill, John Stuart, 51
Minnesota
    eyewitness testimony policies, 112
    Wetterling Act, 245–246, 247, 249
Miranda, Ernesto, 176–177, 185
Miranda rights/ruling, 173–185
    confessions and, 174–177, 180, 182, 185
    criticism of, 184–185
    Ernesto Miranda, 176–177, 185
    issues surrounding, 180–181
    language of Miranda warnings, 178–179
    law prior to, 174–176
    Miranda ruling, 174, 177–180
    subsequent caselaw and, 181–184
    support for, 184
    waivers, 176, 178, 182, 183–184
Miranda v. Arizona, 78, 173, 176, 184
Miranda v. Escobedo, 175

Miranda warning cards, 177
Miranda warnings. *See* **Miranda rights/ruling**
Missouri v. Seibert, 182
mistaken eyewitness testimony, 102, 103, 104, 106, 107–111
mistrials, 38
mitochondrial DNA (mtDNA), 16
    See also **DNA evidence**
M'Naghten, David, 135, 144
M'Naghten test
    cognitive disability and, 135–136, 137
    expert witnesses and, 93, 99
    insanity defense and, 138–139, 140, 142, 144
mock witness procedure, 110
Model Penal Code, 137
money laundering, 6–7, 50, 96
Monroe, Beverly, 23
Montana Department of Revenue v. Kurth Ranch, 39
morphine, 46–47
Munsterberg, Hugo, 102
Mustard, David, 128
Musto, David, 47
Mutt and Jess method, 177

Nadelman, Ethan, 51
Narcotic Control Act, 161
narcotics, 3, 47, 161
    See also **drug laws**
Nardone v. United States, 80
National Academy of Sciences, 207, 208
National Child Sex Offender Registry, 276
National DNA Index (NDIS), 18
National Firearms Act, 121
National Guard, 121
National Highway Traffic Safety Administration (NHTSA), 62
National Household Survey on Drug Abuse, 238
National Instant Criminal Background Check System (NICS) Improvement
    Act, 123
National Institute of Justice, 105
National Institutes of Health, 210

National Research Council, 210
National Rifle Association, 128, 258
National Science Foundation, 210
National Victims Rights Week, 275
Navigation Act, 2–3
needle exchange programs, 55
Netherlands, drug policies, 54
Neufeld, Peter, 22
New Jersey
    eye witness testimony policies, 112
    Megan's Law, 245–246, 249, 254
New Mexico, 207
New York, drug policies, 54
New York criminal statute (1926), 161
New York Times, 52
New York v. Quarles, 174, 181
New York Weekly Journal, 149
New Zealand, 220, 222
Nineteenth Amendment, 150
Nix v. Williams, 81
Nixon, Richard, 46, 48, 180
no compos mentis (no power of mind), 135
norm clarification, 225
Normans, 148
North Carolina, eye witness testimony policies, 112
not guilty by reason of insanity (NGRI), 134–135, 138, 139, 142, 143, 144

Obama, Barack, 54
Obama administration, 53, 56
Ochoa, Christopher, 23
O'Connor, Sandra Day, 261
Old Testament, 40
Omnibus Crime Control and Safe Street Act, 174, 180
On the Witness Stand: Essays on Psychology and Crime (Munsterberg), 102
One 1958 Plymouth Sedan v. Pennsylvania, 11
Operating a Motor Vehicle while Intoxicated (OWI), 63
    See also driving under the influence (DUI) penalties
opiates, 46–47
Oregon, crime victim rights, 275

Oregon v. Elstad, 182
organized crime, 6–7

paint comparison, 93
Palko v. Connecticut, 32–33
Palmer, John, 102
Pam Lychner Sexual Offender Tracking and Identification Act
pardon, 32
parole revocation hearings, 81
patent medicines, 46–47
pattegiamento, 189
penal codes, 137, 163
Pennsylvania Board of Probation and Parole v. Scott, 81
Petersilia, Joan, 52
Petite Policy, 36–37, 41
Petite v. United States, 36–37
petty crimes, 261, 263, 265
photography analysis, 95
physical evidence evaluation, 93–94
physicians, 3, 94
piracy, 3
Pistols Act, 120
plea bargaining, 187–197
    adversarial system of justice and, 197
    coercion and, 190–191
    confessions and, 189, 197
    as contracts, 192–193, 195–196
    development and spread of, 188–189
    as "hawkish," 196
    international examples of, 188–189
    opposition to, 194–197
    substantive justice and, 193–194
    support for, 189–194, 197
    trial cases and, 191–192
Poles, 119
police budgets, asset forfeiture and, 5–6, 7, 8–9
polygraphists, 211
polygraphs, 201–211
    admissibility of in criminal cases, 205–207

confessions and, 204, 205, 208, 210, 211
defined, 201
error rates and, 209–210
history of, 201–202
landmark cases, 205–207
Larson, Reid and, 202
procedures of, 203–204, 211
rehabilitation/recidivism and, 208–209
research standards and, 210–211
support for validity of, 208
use in criminal justice system, 204–205
polymerase chain reaction (PCR), 15
Ponzi schemes, 8
population genetics, 16
Portugal, 54
post-conviction DNA testing, 22–24
postpartum psychosis, 139–140
post-traumatic stress disorder, 139
presumptive sentencing, 237
prison populations
costs of imprisonment, 170
incarceration of drug offenders, 49, 52, 169, 241
mental illness and, 141, 143
social marginality and, 228
waiver of jail time, 39
procedimiento abreviado, 188
Proposition 184 (California), 260
Proposition 36, 53
prosecutorial processes/agencies, xv, 32, 42, 216, 247
Prosecutorial Remedies and Other Tools to end the Exploitation of
    Children Today Act (PROTECT), 247
Protestants, 118
psychiatric/psychological evaluation, 92–93
public health, 25, 50, 51, 55, 128
public justice, 279
public safety
impaired driving laws and, 69–70
mandatory sentencing policies and, 165–166
Miranda rights and, 174

sentencing disparities and, 234–235
sex offender registry and, 254
Purkett v. Elem, 152

quacks, 91, 98

racial discrimination, 25, 26
racial disparity in sentencing (RDS). *See* **sentencing disparities**
racial profiling
    DNA screenings and, 25
    illegal drugs and, 26, 51
racketeering, 6–7
Racketeering Influenced and Corrupt
  Organizations Act (RICO), 3–4, 7
rape
    of children, xiv, 243. *See also* **sex offender registry**
    confessions of, 176–177
    crime victims and, 271
    DNA evidence and, 15, 19, 21, 22, 23, 24, 25, 26
    exoneration for, 23
    by juveniles, 249, 250
    racial profiling and, 26
    of women, 15, 19, 21, 22, 23, 24, 25, 26
    See also **DNA evidence; sex offender registry**; sexual assault
Reagan, Nancy, 48, 55
Reagan, Ronald, 48, 52, 125, 276
Reagan administration, 56, 236
recidivism, 161, 166, 208
rehabilitation, 208
Rehnquist, Judge, 174, 181
Reid, John E., 202, 203, 204
Reilly, Peter, 211
reintegration, 215–216, 217–218, 221, 223, 226
reintegrative shaming, 218
relative judgement, 110–111
Relevant-Irrelevant Test (RIT), 203
restoration to victims, 8
restorative justice, 215–228
    basic premises of, 216–218

community restorative boards, 221, 223
community service and, 223–224, 225, 227
concept of shame and, 217–218
conflict as property and, 217
due process and, 226
fair sentencing and, 227
family group conferencing (FGC), 215, 222
history of, 215, 219–220
indigenous justice and, 220–221
international programs, 220
interventions, 221
opposition to, 226–228
recidivism and, 225
reintegration and, 215–216, 217–218, 221, 223, 226
reintegrative shaming, 218
sentencing circles, 215, 223
support for, 224–225
victim-offender agreements, 225, 227
victim-offender mediation (VOM), 215, 217, 219–220, 222, 227
victim-offender reconciliation programs (VORPs), 219–220
victims' rights movements and, 220–221
Restorative Justice and Peacemaking, 227
re-trials, 38
retribution. *See* **restorative justice**
Revere, Paul, 118
reversible error, 176
Reynolds, Mike, 259
RFLP, 14–15
Rhode Island, crime victim rights, 275
Richter, Max, 14
right to counsel, 173
See also **Miranda rights/ruling**
right to remain silent
See **Miranda rights/ruling**
Roberts (poker player in *Ashe v. Swenson*), 35
Rochin v. California, 77
"Rockefeller era" drug sanctions, 54
Rothstein, Schott, 8
Ryder, Winona, 259

Safe Streets Act. *See* Omnibus Crime Control and Safe Street Act
saliva, 94
    DNA evidence and, 13, 15, 26, 94
    medical/biological evidence evaluation of, 94
Santobello v. New York, 189
Scalia, Antonin, 83, 261
Scheck, Barry, 22
schizophrenia, 140
Schmerber v. California, 65
Schur, Edwin, 45, 50
Scott v. United States, 42
Seattle Times, 258
Second Amendment, 119, 120–122, 129
second-tier trials, 33, 41
securities fraud, 96
semen
    DNA evidence and, 13, 15, 26, 94
    medical/biological evidence evaluation of, 94
sentencing circles, 215, 223
sentencing disparities, 231–241
    African Americans and, 231–232, 235–236, 237–239, 240
    cocaine and, 238–241
    ethnicity and, 235–236
    guidelines and, 236–238
    Hispanics and, 231, 235–236, 238
    methodological flaws in research, 233–234
    negatives outcomes of research, 240–241
    positive outcomes of research, 240
    public safety and, 234–235
    racial disparity in sentencing (RDS), 232–234, 235, 236–237, 238, 240
    research inconsistencies, 232–235
    sentencing and sentencing guidelines, 236–238
    theoretical premises of, 234–235
    three-strikes laws and, 159, 164, 166
    war on crime and, 236–237
    War on Drugs and, 236–240
sentencing equity, 166–167, 168–169
separate sovereignties exception, 35–36
September 11, 2001, 16

serial numbers on guns, 125
Seven Bishop's Trial, 149
Seventh Amendment, 149
Sex Offender Registration and Notification Act (SORNA), 248
sex offender registry, 243–254
   constitutional challenges of, 251–252
   contemporary legislation, 245–250
   crimes against children and, 243
   history of, 244–245
   legality of, 250–252
   Megan's Law and, 245–246, 249, 254
   offender levels, 246–247
   opposition to, 253–254
   procedural inconsistencies, 246
   support for, 252–253
   Tier system, 248–250
   updated legislation, 247–248
   Wetterling Act and, 245–246, 247, 249
sex offenders, polygraphs and, 205, 208–209
sexual assault
   DNA evidence and, 15
   by juveniles, 249, 250
   by strangers, 253
   See also **DNA evidence**; rape
sexual predators. *See* **sex offender registry**
shaming, 217–218
shipping, 2–3
short tandem repeat (STR), 15
showup, 101
Silverthorne Lumber Co. v. United States, 79
Sixth Amendment
   exclusionary rules and, 75, 78–79, 81
   right to counsel, 175
   right to trial by jury, 149, 150–151
skin
   DNA evidence and, 13, 15
   polygraphs and electrical conductivity of, 202
slavery, 276
Smith v. Doe, 251

sobriety checkpoints, 64
Society for Psychophysiological Research, 209
"soft" drugs, 54
South Carolina, crime victim rights, 275
South Dakota v. Neville, 66
sperm DNA, 15
Stalin, Joseph, 119
Star Chamber, 178
stare decisis (deference to previously decided matters), 174, 181
statute of limitations, 24
Stewart, Justice, 185
Strauder v. Virginia, 150
Substance Abuse and Crime Prevention Act (SACPA), 53
substantive justice, 193–194
suppression of evidence. *See* **exclusionary rules**

taint doctrine, 9
Taylor v. Louisiana, 151
temporary licenses, 65
Thiel v. Southern Pacific Co., 150
third party rights violations, 82
Thomas, Clarence, 261
Thompkins (defendant), 183–184
Thornburgh, Dick, 52
Three Strikes and You're Out, 258, 260
three-strikes laws
    California and, 258, 259, 260, 261, 264–265
    costs of, 264–265
    deterrent effect of, 262–263
    history of, 258
    Klaas murder and, 36, 259–260
    legality of, 260–261
    mandatory sentencing and, 159, 164, 166
    opposition to, 264–265
    petty crimes and, 261, 263, 265
    racial disparities and, 264–265
    sentencing disparities and, 159, 164, 166
    support for, 261–263
Tier based sex offender system, 248–250

Timmendequas, Jesse, 245
Tocqueville, Alexis de, 153–154
Tonry, Michael, 52, 164
Tortorici, Ralph, 143
torture, 197
traffic accident reconstruction, 95–96
traffic fatalities, 61–62, 69–70, 71
trafficking of persons, 276
Trafficking Victims Protection Reauthorization Act, 276
treatment-on-demand reforms, 53
trial by battle and ordeal, 147–148
trial by compurgation, 147–148
tribal governments, 36
truth-in-sentencing statutes (TIS), 159
Twelve Angry Men, 147
Twining v. New Jersey, 174
two-tier trial systems, 33
Tyler, Tom, 40

Umbreit, Mark, 227
unanimity requirement, 151–152, 156
Uniform Crime Report, 105
United States Attorneys' Manual, 36
United States v. Bajakajian, 10
United States v. Ballard, 150
United States v. Emerson, 122
United States v. Halper, 38–39
United States v. Havens, 83
United States v. Jacobson, 82
United States v. James Daniel Good Real Property, 10
United States v. Janis, 80–81
United States v. Leon, 41, 81
United States v. Miller, 121
United States v. Scheffer, 206–207
United States v. Ursery, 10
United States v. Verdugo-Urquidez, 82
United States v. Wade, 79
United States v. Wilson, 32, 37
University of California, 202

urine specimens, 64, 65
Ursery, Guy, 10
U.S. Army, 204
U.S. Attorney General, 36–37
U.S. Attorney's Office, 7
U.S. Bureau of Justice Statistics (BJS), 231, 237, 253
U.S. Census Bureau, 235
U.S. Center for Disease Control (CDC), 63
U.S. Constitution, Double Jeopardy Clause and, 32, 34, 41
U.S. Customs Office, 10
U.S. Department of Justice, 7, 36, 104
U.S. Marshals Service, 7
U.S. Olympics, 138
U.S. Parks Police, 7
U.S. Postal Service, 7
U.S. Sentencing Commission, 162–163, 240
U.S. Supreme Court. *See specific cases*

vehicle registration suspension, 67–68
victim rights amendment proposals, 277–281
victim rights and restitution, 269–281
    amendment proposals, 277–278
    fair sentencing and, 271, 279
    federal legislation for, 275–281
    information/notification and, 272
    participation/attendance in justice process and, 273
    reasonable protection and, 272
    restitution overview, 271–272
    return of property and, 273–274
    separate waiting areas and, 272
    services for victims, 274
    state legislation for, 275
    support for constitutional, 278–279
    transportation availability and, 273
    victim compensation, 274
    victims rights overview, 270–271
victimization cycles, 228
victimless crimes, 45
victim-offender agreements, 225, 227

victim-offender mediation (VOM), 215, 217, 219–220, 222, 227
victim-offender reconciliation programs (VORPs), 219–220
Victims Bill of Rights Constitutional Amendment, 276
Victims of Child Abuse Act, 276
Victims of Crime Act, 276
Victims of Crimes Task Force, 276
Victims of Trafficking and Violence Protection Act, 276
Victim's Rights and Restitution Act, 276
Victims Rights Clarification Act, 276
victims' rights movements, 220–221
Victoria, Queen, 135
video recordings, 207
Vignera v. New York, 176
    See also **Miranda rights/ruling**
Violence against Women Act, 276
Violent Crime Control and Law Enforcement Act, 276
violent offender incarceration, 159
Virginia Company Charter, 149
Virginia Tech, 123
voice-stress analysis (VSA), 204, 211
voir dire, 146–147, 152, 154–155
Vollmer, August, 202
von Liszt, Franz, 102
vulnerable populations, 162

waiting periods, 124
waivers
    of jail time, 271
    juveniles into adult criminal court and, 39
    of Miranda rights, 176, 178, 182, 183–184
Wall Street Journal, 49
Walters, John, 49
war on crime
    asset forfeiture and, 1, 7, 17
    sentencing disparities and, 236–237
War on Drugs, 51–52
    asset forfeiture and, 8
    drug laws and, 46, 48, 50–52, 56
    expenditures on, 50

Richard Nixon and, 46, 48
sentencing disparities and, 236–238, 239
Warren, Earl, 173, 180, 185
We, the Jury (Abramson), 153
weapon ownership. *See* **gun control laws**
weapons possession, 161, 163
 See also **gun control laws**
Webb, Richard, 53
Weeks v. United States, 76–77
Weimer Republic, 119
Wells, Gary, 102–103
Westover v. United States, 176
 See also **Miranda rights/ruling**
Wetterling, Jacob, 243, 244
Wetterling Act, 245–246, 247, 249
 See also Megan's Law; **sex offender registry**
Wheeler v. United States, 36
White, Justice, 185
white collar crime, 96
White House Office of National Drug Control Policy, 49
Why People Obey the Law (Tyler), 40
wild beast test, 135
William of Orange (king), 118
Williams v. Florida, 151
Wilson, Kimber, 259
Wilson, Pete, 259
Wisconsin
  concealed weapons, 126
  crime victim rights, 275
  Dahmer murders, 133–134
  eye witness testimony policies, 112
  gun control laws, 127
  mandatory sentencing, 162
Witness and Protection Act, 276
Wolf v. Colorado, 77
women
  female component in DNA testing, 15
  insanity defense and, 144
  jury pools and, 150–151, 152

murder of, 19, 26
rape of, 15, 19, 21, 22, 23, 24, 25, 26
right to vote, 150
violence against, 19, 21, 26, 276
Wong Sun v. United States, 80
work crews, 224
Wrightsman, Laurence, 154–155
wrongful convictions, 22–23

Y chromosome, 15
Yates, Andrea, 139–140
youth offenders. *See* juveniles
Y-STR typing, 15–16

Zehr, Howard, 217, 218, 228
Zeisel, Hans, 155
Zenger, John Peter, 149–150
zero-tolerance laws, 66–67

About the General Editor

William J. Chambliss is professor of sociology at The George Washington University. He has written and edited more than 25 books and numerous articles for professional journals in sociology, criminology, and law. His work integrating the study of crime with the creation and implementation of criminal law has been a central theme in his writings and research. His articles on the historical development of vagrancy laws, the legal process as it affects different social classes and racial groups, and his attempt to introduce the study of state-organized crimes into the mainstream of social science research have punctuated his career.

He is the recipient of numerous awards and honors including a Doctorate of Laws Honoris Causa, University of Guelph, Guelph, Ontario, Canada, 1999; the 2009 Lifetime Achievement Award, Sociology of Law, American Sociological Association; the 2009 Lifetime Achievement Award, Law and Society, Society for the Study of Social Problems; the 2001 Edwin H. Sutherland Award, American Society of Criminology; the 1995 Major Achievement Award, American Society of Criminology; the 1986. Distinguished Leadership in Criminal Justice, Bruce Smith, Sr. Award, Academy of Criminal Justice Sciences; and the 1985 Lifetime Achievement Award, Criminology, American Sociological Association.

Professor Chambliss is a past president of the American Society of Criminology and past president of the Society for the Study of Social Problems. His current research covers a range of lifetime interests in international drug-control policy, class, race, gender and criminal justice and the history of piracy on the high seas.